CASES

IN

CORPORATE

FINANCIAL

REPORTING

CASES

IN

CORPORATE

FINANCIAL

REPORTING

PAUL A. GRIFFIN

University of California, Davis

PRENTICE-HALL, INC., Englewood Cliffs, New Jersey 07632

Editorial/production supervision and interior design by Margaret Rizzi
Cover design by Ben Santora
Manufacturing buyer: Raymond Keating

Printed in the United States of America

10 9 8 7 6 5 4 3 2 1

Prentice-Hall International, Inc., *London*
Prentice-Hall of Australia Pty. Limited, *Sydney*
Editora Prentice-Hall do Brasil, Ltda., *Rio de Janeiro*
Prentice-Hall Canada Inc., *Toronto*
Prentice-Hall of India Private Limited, *New Delhi*
Prentice-Hall of Japan, Inc., *Tokyo*
Prentice-Hall of Southeast Asia Pte. Ltd., *Singapore*
Whitehall Books Limited, *Wellington, New Zealand*

CONTENTS

III. PROPERTY, PLANT, AND EQUIPMENT

IV. INTANGIBLES AND CAPITALIZED EXPENSES

V. ALTERNATIVE VALUATION MODELS

VI. DEBT

VII. LEASES AND PENSIONS

VIII. INCOME TAXES AND INVESTMENT TAX CREDIT

XII. FINANCIAL STATEMENT ANALYSIS FOR COMPANY VALUATION

APPENDIX

APPENDIX

PREFACE

Textbooks that introduce students to the concepts, methods, and uses of financial accounting and reporting often provide little exposure to actual company financial statements. Questions, problem sets, and other assignment material tend to be hypothetical, simplistic, and devoid of the contextual richness of the corporate-reporting milieu. One consequence of such assignment material is that students who have completed the typical introductory course in financial accounting are sometimes bewildered and overwhelmed when confronted with real-world accounting issues. Real-world issues are immersed in a changing and complex environment. Moreover, that environment is all too often characterized by a lack of defined structure, an overabundance of irrelevant data, and an absence of a clear right or wrong answer.

This casebook attempts to bring theory and practice closer together. It stems from a conviction that the learning process is not complete unless the student understands the applications of the concepts and methods of accounting in the real world. Accordingly, the materials explore and analyze the fundamentals of financial accounting in the context of actual annual reports—the primary means of communication by business enterprises to investors, creditors, government, and other users. The overriding thrust of each case is to instill in students a critical ability to *identify* a particular accounting issue or concern and *evaluate* potential alternative treatments of that issue or concern. However, most of the cases go further. They enable students to examine certain financial and economic *consequences* of accounting treatments and assess or conjecture on what *motivates* preparers of financial statements to choose particular accounting treatments.

This book is best used as a supplement to one of the standard textbooks in financial accounting. However, it could also be used by itself or accompanied by readings to study many topical and sometimes controversial aspects of accounting and financial reporting. The cases are aimed at students with some prior exposure to the concepts and methods of accounting. Such students could, for example, be undergraduates at the intermediate level. Master's students and business executives, on the other hand, should find the materials appropriate at several levels. To guide instructors in using this text, the cases are ranked by degree of difficulty and expected time for completion. Also, an appendix (Appendix A) is provided showing the assignment of cases to chapters in selected introductory and intermediate accounting texts.

One last aspect of the text should be mentioned. Numerous cases adopt the perspective that accounting statements are the product of managerial decisions about the measurement and disclosure of financial information. As such, these materials may be used to cover issues of policy, management's motivations, and the economic effects of accounting choices. Since accounting researchers have studied such issues most comprehensively in recent years, an excellent opportunity is provided to introduce the results of academic research into the classroom.

In assembling the materials, master's candidate David L. Bauer of the Davis Graduate School of Administration provided competent research and technical assistance. I am grateful for his tireless efforts in reviewing company financial statements in order to identify interesting and challenging issues. Also, I wish to thank my former colleagues at Stanford's Graduate School of Business, whose pedagogical philosophies have no doubt shaped my thinking in preparing certain cases. Cases based on materials prepared by Robert K. Jaedicke, James M. Patell, and Mark A. Wolfson are included. My thanks to the reviewers of this text, Professor Thomas J. Burns, Ohio State University; Professor Trini U. Melcher, California State University; and Dr. Blaine A. Ritts, Bowling Green State University. Finally, I extend special thanks to John Grant Rhode, University of San Francisco, who class-tested a draft of the text; Linda Walters, who typed the manuscript; and Jack Ochs and Elinor Paige, Prentice-Hall, Inc., for their steady support and encouragement. Of course, I alone am responsible for any remaining errors.

The contents of this book are listed by topic. Apart from the cases in Section 1—on fundamental accounting relationships—the sequencing of the materials is up to the instructor. Instructors should carefully review all the cases before they are assigned to students to ensure that adequate coverage of the accounting issues involved has been given in class. Many cases, for instance, rely on information provided in the statement of changes in financial position. In this situation it is desirable, though not necessary, that some treatment of the statement of changes in financial position be given early in the course. A solutions manual containing detailed numerical solutions, as well as teaching suggestions, is available for instructors. Check figures are listed in Appendix B to this text.

Paul A. Griffin
Graduate School of Administration
Davis, California

1.1. THE LTV CORPORATION

The accounting equation, articulating the income statement and balance sheet. (Straightforward: 30 minutes)

The LTV Corporation is a conglomerate engaged in five basic industries: steel, energy products and services, aerospace, meat and food products, and ocean shipping. It conducts its operations through Jones & Laughlin Steel Corporation and Youngstown Sheet and Tube Company, Continental Emsco Company, Vought Corporation and Kentron International, Wilson Foods Corporation, and Lykes Bros. Steamship Co. Headquarters are in Dallas.

Study LTV's 1979–80 Statements of Consolidated Financial Position and 1978–80 Statements of Consolidated Income.

1. Reconcile the 1979 and 1980 Statements of Income to show that Net Income = (Revenues − Expenses) + (Gains − Losses). Explain your treatment of cumulative effect on prior years of accounting change.

2. Reconcile the 1979 and 1980 Statements of Financial Position to show that Assets = Liabilities + Shareholders' Equity.

3. Compute dividends declared for 1980.

4. If noncurrent liabilities increased, we usually say that working capital has increased as a result. Working capital might also increase from (1) increases in shareholders' equity and (2) decreases in noncurrent assets, as in the sale of property, plant, and equipment.

   a. Calculate the change in working capital from 1979 to 1980.

   b. Show how that change in working capital is reflected in changes in shareholders' equity, changes in noncurrent assets, and changes in noncurrent liabilities.

5. Comment on the display of LTV's assets and liabilities. Do you find their presentation easier to understand than the conventional, more orthodox presentation used by most companies?

I. FUNDAMENTALS

STATEMENT OF CONSOLIDATED FINANCIAL POSITION

The LTV Corporation and Subsidiaries
December 31
(In thousands)

	1980	1979 (1)
Current Assets		
Cash and short-term securities	$ 78,230	$ 90,481
Receivables	853,955	807,947
Inventories	1,047,105	983,451
Prepaid expenses	50,413	52,344
Total Current Assets	2,029,703	1,934,223
Current Liabilities		
Notes payable to banks	50,630	75,500
Accounts payable	536,621	499,130
Accrued liabilities	618,018	537,898
Current portion of long-term debt and		
capitalized lease obligations	21,708	20,131
Total Current Liabilities	1,226,977	1,132,659
Working capital	802,726	801,564
Investments and other assets	258,667	208,031
Property, plant and equipment	1,741,299	1,702,945
Total Assets Less Current Liabilities	2,802,692	2,712,540
Less Noncurrent Liabilities and Other Items		
Long-term debt	1,418,996	1,476,644
Capitalized lease obligations	70,157	74,564
Employee compensation and benefits	363,053	372,468
Deferred income taxes	27,252	8,324
Other noncurrent liabilities	83,520	62,774
Preferred stock with mandatory redemption	20,768	20,768
Total Noncurrent Liabilities and Other Items	1,983,746	2,015,542
Other Preferred Stock, Common Stock and Other Shareholders' Equity	$ 818,946	$ 696,998
Other Preferred Stock, Common Stock and Other Shareholders' Equity		
$2.60 Series B preferred stock	$ —	$ 4,438
Series 1 participating preference stock	1,000	513
Special stock, class AA	352	432
Common stock	17,896	12,322
Additional capital	501,038	498,300
Retained earnings	318,398	200,731
Less excess of redemption value over par		
value of $5 Series A preferred stock	(19,738)	(19,738)
Total Other Preferred Stock, Common Stock and Other Shareholders' Equity	$ 818,946	$ 696,998

The LTV Corporation

STATEMENT OF CONSOLIDATED INCOME

The LTV Corporation and Subsidiaries
Years Ended December 31
(In thousands except per share data)

	1980	1979	1978
Net sales and revenues	**$8,009,958**	$7,996,809	$5,260,537
Operating costs and expenses:			
Cost of products sold	7,277,216	7,230,599	4,886,561
Depreciation and amortization	128,830	132,441	83,257
Selling, administrative and general expenses	388,848	351,996	195,206
Interest expense and debt discount	151,305	160,639	105,694
Interest and other income	(55,947)	(36,180)	(12,622)
Gains from early extinguishment of debt	(31,187)	(13,890)	(4,922)
Unusual credits	—	—	(16,721)
Total Costs and Expenses	**7,859,065**	7,825,605	5,236,453
Income from continuing operations before income taxes	150,893	171,204	24,084
Income taxes	(23,000)	(24,600)	(4,100)
Income from continuing operations	127,893	146,604	19,984
Discontinued operations — credit	—	5,500	6,500
Income before extraordinary credit and accounting change	127,893	152,104	26,484
Extraordinary credit — tax benefit of operating loss carryforward	—	7,100	—
Cumulative effect on prior years of accounting change	—	14,323	13,119
Net Income	**$ 127,893**	$ 173,527	$ 39,603
Earnings per share:			
Fully diluted:			
Continuing operations	$ 2.96	$ 3.62	$ 1.09
Discontinued operations	—	0.13	0.33
Before extraordinary credit and accounting change	2.96	3.75	1.42
Extraordinary credit	—	0.17	—
Accounting change	—	0.35	0.67
Net Income	$ 2.96	$ 4.27	$2.09
Primary:			
Continuing operations	$ 3.95	$ 5.02	$ 1.07
Discontinued operations	—	0.21	0.42
Before extraordinary credit and accounting change	3.95	5.23	1.49
Extraordinary credit	—	0.26	—
Accounting change	—	0.54	0.84
Net income	$ 3.95	$ 6.03	$ 2.33
Pro Forma Data:			
Pro forma amounts, assuming retroactive application of 1979 and 1978 cumulative effect of accounting change:			
Net Income		$ 159,204	$ 35,537
Earnings per share:			
Fully diluted		3.92	1.88
Primary		5.49	2.07

I. FUNDAMENTALS

1.2. WHAT SHOULD MISS ANNIE DO?

Performance evaluation of J.P. and Ronnie's oil production, basic principles. (Moderate: 45 minutes)

J.P. and Ronnie (Tex) Richards are in competition to take over Richards Oil. J.P. told Ronnie, "This oil company ain't big enough for the both of us." The Richards have run out of money and, with the oil glut, there isn't much of a market for oil. However, they can sell crude to buy oil-drilling equipment. In Jack's (the recently deceased father of J.P. and Ronnie) will, J.P. and Ronnie were each left 12,000 barrels of oil and some land. J.P.'s parcel of land is smaller (15 acres) than Ronnie's (20 acres) because Ronnie was Jack's favorite. According to the will, Miss Annie must hand over the controlling rights to the son who does relatively better. Neither of the boys has enough oil to purchase drilling equipment outright, but arrangements can be made for payment after the wells produce. The boys have exactly one year to start the wells and produce the crude for comparison.

One year later, J.P.'s wells have produced 82,500 barrels of oil. He made arrangements to buy 10,000 barrels' worth of drilling equipment. The equipment is now capable of producing only 247,500 more barrels of oil. Of the original 12,000 barrels given to J.P. by Jack, he used 8,000 barrels for drilling expenses. At the end of the year, Ronnie had 115,000 barrels of oil. He made arrangements to purchase 15,000 barrels' worth of equipment, but after a fire at the beginning of the year, he found that he only had 5,000 barrels' worth. The equipment had not been insured. What remains of the equipment has 180,000 barrels of production capability left. Ronnie used up all of his original 12,000 barrels allotted for drilling. During the year, however, Ronnie, having a soft heart for Miss Annie, did send 5,000 barrels of produced oil to Miss Annie so that she could go to camp. But upon hearing what Ronnie did, at the end of the year J.P. sent Miss Annie a brand new Mercedes-Benz valued at 12,000 barrels of produced oil. Miss Annie was charmed by both her son's gifts.

Now Miss Annie must determine which son did better so that she can hand over to him the controlling rights to run Richards Oil, and kiss the other son good-bye.

1.3. ANOTHER IMPROBABLE OCCURRENCE*

Evaluation of performance with wheat production, preparation of basic statements. (Moderate: 30 minutes)

Once upon a time many, many years ago, there lived a feudal landlord in a small province of Central Europe. The landlord, called the Red Bearded Baron, lived in a castle high on a hill, and this benevolent fellow was responsible for the well-being of many peasants who occupied the lands surrounding his castle. Each spring, as the snow began to melt and thoughts of other, less influential men turned to matters other than business, the Baron would decide how to provide for all his serf-dependents during the coming year.

One spring, the Baron was thinking about the wheat crop of the coming growing season. "I believe that 30 acres of my land, being worth five bushels of wheat per acre, will produce enough wheat for next winter," he mused, "but who should do the farming? I believe I'll give Ivan the Indefatigable and Igor the Immutable the task of growing the wheat." Whereupon Ivan and Igor, two gentry noted for their hard work and not overly active minds, were summoned for an audience with the Landlord.

"Ivan, you will farm on the twenty acre plot of ground and Igor will farm the ten acre plot," the Baron began. "I will give Ivan 20 bushels of wheat for seed and 20 pounds of fertilizer. (Twenty pounds of fertilizer are worth two bushels of wheat.) Igor will get ten bushels of wheat for seed and ten pounds of fertilizer. I will give each of you an ox to pull a plow but you will have to make arrangements with Feyador, the Plowmaker, for a plow. The oxen, incidentally, are only three years old and have never been used for farming, so they should have a good ten years of farming ahead of them. Take good care of

---

*Written by W. T. Andrews, Texas A&M University, reprinted with permission from the *Accounting Review*, April 1974, pp. 369–70.

them, because an ox is worth 40 bushels of wheat. Come back next fall and return the oxen and the plows along with your harvest."

Ivan and Igor genuflected and withdrew from the Great Hall, taking with them the things provided by the Baron.

The summer came and went and after the harvest Ivan and Igor returned to the Great Hall to account to their master for the things given them in the spring. Ivan, pouring 223 bushels of wheat onto the floor, said, "My Lord, I present you with a slightly used ox, a plow, broken beyond repair, and 223 bushels of wheat. I, unfortunately, owe Feyador, the Plowmaker, three bushels of wheat for the plow I got from him last fall. And, as you might expect, I used all the fertilizer and seed you gave me last spring. You will also remember, my Lord, that you took 20 bushels of my harvest for your own personal use."

Igor, who had been given 10 acres of land, 10 bushels of wheat and 10 pounds of fertilizer, spoke next. "Here, my Lord, is a partially used-up ox, the plow for which I gave Feyador, the Plowmaker, three bushels of wheat from my harvest and 105 bushels of wheat. I, too, used all my seed and fertilizer last spring. Also, my Lord, you took 30 bushels of wheat several days ago for your own table. I believe the plow is good for two more seasons."

"Knaves, you did well," said the Red Bearded Baron. Blessed with this benediction and not wishing to press their luck further, the two serfs departed hastily.

After the servants had taken their leave, the Red Bearded Baron, watching the two hungry oxen slowly eating the wheat piled on the floor, began to contemplate what had happened. "Yes," he thought, "they did well, but I wonder which one did better?"

1.4. CAMPBELL SOUP COMPANY—I

Accounting transactions, using T-accounts to compute end-of-year balances. (Moderate: 60 minutes)

The Campbell Soup Company is a diversified grower, producer, and processor of consumer food products. Well known for its soups, Campbell's operations also include Pepperidge Farm, Swanson Foods, Godiva chocolates, and Vlasic Foods (pickles).

Study the 1980 Consolidated Balance Sheets and the 1979–81 Consolidated Statements of Earnings for the Campbell Soup Company. Other information is supplied below.[1] All numbers are in thousands of dollars.

1. Assume that all sales were on credit; cash received from customers amounted to $2,786,108.

2. All expenses except interest and depreciation (see part 7 below) were charged to current liability accounts. Cash payments made to reduce the various current liability accounts amounted to $2,541,646.

3. Prepaid expenses were for interest only. Cash payments for interest during the year amounted to $37,123.

4. Temporary investments were sold for $18,469 cash. No gain or loss was made.

5. Using better management techniques, inventories were reduced by $16,819. Such reductions "released" cash for use elsewhere in the business.

6. Other assets purchased for cash amounted to $34,798.

---

[1]The amounts stated are estimates based on simplifying assumptions. As such, they do not necessarily approximate the actual cash flows experienced by Campbell Soup Company.

7. Depreciation on plant assets amounted to $75,118.

8. Plant assets purchased for cash amounted to $166,433.

9. Cash generated by increased long-term debt and other liabilities amounted to $32,364.

10. No transactions occurred involving deferred taxes.

11. A dividend of $66,298 was paid in cash.

12. Other than the dividend in part 11, stockholders' equity transactions involved only cash purchases of treasury stock amounting to $21,352.

Using the financial reports and the information above, compute the following account balances as of August 2, 1981:

a.	Temporary investments	h.	Current liabilities (one number)
b.	Accounts receivable	i.	Long-term debt and other liabilities (one number)
c.	Inventories		
d.	Prepaid expenses	j.	Deferred income taxes
e.	Other assets	k.	Capital stock
f.	Plant assets	l.	Capital surplus
g.	Cash	m.	Earnings retained in the business
		n.	Capital stock in treasury

Consolidated Balance Sheets
CAMPBELL SOUP

	August 2, 1981	August 3, 1980
	(000 omitted)	
Current assets		
Cash		$ 26,105
Temporary investments, at cost, which approximates market		97,165
Accounts receivable		204,891
Inventories		501,013
Prepaid expenses		32,671
		861,845
Other assets		77,715
Plant assets, net of depreciation		688,005
		$1,627,565
Current liabilities		
Notes payable		$ 128,663
Payable to suppliers and others		204,966
Accrued payrolls, taxes, etc.		82,459
Accrued income taxes		40,129
		456,217
Long-term debt		137,879
Other liabilities		5,273
Deferred income taxes		69,753
Stockholders' equity		
Capital stock		20,343
Capital surplus		35,413
Earnings retained in the business		936,547
Capital stock in treasury, at cost		(33,860)
		958,443
		$1,627,565

Consolidated Statement of Earnings
CAMPBELL SOUP

	1981 (52 weeks)	1980 (53 weeks) (000 omitted)	1979 (52 weeks)
Net sales	**$2,797,663**	$2,560,569	$2,248,692
Costs and expenses			
Cost of products sold	**2,172,806**	1,976,754	1,719,134
Marketing and sales expenses	**256,726**	213,703	181,229
Administrative and research expenses	**93,462**	102,445	94,716
Interest—net	**30,302**	10,135	1,169
	2,553,296	2,303,037	1,996,248
Earnings before taxes	**244,367**	257,532	252,444
Taxes on earnings	**114,650**	122,950	119,700
Earnings before prior year effect of change in accounting principle	**129,717**	134,582	132,744
Prior year effect of change to LIFO method of inventory accounting		(12,927)	
Net earnings	**$ 129,717**	$ 121,655	$ 132,744
Per share (based on average shares outstanding):			
Earnings before prior year effect of change in accounting principle	**$4.00**	$4.08	$3.98
Prior year effect of change to LIFO method of inventory accounting		(.39)	
Net earnings	**$4.00**	$3.69	$3.98
Pro Forma Net Earnings			

Although in accordance with generally
  accepted accounting principles the
  prior year could not be restated for
  the change to LIFO, these amounts
  report earnings as though the
  restatement had been made			

Net earnings	**$ 129,717**	$ 134,582	$ 119,817
Net earnings per share	**$4.00**	$4.08	$3.59

             I. FUNDAMENTALS

1.5. WRATHER CORPORATION AND SUBSIDIARIES

Journal entries and construction of statements.
(Moderate: 75 minutes)

Wrather Corporation is a diversified company operating principally in the hotel, oil and gas, and motion picture industries. Wrather operates the Queen Mary and Spruce Goose in Long Beach, California, and produced the remake of the *Legend of the Lone Ranger.*

Study the 1979 Consolidated Balance Sheet and the 1978–80 Consolidated Statements of Income. Other information is provided below. All numbers are in thousands of dollars.

ADDITIONAL INFORMATION

- All 1979 prepaid expenses were used in 1980. Prepaid expenses purchased for cash in 1980 amounted to $1,988.
- Interest expense was paid in cash.
- Depreciation on property, plant, and equipment amounted to $3,173; depletion and amortization on oil and gas properties amounted to $3,251.
- All expenses other than prepaid expenses, depreciation, taxes on income, and interest were charged to various liability accounts. Film distribution costs incurred in 1980 amounted to $5,000; costs incurred associated with accrued liabilities amounted to $5,000; the remaining expenses on account were charged to accounts payable. Cash payments in 1980 for film distribution costs, accrued liabilities, and accounts payable were $4,956, $2,110, and $37,760, respectively.
- The credit for income taxes ($1,860) comprised current taxes payable of $3, which was credited to the account Other Liabilities, a loss carry forward of $1,157, and a reduction in de-

ferred taxes of $706. Cash payments for Other Liabilities amounted to $88.

- All sales were on credit. Cash received from customers, $60,977.
- Property, plant, and equipment purchased for cash, $8,145; oil and gas properties purchased for cash, $6,173; cash investments in *Lone Ranger* motion picture, $6,642.
- Certain other assets were sold at their book value for $60.
- Common stock issued for cash amounted to $192.
- A dividend was paid in cash.
- Long-term debt repayments of $2,186 were made, and $1,156 of long-term debt became payable in 1981. Cash received from issuance of bank notes and mortgages amounted to $20,964.
- Other current assets were purchased for cash, $699.

1. Prepare journal entries for all transactions in 1980. Use only the accounts indicated in the 1979–80 statements.

2. Prepare the 1980 Consolidated Balance Sheet.

(*Note:* All expenses other than depreciation and amortization, and interest, should be treated as *general* expenses.)

Consolidated Balance Sheets

December 31, 1980 and 1979

	1980	1979
ASSETS		
Current Assets:		
Cash	$	$ 336,000
Accounts and notes receivable		4,770,000
Prepaid expenses		1,813,000
Other current assets		1,463,000
Net operating loss carryforward		
Total current assets		8,382,000
Teleprompter Corporation Common Stock, at cost		10,023,000
Property, Plant and Equipment, at cost		72,936,000
Less accumulated depreciation and amortization		16,728,000
Property—net		56,208,000
Oil and Gas Properties (under full cost method)—net		11,127,000
Investment in Lone Ranger Feature Joint Venture		450,000
Land and Other Assets		5,545,000
Total		$91,735,000

	1980	1979
LIABILITIES AND STOCKHOLDERS' EQUITY		
Current Liabilities:		
Current portion of long-term debt	$	$ 2,186,000
Accounts payable		1,948,000
Accrued film distribution costs		810,000
Accrued liabilities		3,515,000
Total current liabilities		8,459,000
Long-Term Debt		66,203,000
Deferred Income Taxes		2,205,000
Other Liabilities		874,000
Commitments and Contingent Liabilities		
Stockholders' Equity:		
Preferred stock, $1 par value—authorized 1,000,000 shares; issued, none		
Common stock, no par value—authorized 10,000,000 shares; issued and outstanding shares; 1980, 2,328,180; 1979, 2,271,030		7,552,000
Retained earnings		6,442,000
Stockholders' equity		13,994,000
Total		$91,735,000

Consolidated Statements of Income

For the years ended December 31, 1980, 1979 and 1978   WRATHER CORPORATION AND SUBSIDIARIES

	1980	1979	1978
Revenues:			
Hotel room revenues	$27,500,000	$23,923,000	$19,245,000
Food and beverage	22,528,000	18,412,000	18,233,000
Other	12,457,000	10,075,000	5,937,000
	62,485,000	52,410,000	43,415,000
Expenses:			
Operating expenses	29,080,000	23,833,000	18,651,000
Cost of sales	7,926,000	6,506,000	5,209,000
Selling, general and administrative expenses	14,603,000	10,752,000	9,767,000
Depreciation, depletion and amortization	6,424,000	4,441,000	4,162,000
Interest expense	10,888,000	8,026,000	4,673,000
	68,921,000	53,558,000	42,462,000
Income (Loss) Before Income Taxes and Extraordinary Item	(6,436,000)	(1,148,000)	953,000
Income Taxes (Credit)	(1,860,000)	(314,000)	(48,000)
Income (Loss) Before Extraordinary Item	(4,576,000)	(834,000)	1,001,000
Extraordinary Item		(191,000)	(118,000)
Net Income (Loss)	$(4,576,000)	$(1,025,000)	$ 883,000
Per Common Share:			
Income (loss) before extraordinary item	$ (1.98)	$ (.37)	$ .43
Extraordinary item		(.09)	(.05)
Net income (loss)	$ (1.98)	$ (.46)	$ .38

Consolidated Statements of Retained Earnings

For the years ended December 31, 1980, 1979 and 1978   WRATHER CORPORATION AND SUBSIDIARIES

	1980	1979	1978
Retained Earnings—Beginning of Year	$6,442,000	$7,581,000	$6,810,000
Net Income (Loss)	(4,576,000)	(1,025,000)	883,000
Cash Dividend ($.05 Per Share)	(116,000)	(114,000)	(112,000)
Retained Earnings—End of Year	$1,750,000	$6,442,000	$7,581,000

1.6. BLUE BELL, INC.

Introduction to the Statement of Changes in Financial
Position, working-capital concept of flow of funds.
(Moderate: 45 minutes)

Blue Bell is primarily a clothing manufacturer. Its well-known brands include Wrangler, Jantzen, Sedgefield, Red Kap, Big Ben, Maverick, Rustler, and Lucchese.

Using the accompanying 1981 Statement of Consolidated Income and Retained Earnings and the 1980 and 1981 Consolidated Balance Sheets, compute the unknowns (a, b, c, etc.) on the 1981 Statement of Changes in Consolidated Financial Position.

The following assumptions should be made:

1. A working-capital concept of funds is used.

2. Property was sold during the year for book value. No gain or loss on sale was recorded.

3. Deferred income taxes relate to differences in timing of the recognition of foreign subsidiaries' earnings. In 1981, $13,488,000 was included in consolidated net income.

Statements of Consolidated Income and Retained Earnings

For the years ended September 30
In thousands*

	1981	1980	1979
Net Sales	$1,427,164	$1,397,760	$1,029,453
Cost and Expenses:			
Cost of goods sold	1,025,812	983,295	710,342
Marketing, administrative and general expenses	295,981	272,457	195,033
Interest expense	33,052	25,563	8,803
Interest income	(2,900)	(5,916)	(7,659)
Miscellaneous income — net (Note 9)	(14,338)	(1,720)	(586)
Total	1,337,607	1,273,679	905,933
Income Before Income Taxes	89,557	124,081	123,520
Income Taxes (Note 10)	42,881	56,171	56,237
Net Income	46,676	67,910	67,283
Retained Earnings, Beginning of Year	344,351	298,999	251,755
Total	391,027	366,909	319,038
Cash Dividends Declared (1981 and 1980, $1.80 per share; 1979, $1.60 per share)	22,765	22,558	20,039
Retained Earnings, End of Year (Note 6)	$ 368,262	$ 344,351	$ 298,999
Average Number of Shares Outstanding	12,632	12,583	12,549
Earnings Per Share	$3.70	$5.40	$5.36

*Except per share data.

Consolidated Balance Sheets

September 30 In thousands*	1981	1980
ASSETS **Current Assets:**		
Cash (Note 4)	$ 7,475	$ 8,451
Receivables, principally trade accounts, less allowances		
(1981, $2,994; 1980, $3,149)	271,088	297,378
Inventories (Note 3)	372,131	410,050
Prepaid and other	16,951	14,823
Total Current Assets	667,645	730,702
Property, at cost (Note 5):		
Land and land improvements	7,419	7,116
Buildings	82,414	67,345
Machinery and equipment	144,138	130,420
Improvements to leased property	18,707	17,361
Total	252,678	222,242
Less accumulated depreciation and amortization	115,700	98,060
Property, net	136,978	124,182
Note Receivable, 7¾% — Due May 1990	5,000	5,000
Other Assets	9,283	8,890
Total	$818,906	$868,774
LIABILITIES **Current Liabilities:**		
Notes payable — Banks and other (Note 4)	$135,419	$171,134
Current maturities of long-term debt (Note 6)	3,664	3,617
Accounts payable, principally trade	120,697	124,790
Dividends payable	5,756	5,640
Accrued liabilities:		
Compensation	23,620	25,287
Pension and profit sharing (Note 11)	4,981	8,453
Income taxes	21,624	30,128
Taxes — Other than income	8,028	10,856
Interest	3,534	6,034
Other	7,983	9,916
Total Current Liabilities	335,306	395,855
Long-term Debt (Note 6)	54,324	58,587
Deferred Income Taxes (Note 10)	—	13,488
Shareholders' Equity (Notes 11 and 12):		
Common stock — $3.33⅓ par value		
(authorized — 30,000,000 shares;		
issued: 1981 — 12,751,685 shares; 1980 — 12,545,448 shares)	42,506	41,818
Additional paid-in capital	18,666	14,833
Retained earnings (Note 6)	368,262	344,351
Total	429,434	401,002
Less treasury stock — at cost (12,158 shares)	158	158
Shareholders' Equity	429,276	400,844
Total	$818,906	$868,774

*Except share data.

I. FUNDAMENTALS

Statements of Changes in Consolidated Financial Position

For the years ended September 30
In thousands

	1981	1980	1979
Sources of Funds:			
Net Income	a	$ 67,910	$67,283
Add (deduct) amounts not affecting working capital:			
Depreciation and amortization	21,860	18,396	13,330
Deferred income taxes — noncurrent portion	b	6,734	(9,812)
Other	470	253	285
Working Capital Provided from Operations	c	93,293	71,086
Debt Assumed from Acquired Company (Note 2)	0	14,116	
Long-term Borrowings	1,317	6,200	2,403
Issuance of Common Stock (Note 11)	d	165	14
Other	(760)	1,569	145
Total	$60,596	$115,343	$73,648
Applications of Funds:			
Increase (Decrease) in Working Capital Components:			
Cash and short-term investments	e	$ (60,943)	$13,423
Receivables	f	81,099	61,090
Inventories	g	128,684	62,778
Notes and accounts payable	h	(123,961)	(88,549)
Income taxes	i	18,543	(20,342)
Other accrued liabilities	j	(15,150)	(11,542)
Other, net	k	3,997	1,609
Increase (Decrease) in Working Capital	l	32,269	18,467
Cash Dividends Declared	m	22,558	20,039
Net Noncurrent Assets of Acquired Company (Note 2):			
Property	0	17,126	6,846
Other, net			3,641
Additions to Property, Net	n	37,267	18,761
Reductions of Long-term Debt	o	4,149	4,073
Other	103	1,974	1,821
Total	p	$115,343	$73,648

2.1. CRANE COMPANY AND SUBSIDIARIES

Investments at cost vs. market value.
(Moderate: 60 minutes)

Crane Company is a diversified manufacturer of products for basic industry. Principal products include steel, cement, fluid and pollution control equipment, building products, and aircraft and aerospace systems.

Study (1) the assets section of Crane's Consolidated Balance Sheet at December 31, 1980, (2) Crane's 1980 Consolidated Statement of Changes in Financial Position (this statement shows Crane's purchases and sales of long-term investments, among other items), and (3) a note to the financial statements explaining various "miscellaneous items" in the Statement of Income. Crane's "net income before taxes," but after including $7,312,023 for miscellaneous items, totaled $62,723,486.

If Crane had used market values instead of cost in accounting for its "investments" and had included any unrealized market appreciation as an item in calculating net income before taxes:

1. At what amount would investments have been reported as of 1979 and 1980?

2. Prepare a journal entry to convert Crane's accounting system from historical cost to market values as of January 1, 1980.

3. Assume that the long-term investments were sold in the market for cash (cost was $1,638,289) on January 2, 1980 (the New York Stock Exchange was closed on New Year's Day). Prepare journal entries to record the sale, assuming a historical-cost accounting system.

4. Given the assumed sale in part 3, state net income before taxes for 1980 on a market-value basis.

5. What entry or entries are necessary to maintain the investments account on a market-value basis throughout the year, including December 31, 1980?

Consolidated Balance Sheet

At December 31	1980	1979
Assets		
Current Assets:		
Cash	$ 20,674,488	$ 31,367,545
Short-term investments, at lower of cost or market	93,286,903	70,535,634
Accounts receivable, less allowances of $3,303,487 ($3,472,642 in 1979)	178,755,201	175,112,126
Inventories, at lower of cost, principally last-in, first-out, or market.		
LIFO reserves amounted to $88,914,390 ($83,372,559 in 1979):		
Finished goods	86,812,759	84,660,137
Work in process	45,848,137	53,316,042
Raw materials and supplies	33,370,982	38,900,550
	166,031,878	176,876,729
Prepaid expenses	4,029,373	3,996,853
Total Current Assets	462,777,843	457,888,887
Investments and Other Assets:		
Investments (Market $142,580,000; $82,395,000 in 1979) (see page 9)	57,849,696	45,811,803
Unamortized debt discount	6,163,187	8,240,982
Construction fund	2,088,840	4,293,119
Outlying lands	1,224,283	1,224,283
Other assets	3,995,831	6,057,722
	71,321,837	65,627,909
Property, Plant and Equipment at Cost:		
Land	32,725,441	34,799,160
Buildings and improvements	200,439,399	208,387,435
Machinery and equipment	845,912,255	856,244,060
	1,079,077,095	1,099,430,655
Less accumulated depreciation	609,059,683	580,693,139
	470,017,412	518,737,516
	$1,004,117,092	$1,042,254,312

Miscellaneous—Net

	Components		
	1980	1979	1978
	(in thousands)		
Gain on investments—net	$5,015	$2,547	$8,079
Disposal of capital assets—net	2,690	(1,379)	969
Termination of certain operations	(1,084)	(1,427)	(5,243)
Gain (loss) on repurchase of debentures	984	(178)	(168)
Minority interest	(1,076)	(1,733)	(701)
Foreign exchange adjustments	931	485	(659)
Other	(148)	(328)	(74)
	$7,312	$(2,013)	$2,203

Consolidated Statement of Changes in Financial Position

CRANE CO. AND SUBSIDIARIES

For Years Ended December 31	1980	1979	1978
Source of Funds:			
Operations:			
Net Income	$ 42,596,095	$ 55,028,771	$ 35,355,414
Depreciation	81,672,886	73,868,510	51,188,976
Amortization of debt discount	2,077,795	3,645,777	2,082,257
Other, net	1,110,050	(18,049)	2,254,712
	127,456,826	132,525,009	90,881,359
Increase in long-term debt	334,220	114,920,550	34,250,000
Increase in capital leases—net	6,579,982	6,808,922	10,649,431
Conversion of debt to common stock	612,075	729,200	1,213,400
Decrease in long-term investments	1,638,289	61,180,342	32,361,349
Disposals of property, plant and equipment	22,043,664	10,412,786	5,883,953
	158,665,056	326,576,809	175,239,492
Application of Funds:			
Additions to property, plant and equipment	55,079,618	85,314,963	57,403,054
Acquisition of Medusa Corp. property, plant			
and equipment—net	—	141,665,000	—
Increase in long-term investments	13,676,182	2,394,803	61,180,342
Increase (decrease) in other assets—net	(1,611,228)	10,231,300	5,486,166
Decrease in reserves and other liabilities	2,993,746	1,957,375	10,475,934
Reduction in long-term debt	64,619,635	38,236,706	31,959,312
Reacquisition of shares, less options exercised	2,322,854	5,349,113	12,987,865
Cash dividends	16,298,361	14,562,512	14,131,846
	153,379,168	299,711,772	193,624,519
Net Source (Application) of Funds	$ 5,285,888	$ 26,865,037 *	$(18,385,027)

* Includes Medusa's working capital of $31,202,000 at March 31, 1979 less cash tender cost of $17,232,000.

Increase (Decrease) in Components of Working Capital:			
Current assets:			
Cash and short-term investments	$ 12,058,212	$ 1,875,951	$(24,008,030)
Accounts receivable	3,643,075	38,747,791	(5,594,022)
Inventories	(10,844,851)	30,365,477	1,810,676
Prepaid expenses	32,520	1,481,183	312,440
	4,888,956	72,470,402	(27,478,936)
Current liabilities:			
Current maturities of long-term debt	3,791,009	(3,791,285)	(6,701,215)
Loans payable to banks	531,986	2,610,047	(5,711,708)
Accounts payable	1,056,613	12,773,091	3,989,285
Accrued liabilities	(9,996,342)	26,080,445	(2,524,913)
U.S. and foreign taxes on income	4,219,802	7,933,067	1,854,642
	(396,932)	45,605,365	(9,093,909)
Increase (Decrease) in Working Capital	$ 5,285,888	$ 26,865,037	$(18,385,027)

II. CURRENT ASSETS

2.2. NATIONAL SEMICONDUCTOR CORPORATION

Receivables, allowance for doubtful debts, bad debts
written off. (Straightforward: 45 minutes)

National Semiconductor Corporation designs, manufactures, and markets semiconductor devices and related technologies. The company is one of the largest (merchant) manufacturers of integrated circuits in the world.

Study National Semiconductor's 1980–81 Consolidated Statements of Operations and a note relating to receivables explaining the amounts reported in the consolidated balance sheets.

1. Assume that National Semiconductor estimates returns and allowances on 1981 and 1982 sales to be $50 million. Also, assume that the company estimates that doubtful debts will be 1 percent of 1982 gross sales and that doubtful debts allowances are charged as expenses rather than as reductions of sales revenues. Calculate the amount paid by customers (trade and other) to the company during the fiscal year ended May 31, 1982.

2. Of the amount estimated in part 1 above, assume that on May 31, 1982, $2 million was received from customers whose accounts had been viewed as doubtful on May 31, 1980, and whose accounts had been written down as only 25 percent collectible on May 31, 1981. Prepare journal entries to record all three transactions.

3. Comment on the trend in the collectibility of the company's receivables. Use year-end balances in your calculation of average collection period. Assume that all sales are on credit.

Consolidated Statements of Operations

For the years ended May 31 (in thousands, except per share amounts)	1982	1981	1980
Net sales	$1,104,095	$1,110,053	$910,113
Costs and expenses:			
Cost of sales	846,865	763,104	618,691
Research and development	109,056	96,043	80,117
Selling, general, and administrative	159,839	150,157	122,463
Interest, net	5,584	5,833	11,118
Total costs and expenses	1,121,344	1,015,137	832,389
Earnings (Loss) before income taxes	(17,249)	94,916	77,724
Income taxes (credit)	(6,555)	41,953	34,354
Net earnings (loss) from continuing operations	(10,694)	52,963	43,370
Earnings (Loss) from discontinued operations,			
net of income taxes	—	(537)	1,673
Net earnings (loss)	$ (10,694)	$ 52,426	$ 45,043
Earnings (Loss) per common and			
common equivalent share:			
Continuing operations	$(0.47)	$2.40	$2.14
Discontinued operations	—	(.03)	.08
Net earnings (loss)	$(0.47)	$2.37	$2.22
Weighted average common and			
common equivalent shares	22,869	22,086	20,308

3. Receivables

Receivables comprise:

At May 31 (in thousands)	1982	1981
Trade	$196,534	$198,340
Other	12,193	11,798
Total	208,727	210,138
Less allowances:		
Doubtful accounts	4,792	5,980
Returns and allowances	14,051	10,529
Total	18,843	16,509
Net receivables	$189,884	$193,629

II. CURRENT ASSETS

2.3. ELGIN NATIONAL INDUSTRIES, INC.

Construction receivables, revenue recognition.
(Moderate: 45 minutes)

Elgin National Industries' business is concentrated in two basic areas: (1) specialized engineering, manufacturing, and construction and (2) clocks and watches. Elgin is the official manufacturer and distributor of Mickey Mouse and other Disney fanciful character watches and clocks.

Study Elgin's Consolidated Statements of Income for 1978–80, Balance Sheets for 1979–80, and Notes 1 and 2 to the financial statements.

1. What method of accounting for construction costs does Elgin use for financial-reporting purposes? In what way might that method illustrate the concept of conservatism?

2. Does Elgin use the same method of accounting for construction costs for computing income taxes? Suggest why Elgin would adopt such a method.

3. Assume that Elgin's costs of production and construction average 80 percent of sales and construction revenues and that other expenses—such as selling, general, administrative, and interest expenses—are comparatively fixed. Calculate what Elgin's 1980 Income before Taxes on Income would have been had the company used for reporting purposes the method of accounting for construction contracts used for tax purposes. Provide journal entries that would restate profits on the alternative basis.

Elgin National Industries, Inc. and Subsidiaries

	Year Ended December 31,		
	1980	1979	1978
Net sales and construction revenues including agency sales (Note 1)	$210,768,316	$229,862,379	$208,616,421
Revenues:			
Net sales and construction revenues	$200,346,720	$207,527,696	$189,282,849
Interest income	3,677,064	1,070,431	276,970
Other income	415,239	145,209	—
	$204,439,023	$208,743,336	$189,559,819
Costs and expenses:			
Cost of sales and cost of construction	$162,588,944	$171,109,354	$153,069,273
Selling, general and administrative expenses	21,831,209	20,110,901	19,228,221
Interest expense	373,921	315,055	655,150
	$184,794,074	$191,535,310	$172,952,644
INCOME BEFORE TAXES ON INCOME	$ 19,644,949	$ 17,208,026	$ 16,607,175
Tax provision on above income (Note 7)	9,297,000	7,924,000	8,319,000
NET INCOME	$ 10,347,949	$ 9,284,026	$ 8,288,175
Primary income per share	$3.46	$3.13	$2.83
Fully diluted income per share	$3.37	$3.03	$2.71

See notes to consolidated financial statements.

II. CURRENT ASSETS

Elgin National Industries, Inc. and Subsidiaries

CONSOLIDATED BALANCE SHEETS

	December 31,	
	1980	**1979**
ASSETS		
CURRENT ASSETS:		
Cash	$ 2,316,939	$ 7,363,746
Short-term investments (at cost which approximates market)	29,200,000	21,900,000
Accounts and notes receivable (Note 2)	46,529,208	50,611,335
Receivable — sale of companies (Note 4)	605,000	—
Inventories (Note 3)	16,900,866	16,237,155
Prepaid expenses and other current assets	576,845	728,903
TOTAL CURRENT ASSETS	$ 96,128,858	$ 96,841,139
PROPERTY, PLANT AND EQUIPMENT (Note 5)	$ 9,492,770	$ 9,686,583
OTHER ASSETS:		
Receivable — sale of companies (Note 4)	$ 258,000	$ 508,000
Excess of cost over net assets acquired (Note 1)	6,153,046	6,322,750
Other	478,563	530,443
	$ 6,889,609	$ 7,361,193
	$112,511,237	$113,888,915
LIABILITIES AND STOCKHOLDERS' INVESTMENT		
CURRENT LIABILITIES:		
Trade payables	$ 9,740,429	$ 12,548,026
Accrued liabilities and taxes (Note 6)	26,285,230	27,896,022
Federal income taxes payable:		
Current	4,335,000	3,965,000
Deferred (Note 1)	14,387,333	16,783,598
Current portion of long-term debt (Note 9)	498,780	440,736
TOTAL CURRENT LIABILITIES	$ 55,246,772	$ 61,633,382
LONG-TERM DEBT (Note 9)	$ 2,438,128	$ 3,319,604
LOAN GUARANTEE — EMPLOYEE STOCK OWNERSHIP TRUST (Notes 9 and 10)	$ 5,203,582	$ 6,562,370
CONTINGENT LIABILITIES (Note 12)		
STOCKHOLDERS' INVESTMENT (Note 9):		
Preferred stock, par value $1 per share; authorized 1,000,000 shares; none issued	$ —	$ —
Common stock, par value $1 per share; authorized 7,500,000 shares; issued 4,621,724 in 1980, 4,599,008 in 1979	4,621,724	4,599,008
Paid-in surplus	51,486,105	51,168,485
Retained earnings	13,659,465	8,109,393
	$ 69,767,294	$ 63,876,886
Less:		
Cost of 1,612,894 shares of common stock in treasury	14,940,957	14,940,957
Deferred charge — Employee Stock Ownership Trust (Notes 9 and 10)	5,203,582	6,562,370
	$ 49,622,755	$ 42,373,559
	$112,511,237	$113,888,915

Elgin National Industries, Inc. and Subsidiaries

Notes to Consolidated Financial Statements

1. Summary of significant accounting and reporting policies:

(a) **Principles of consolidation**—The consolidated financial statements include the accounts of the Company and its wholly-owned subsidiaries. All significant intercompany profits, transactions and balances have been eliminated in consolidation.

(b) **Accounting for construction contracts**—The length of the Company's construction contracts varies but is typically longer than one year. Therefore, contract related assets and liabilities are classified as current in the accompanying consolidated balance sheets. For financial statement purposes, profits on uncompleted contracts are determined by applying the percentage of completion to the engineering estimate of total profit on each contract. The percentage of completion is determined by comparing costs incurred to date with total estimated costs on each project. The Company's contract cost estimates include amounts related to plant start-up, customer acceptance, and other construction uncertainties. Favorable adjustments to these estimates are made and the effect on income is recorded only when construction progress reaches the point where experience is sufficient to estimate final results with reasonable accuracy; unfavorable adjustments are recorded as soon as they are apparent. Other adjustments of cost estimates, if required, are recorded in the periods when they become known. Estimated losses on uncompleted contracts are provided in full.

2. Accounts and notes receivable:

Accounts and notes receivable consist of the following:

	December 31,	
	1980	**1979**
Trade accounts	$12,944,961	$ 9,649,369
Construction contracts:		
Billed	$16,278,687	$25,806,240
Recoverable costs and accrued profits on contracts in process — unbilled	2,608,519	1,986,061
Retainage due upon completion of contracts	14,572,109	12,614,155
	$33,459,315	$40,406,456
Other	$ 989,385	$ 1,198,502
	$47,393,661	$51,254,327
Less allowance for doubtful accounts	864,453	642,992
	$46,529,208	$50,611,335

It is estimated that approximately $13,500,000 of the retainage balance at December 31, 1980, will be collected in 1981.

The unbilled recoverable costs and accrued profits on contracts in process represent revenues which have been recognized in the financial statements because the related costs have been incurred but which were not yet billed to customers under the terms of the contract.

Deferred contract revenues are included in accrued liabilities.

2.4. CHAMPION SPARK PLUG COMPANY

FIFO vs. LIFO inventory valuation, cumulative and specific year effects. (Straightforward: 45 minutes)

Champion Spark Plug Company is a worldwide firm involved principally in the manufacture, distribution, and marketing of spark plugs, windshield wipers, and other automotive components. Through subsidiaries, Champion is also engaged in manufacturing coating application equipment, health-care equipment, and cold-drawn steel. Champion makes more than 850 types of spark plugs, diesel-starting glow plugs, and related items for a wide array of power-driven devices.

Study Champion's Consolidated Statements of Earnings for 1978–80, Consolidated Balance Sheets for 1979–80 and 1978–79 (assets section only), and note to the 1980 Financial Statements, "Inventories: Change to LIFO in 1979."

1. Using the financial statements provided, identify the unknowns in the table below. Assume that the effective tax rate for Champion during 1979 and 1980 was 46 percent. (Since it is actually a fraction less than 46 percent, any minor "unexplained" differences can be attributed to rounding errors.)

	1980	1979	1978
Inventories on LIFO basis	a	b	N.A.*
Inventories on FIFO basis	c	d	e
Cumulative impact of switch to LIFO as of December 31 on pretax basis	f	g	N.A.
Specific-year impact of switch to LIFO on pretax basis	h	N.A.	N.A.
Specific-year impact of switch to LIFO on after-tax basis	i	N.A.	N.A.

*N.A. = not available.

2. Provide a journal entry to change Champion's method of pricing

inventory from FIFO to LIFO; assume the entry was made on December 31, 1979. How does this entry affect Champion's 1978 Balance Sheet and Statement of Earnings?

3. Champion's operating earnings decreased slightly from $118.2 million in 1978 to $114.1 million in 1979. After fully recognizing the effects of the switch to LIFO on 1978 and 1979 income, assess the extent of change in operating earnings. In other words, of the earnings change, how much appears to be due to change in accounting rules for inventories and how much appears to be due to economic activity? (*Note:* A precise numerical solution is not possible.)

4. In nontechnical language, explain what the company is trying to tell its stockholders in the third paragraph of the note entitled "Inventories: Change to LIFO in 1979."

Consolidated Statements of Earnings

CHAMPION SPARK PLUG COMPANY

Years ended December 31, 1980, 1979 and 1978 *(In millions, except per share)*	1980	1979	1978
Net sales	$799.8	$806.5	$692.6
Costs and expenses:			
Cost of goods sold	535.9	516.0	421.4
Selling, administrative and general expenses	190.6	176.4	153.0
	726.5	692.4	574.4
Operating earnings	73.3	114.1	118.2
Other income:			
Interest and dividends	4.5	6.0	4.3
Sundry—net	2.9	1.5	.8
	7.4	7.5	5.1
	80.7	121.6	123.3
Other deductions:			
Interest expense	11.4	7.3	6.3
Amortization of goodwill	.8	.8	.7
Prior year loss arising from translation of a capitalized foreign lease	—	—	1.3
Net loss due to foreign currency fluctuations	1.9	.9	.1
	14.1	9.0	8.4
Earnings before taxes based on income	66.6	112.6	114.9
State and local taxes based on income	2.2	5.0	5.2
Earnings before federal and foreign income taxes	64.4	107.6	109.7
Federal and foreign income taxes	25.5	49.0	52.9
Net earnings before minority interests	38.9	58.6	56.8
Minority interests in net earnings of consolidated subsidiaries	2.0	1.7	1.5
Net earnings	$ 36.9	$ 56.9	$ 55.3
Net earnings per share	$ .96	$1.49	$1.45

Consolidated Balance Sheets

CHAMPION SPARK PLUG COMPANY

ASSETS *December 31, 1980 and 1979* *(Dollars in millions)*	1980	1979
Current Assets:		
Cash	$ 8.1	$ 10.6
Marketable securities, at cost which approximates market	12.4	32.8
Accounts receivable, less allowances of $4.1 million and $3.1 million	136.0	125.8
Current portion of notes receivable	1.3	1.3
Inventories	261.4	240.8
Prepaid expenses	8.9	5.9
Total current assets	428.1	417.2
Notes receivable and other assets	9.5	11.1
Property, plant and equipment, at cost:		
Land and land improvements	8.3	8.2
Buildings	105.0	94.1
Machinery and equipment	188.5	175.6
Construction in progress	17.6	9.2
	319.4	287.1
Less accumulated depreciation and amortization	138.1	122.6
Net property, plant and equipment	181.3	164.5
Intangible assets, at amortized cost	17.3	18.0
	$636.2	$610.8

II. CURRENT ASSETS

LIABILITIES AND STOCKHOLDERS' EQUITY _(Dollars in millions)_	1980	1979
Current liabilities:		
Notes payable to banks...	$ 40.9	$ 19.3
Current portion of long-term debt	5.4	5.0
Accounts payable	52.3	52.3
Accrued expenses:		
Salaries and wages...	14.4	12.9
Taxes, other than federal and foreign income taxes	9.1	9.8
Pension and other	26.2	20.9
Federal and foreign income taxes	14.6	19.7
Total current liabilities	162.9	139.9
Non-current portion of long-term debt:		
5⅞% debentures due September 15, 1992 (net of $4.1 million and $5.5 million reacquired)	13.9	14.0
Unsecured notes payable	6.0	9.0
Capital lease obligations and other...................................	21.5	21.4
Total non-current portion of long-term debt	41.4	44.4
Deferred income	7.3	8.1
Deferred federal and foreign income taxes	10.6	12.7
Minority interests in subsidiary companies	8.1	6.5
Stockholders' equity:		
Common stock of 30¢ par value per share.		
Authorized 40,000,000 shares; issued 38,292,757 and 38,260,728 shares	11.5	11.5
Capital in excess of par value	18.4	18.0
Retained earnings	376.0	369.7
Total stockholders' equity	405.9	399.2
	$ 636.2	$ 610.8

Consolidated Balance Sheets

CHAMPION SPARK PLUG COMPANY

ASSETS	1979	1978
Current Assets:		
Cash	$ 10,594,055	$ 12,137,198
Marketable securities, at cost which approximates market	32,776,831	32,183,253
Accounts receivable, less allowances of $ 3,126,000 and $ 2,488,000	125,825,970	113,110,560
Current portion of notes receivable	1,246,400	1,246,400
Inventories	240,812,523	227,091,343
Prepaid expenses	5,938,104	5,801,327
Total current assets	417,193,883	391,570,081
Notes receivable and other assets	11,098,313	9,469,437
Property, plant and equipment, at cost:		
Land and land improvements	8,232,174	8,174,386
Buildings	94,085,302	89,513,229
Machinery and equipment	175,611,880	164,182,022
Construction in progress	9,160,076	5,980,900
	287,089,432	267,850,537
Less accumulated depreciation and amortization	122,605,393	108,800,675
Net property, plant and equipment	164,484,039	159,049,862
Intangible assets, at amortized cost	18,022,323	20,043,789
	$ 610,798,558	$ 580,133,169

II. CURRENT ASSETS

In 1979 the Company adopted the last-in, first-out (LIFO) method of determining costs for substantially all of its U. S. inventories. In prior years, inventory values were principally computed under the lower of cost or market, first-in, first-out (FIFO) method. The effect of the change on the operating results for 1979 was to reduce net earnings by $5.8 million, or $.15 per share.

Inventory balances at December 31, 1980 and 1979 would have been $26.8 million and $ 10.7 million higher respectively if U. S. inventory costs had continued to be determined principally under FIFO rather than LIFO. Net earnings on a primarily FIFO method basis would have been $45.6 million or $ 1.19 per share compared to $62.7 million or $ 1.64 per share in 1979.

During 1980 certain inventory balances declined below below the levels at the beginning of the year resulting in a smaller increase in the LIFO reserve than would have occurred if these inventory levels had not declined. Net earnings in 1980 would have been $ 1.3 million ($.03 per share) lower had the LIFO reserve addition not been affected by reduced inventories.

It was not practical to determine prior year effects of retroactive LIFO application.

2.5. TEXACO INC. AND SUBSIDIARY COMPANIES

Inventory valuation and unrealized holding gains.
(Moderate: 45 minutes)

Texaco Inc., together with subsidiary and nonsubsidiary companies (those companies owned 50 percent or less), is engaged in the world-wide exploration for and production, transportation, refining, and marketing of crude oil and its products, including petrochemicals. In 1980, Texaco achieved the highest earnings in its seventy-eight-year history.

Study the comparative Statements of Consolidated Income and Retained Earnings for 1978–80 and the assets section of the Consolidated Balance Sheet as of December 31, 1979–80. Notes 1, 2, and 4 to those consolidated statements are also given.

1. Determine the unrealized holding gains (losses) associated with the "Crude Oil, Petroleum Products and Other Merchandise" inventories as of December 31, 1979 and 1980.

2. If Texaco had used current replacement-cost accounting for "Crude Oil, Petroleum Products and Petrochemicals" inventories, what would have been reported as Net Income? (Assume that all other asset and liability values are "in line" with replacement cost.)

3. What was the impact of the LIFO extension by Texaco and Caltex on 1979 net income (ignore tax effects)? What was the impact on 1980 net income? Explain why the 1979 and 1980 effects of switching to LIFO differ in magnitude and direction of impact on profit.

4. Was the LIFO method reported consistently for 1978, 1979, and 1980? Explain the essential differences, if any.

Statements of Consolidated Income and Retained Earnings

For the years ended December 31, 1980, 1979, and 1978

	1980	1979	1978
Revenues:			
Sales and services (includes sales to a significant nonsubsidiary company of $8 billion in 1980, $5.1 billion in 1979, and $4 billion in 1978)	$51,195,830,000	$38,350,370,000	$28,607,521,000
Equity in net income of nonsubsidiary companies, dividends, interest, and other income	1,288,810,000	745,074,000	516,622,000
	$52,484,640,000	$39,095,444,000	$29,124,143,000
Deductions:			
Costs and operating expenses (includes purchases from significant nonsubsidiary companies of $25.1 billion in 1980, $16.3 billion in 1979, and $10.9 billion in 1978)	$43,888,794,000	$31,839,520,000	$23,992,642,000
Selling, general and administrative expenses	1,252,134,000	1,145,561,000	976,467,000
Maintenance and repairs	713,948,000	470,215,000	419,866,000
Dry hole expenses	158,020,000	154,733,000	108,253,000
Depreciation, depletion, and amortization	1,105,915,000	1,086,158,000	969,871,000
Interest charges—indebtedness	146,593,000	263,896,000	271,461,000
—capital lease obligations	73,922,000	76,635,000	81,984,000
Taxes other than income taxes*	987,990,000	561,450,000	482,460,000
Provision for income taxes—current	1,946,100,000	1,589,100,000	682,200,000
—deferred	(68,412,000)	118,697,000	271,195,000
Minority interest in net income	39,397,000	30,410,000	15,283,000
	$50,244,401,000	$37,336,375,000	$28,271,682,000
Net Income:			
Net income before extraordinary credit	$ 2,240,239,000	$ 1,759,069,000	$ 852,461,000
Extraordinary credit—Gain on sale of interest in Belridge Oil Company less applicable income taxes of $186.2 million	402,303,000	—	—
Net income	$ 2,642,542,000	$ 1,759,069,000	$ 852,461,000
Net income per share before extraordinary credit	$8.31	$6.48	$3.14
Extraordinary credit per share	1.48	—	—
Net income per share	$9.79	$6.48	$3.14
(Based on average number of shares outstanding: 1980—269,791,000; 1979—271,446,000; and 1978—271,454,000)			
Retained Earnings:			
Balance at beginning of year	$ 8,363,536,000	$ 7,179,925,000	$ 6,870,372,000
Add: Net income for the year	2,642,542,000	1,759,069,000	852,461,000
Deduct: Cash dividends—$2.45 per share in 1980, $2.12 per share in 1979, and $2.00 per share in 1978	661,136,000	575,458,000	542,908,000
Balance at end of year	$10,344,942,000	$ 8,363,536,000	$ 7,179,925,000

*In addition, motor fuel, value added, and other taxes collected from consumers for governmental agencies in the United States and abroad amounted to $3,512,166,000 during 1980, $3,116,214,000 during 1979, and $2,631,320,000 during 1978.

Consolidated Balance Sheet

As of December 31, 1980 and 1979

Assets	1980	1979
Current Assets:		
Cash	$ 333,982,000	$ 456,238,000
Cash investments and marketable securities—at cost	2,685,834,000	1,568,817,000
Accounts and notes receivable (includes receivables from significant nonsubsidiary companies of $684.9 million in 1980 and $859.1 million in 1979), less allowance for doubtful accounts of $26.5 million in 1980 and $31.1 million in 1979	5,856,472,000	5,109,281,000
Inventories	3,319,056,000	3,253,429,000
Prepaid expenses and deferred income taxes	324,287,000	91,631,000
Total current assets	$12,519,631,000	$10,479,396,000
Investments and Advances	$ 1,746,806,000	$ 1,775,189,000
Properties, Plant, and Equipment—at Cost:		
Producing	$10,937,022,000	$ 9,539,016,000
Manufacturing	3,676,569,000	3,538,248,000
Petrochemical	1,119,309,000	963,619,000
Marketing	2,434,636,000	2,379,696,000
Marine	1,462,253,000	1,422,320,000
Pipe lines	375,335,000	367,267,000
Other	369,527,000	311,390,000
	$20,374,651,000	$18,521,556,000
Less—Depreciation, depletion, and amortization	8,617,053,000	7,738,327,000
Net properties, plant, and equipment	$11,757,598,000	$10,783,229,000
Deferred Charges	$ 406,320,000	$ 260,046,000
Total	$26,430,355,000	$23,297,860,000

Certain balance sheet accounts have been reclassified to conform with the 1980 presentation.
Texaco follows the "successful efforts" method of accounting for its oil and gas exploration and producing operations.

II. CURRENT ASSETS

Notes to Consolidated Financial Statements

Note 1.
Revisions in Accounting Policies

During the first quarter of 1980, Texaco revised its method of accounting for periodic maintenance and repairs applicable to marine vessels and manufacturing facilities from an incurred to an accrual basis. This change was made to provide a better matching of costs and revenues. Normal maintenance and repairs of all other properties, plant, and equipment are charged to expense as incurred. The cumulative effect of this accounting change for periods prior to January 1, 1980, which has been reflected as a reduction in 1980 net income, amounted to $66,300,000, net of income taxes, or $.25 per share.

In accordance with Financial Accounting Standards Board Statement No. 34, which was effective as of January 1, 1980, Texaco capitalized interest costs during 1980 on major construction and development projects in progress. Of the $276,154,000 worldwide interest costs on indebtedness and capital lease obligations incurred by Texaco during 1980, $55,639,000 was capitalized as part of the costs of major projects in progress and, after applicable income taxes, 1980 net income was increased $38,873,000, or $.14 per share.

Effective January 1, 1979, Texaco revised its method of accounting for inventories of crude oil, petroleum products, and petrochemicals by extending the last-in, first-out (LIFO) accounting method to virtually all such inventories outside the United States. Under the LIFO method, the effect of increased costs on earnings is recognized more promptly than under the first-in, first-out (FIFO) method previously followed. The extension of the LIFO method to areas outside the United States reduced net income for the year 1979 by $732,200,000, or $2.70 per share.

The Caltex Petroleum Corporation (Caltex), a 50% owned company, also extended the LIFO accounting method to inventories of crude oil, petroleum products, and petrochemicals of virtually all of its subsidiary companies as well as its interests in the inventories of its principal nonsubsidiary companies, effective January 1, 1979. This extension of the LIFO method resulted in a decrease of $116,000,000, or $.43 per share, in the 1979 consolidated net income of Texaco, which accounts for its investment in Caltex on the equity method.

With respect to the extension of the LIFO method by both Texaco and Caltex in 1979, the net income of prior years is not affected, because under generally accepted accounting principles a change of accounting to adopt LIFO is not applied retroactively to prior years.

Note 2.
Extraordinary Credit

On December 10, 1979, a majority of the shareholders of Belridge Oil Company (Belridge), in which Texaco owned a capital stock interest of 17.04%, approved a merger offer of Shell Oil Company to acquire the outstanding shares of Belridge for $3,665 per share. Texaco voted its 17.04% capital stock interest in Belridge against the merger offer.

As of December 31, 1979 and until January 11, 1980, at which time Texaco delivered its shares in Belridge, Texaco remained a shareholder in Belridge entitled to the rights and privileges of a shareholder.

On January 17, 1980, Texaco received $3,665 per share for its interest in Belridge, or a total of $622,600,000. The effect of this extraordinary credit was an increase in net income for the year 1980 of $402,303,000, or $1.48 per share, after provision for applicable income taxes of $186,200,000.

Note 4.
Inventories

The inventories of Texaco Inc. and subsidiary companies were as follows:

As of December 31,	1980	1979
Crude oil	$1,264,181,000	$1,315,182,000
Petroleum products and other merchandise	1,756,326,000	1,728,932,000
	$3,020,507,000	$3,044,114,000
Materials and supplies	298,549,000	209,315,000
Total	$3,319,056,000	$3,253,429,000

The excess of estimated current cost over the LIFO value of crude oil, petroleum products, and petrochemicals was approximately $4,874,000,000 and $2,613,000,000 at December 31, 1980 and 1979, respectively.

As of December 31, 1980, worldwide inventories accounted for on the LIFO basis were partially liquidated, resulting in inventory costs prevailing in prior years, which were lower than current year's costs, being charged to 1980 cost of sales. These lower costs increased 1980 net income by approximately $98,900,000, after applicable income taxes.

2.6.   U & I INCORPORATED AND SUBSIDIARIES*

LIFO vs. FIFO, disposal of inventory.
(Difficult: 75 minutes)

U & I Incorporated operates in two principal industries: farming and related processing, and warehousing and distribution. Previously involved in sugar-processing operations, the company announced in November 1978 that its sugar factories and terminals were for sale. Sugar inventories were liquidated mainly during the fiscal years 1980 and 1981.

Study the accompanying portions of U & I Incorporated's statements: (1) Consolidated Statements of Financial Position for 1974–75 and 1975–76, and Notes D and B to those respective statements; (2) Consolidated Statements of Earnings and Earnings Retained for Use in the Business for 1974–75 and 1975–76; and (3) Consolidated Statements of Financial Position and Operations for 1980–81, together with Notes B, D, and I to those statements.

1. Identify or compute the end-of-year values for inventories on the LIFO and FIFO accounting methods. Prepare your answer in a tabular format such as the following:

	YEAR ENDED FEBRUARY 28(29)th		
Inventories	1976	1975	1974
FIFO valuation			
LIFO valuation			
Difference (FIFO–LIFO)			

---

*Based on earlier cases by Robert K. Jaedicke and James M. Patell.

2. a. If U & I had used FIFO instead of LIFO for the granulated sugar part of the inventory, what effect would this have had on the 1975 and 1976 Statements of Financial Position? Ignore tax effects.

   b. If U & I had used FIFO instead of LIFO for the granulated sugar part of the inventory, what effect would this have had on the 1975 and 1976 Earnings before Taxes? Ignore tax effects.

3. a. Assume that U & I pays taxes on profits at the rate of 40 percent. What effect would the use of FIFO have on the 1975 and 1976 Statements of Financial Position? (Note: This is the same question as 2a except that the tax rate is assumed to be 40 percent.)

   b. Assume that U & I pays taxes on profits at the rate of 40 percent. What effect would the use of FIFO have on the 1975 and 1976 Earnings before Taxes, Taxes, and Earnings after Taxes?

4. Comment on the nature and impact of sugar price movements during 1974–76. Did U & I make a sound business decision to adopt the LIFO method for valuing sugar inventories prior to 1974? Aside from tax considerations, what other factors might have influenced the firm's decision at the time?

5. From 1976 to 1981, U & I reduced its inventories of sugar and sugar-related products substantially. In 1976, for instance, sugar inventories on a LIFO basis were $38,505,138, whereas in 1980 and 1981 sugar inventories on a LIFO basis were $1,585,000* and $900,000, respectively (*this excludes inventories of $5,455,000 relating to discontinued operations). If U & I had used FIFO consistently during 1976–81, how much different would "cumulative earnings before taxes" have been as of February 28, 1981? Cumulative earnings represents the sum of earnings for those years. However, it is not necessary to calculate each year's change individually.

6. a. If U & I had used FIFO during 1981 and earlier, what would the Gain (Loss) on Disposal before Income Taxes have been? See Note B, "Discontinuance of Sugar Processing Operations." Use a 35 percent tax rate, excluding investment tax recapture of $1,244,000, assumed to remain unchanged if the gain (loss) is reported on a FIFO basis.

   b. Restate 1981 Net Earnings (Loss) on the FIFO basis (assuming that FIFO had been used during 1980, 1981, and earlier).

Consolidated Statements of Financial Position

UTAH-IDAHO SUGAR COMPANY
AND SUBSIDIARIES

ASSETS	February 28 1975	February 28 1974 Restated Note C
Current Assets		
Cash	$ 2,658,528	$ 2,425,768
Trade and other receivables, less allowances for doubtful accounts, and discounts of $323,552 in 1975 and $312,911 in 1974	11,495,101	11,502,218
Claims for income tax refunds	1,113,602	
Inventories (first-in, first-out method would be $105,466,988 higher in 1975 and $18,723,033 higher in 1974)—Note D	44,846,014	42,114,796
Prepaid expenses	2,865,375	1,281,290
Total Current Assets	62,978,620	57,324,072
Other Assets—principally investments— at cost	1,940,736	943,977
Property, Plant, and Equipment—at cost less allowances for depreciation— Note E	77,208,214	56,197,911
	$142,127,570	$114,465,960

II. CURRENT ASSETS

Consolidated Statements of Earnings and Earnings Retained for Use in the Business

UTAH-IDAHO SUGAR COMPANY
AND SUBSIDIARIES

	Year Ended 1975	February 28 1974
		Restated—Note C
Revenues		
Sales of refined sugar and other products	**$237,429,801**	$142,560,928
Interest and other revenues	**1,367,918**	572,299
Total Revenues	**238,797,719**	143,133,227
Costs and Expenses		
Cost of sales	**209,330,935**	111,175,068
Selling expenses and excise tax on sugar	**18,046,596**	19,668,936
Interest, including $1,491,887 in 1975 and		
$1,396,585 in 1974 on long-term debt	**2,221,166**	2,031,706
	229,598,697	132,875,710
Earnings Before Income Taxes	**9,199,022**	10,257,517
Income taxes		
Current federal and state income taxes	**2,698,503**	4,305,825
Deferred federal income taxes	**759,623**	517,963
	3,458,126	4,823,788
Net Earnings	**5,740,896**	5,433,729
Earnings Retained for Use in the Business		
Dividends paid on Preferred Stock:		
Class A—$1.265 per share in 1975 and 1974	**124,501**	124,501
Class B—$1.265 per share in 1975 and 1974	**124,508**	124,508
Earnings Available to Common Stock	**5,491,887**	5,184,720
Amount at beginning of year as previously reported		29,197,096
Restatement to show settlement with Internal Revenue Service—Note C		(851,714)
Amount at beginning of year as restated	**32,722,030**	28,345,382
Dividends paid on Common Stock—$.80 per share in 1975 and $.35 per share in 1974	**1,832,046**	808,072
Retained Earnings at End of Year	**$ 36,381,871**	$ 32,722,030

Consolidated Statements of Financial Position

U and I INCORPORATED AND SUBSIDIARIES

Assets	February 29 1976	February 28 1975 Restated
CURRENT ASSETS		
Cash	$ 4,269,384	$ 2,658,528
Trade and other receivables, less allowances for doubtful accounts and discounts of $325,000 in 1976 and $324,000 in 1975	13,223,751	11,495,101
Claims for income tax refunds		1,113,602
Inventories (first-in, first-out method would be $49,788,076 higher in 1976 and $105,466,988 higher in 1975)—Note B	55,772,773	44,846,014
Prepaid expenses	2,450,604	2,865,375
TOTAL CURRENT ASSETS	75,716,512	62,978,620
OTHER ASSETS	2,413,291	1,940,736
PROPERTY, PLANT, AND EQUIPMENT—at cost less allowances for depreciation—Note E	84,170,519	77,208,214
	$162,300,322	$142,127,570

II. CURRENT ASSETS

Consolidated Statements of Earnings and Retained Earnings

U and I INCORPORATED AND SUBSIDIARIES

	Year Ended	
	February 29 1976	February 28 1975 Restated
REVENUES		
Sales of refined sugar and other products	**$199,965,391**	$237,429,801
Interest and other revenues	**698,225**	1,367,918
TOTAL REVENUES	**200,663,616**	238,797,719
COSTS AND EXPENSES		
Cost of sales	**159,651,588**	209,330,935
Selling expenses including excise tax on sugar	**20,162,600**	18,046,596
Interest, including $1,714,393 in 1976 and		
$1,491,887 in 1975 on long-term debt	**2,164,727**	2,221,166
	181,978,915	229,598,697
EARNINGS BEFORE INCOME TAXES	**18,684,701**	9,199,022
INCOME TAXES		
Current federal and state income taxes	**7,429,810**	2,698,503
Deferred federal income taxes	**579,869**	759,623
	8,009,679	3,458,126
NET EARNINGS	**10,675,022**	5,740,896
RETAINED EARNINGS		
Dividends paid on Preferred Stock:		
Class A—$1.265 per share	**124,501**	124,501
Class B—$1.265 per share	**124,508**	124,508
EARNINGS AVAILABLE TO		
COMMON STOCK	**10,426,013**	5,491,887
Amount at beginning of year as previously reported		32,722,030
Restatement to record change in accounting		
for self-insurance—Note C		1,179,430
Amount at beginning of year as restated	**37,561,301**	33,901,460
Dividends paid on Common Stock—$1.65 per		
share in 1976 and $.80 per share in 1975	**3,746,987**	1,832,046
RETAINED EARNINGS AT END		
OF YEAR	**$ 44,240,327**	$ 37,561,301

Notes to Consolidated Financial Statements

UTAH-IDAHO SUGAR COMPANY
AND SUBSIDIARIES

Years ended February 28, 1975 and 1974

NOTE D—Inventories and Change in Accounting Principle

	1975	1974
Granulated sugar, thick juice, beets and molasses —at lower of cost (last-in, first-out method) or market	$30,210,363	$31,625,017
Dried beet pulp, operating materials and supplies, farm products and other inventories—at lower of cost (first-in, first-out method) or market	14,635,651	10,489,779
	$44,846,014	$42,114,796

Effective March 1, 1974, the Company changed to the dollar-value method (from the specific-goods method) of determining last-in, first-out (LIFO) inventory valuations.

Notes to Consolidated Financial Statements

U and I INCORPORATED AND SUBSIDIARIES

Years ended February 29, 1976 and February 28, 1975

NOTE B—INVENTORIES

Inventories at each year end were as follows:

	1976	1975
Granulated sugar, thick juice, beets and molasses—at lower of cost (last-in, first-out method) or market	$38,505,138	$30,210,363
Dried beet pulp, operating materials and supplies, farm products and other inventories—at lower of cost (first-in, first-out method) or market	17,267,635	14,635,651
	$55,772,773	$44,846,014

II. CURRENT ASSETS

Consolidated Statements of Operations

U and I INCORPORATED AND SUBSIDIARIES

	Year Ended		
	February 28 1981	February 29 1980	February 28 1979
REVENUES:			
Net sales	**$79,928,000**	$64,333,000	$58,545,000
Gain on sale of farm real estate	**6,547,000**		
Other income	**1,085,000**	689,000	122,000
	87,560,0000	65,022,000	58,667,000
COSTS AND EXPENSES:			
Cost of sales	**79,640,000**	63,450,000	52,998,000
Selling expenses	**2,649,000**	2,794,000	2,232,000
Interest—Note C	**3,399,000**	2,336,000	1,920,000
	85,687,000	68,580,000	57,150,000
EARNINGS (LOSS) FROM CONTINUING OPERATIONS BEFORE INCOME TAXES (CREDITS)	**1,873,000**	(3,558,000)	1,517,000
INCOME TAXES (CREDITS)—Note I:	**(2,408,000)**	(2,900,000)	700,000
EARNINGS (LOSS) FROM CONTINUING OPERATIONS	**4,281,000**	(658,000)	817,000
DISCONTINUED SUGAR PROCESSING OPERATIONS—Notes B and 1:			
Loss from operations, less applicable income tax credits			(8,852,000)
Gain on disposal, less provision for estimated additional phase-out costs and applicable income taxes	**802,000**		
NET EARNINGS (LOSS)	**$ 5,083,000**	$ (658,000)	$ (8,035,000)

Consolidated Statements of Financial Position

U and I INCORPORATED AND SUBSIDIARIES

	February 28 1981	February 28 1980
ASSETS		
Assets Applicable To Continuing Operations		
CURRENT ASSETS		
Cash	$ 4,660,000	$ 974,000
Short-term investments		9,000,000
Trade and other receivables	6,894,000	12,742,000
Inventories—Notes D and E	24,872,000	15,530,000
Prepaid expenses and other current assets	5,741,000	3,590,000
	42,167,000	41,836,000
PROPERTY, PLANT, AND EQUIPMENT—		
Notes C and H		
Land and canals	15,580,000	15,985,000
Plant and equipment	75,784,000	58,382,000
Less allowances for depreciation	(24,205,000)	(21,468,000)
	67,159,000	52,899,000
TOTAL ASSETS APPLICABLE TO CONTINUING OPERATIONS	109,326,000	94,735,000
Assets Applicable to Discontinued Operations—Note B		
Inventories		5,455,000
Property, plant, and equipment:		
Land		2,209,000
Plant and equipment		83,621,000
Less net proceeds from assets sold and allowances for depreciation		(73,981,000)
		11,849,000
TOTAL ASSETS APPLICABLE TO DISCONTINUED OPERATIONS		17,304,000
	$109,326,000	$112,039,000

II. CURRENT ASSETS

	February 28 1981	February 28 1980
LIABILITIES AND STOCKHOLDERS' EQUITY		
Liabilities Applicable To Continuing Operations		
CURRENT LIABILITIES		
Notes payable—Note E	**$ 13,338,000**	$ -0-
Accounts payable and accrued expenses— Note F	**9,577,000**	14,452,000
Accrued phase-out costs—Note B	**3,073,000**	
Current portion of long-term debt	**2,871,000**	2,280,000
	28,859,000	16,732,000
LONG-TERM DEBT, less current portion— Note G	**25,292,000**	27,800,000
DEFERRED INCENTIVE COMPENSATION	**1,364,000**	1,381,000
MINORITY INTEREST IN SUBSIDIARIES	**330,000**	462,000
TOTAL LIABILITIES APPLICABLE TO CONTINUING OPERATIONS	**55,845,000**	46,375,000
Liabilities Applicable to Discontinued Operations—Note B		
Notes payable		7,058,000
Accounts payable and accrued expenses		2,323,000
Deferred federal income taxes		7,636,000
TOTAL LIABILITIES APPLICABLE TO DISCONTINUED OPERATIONS		17,017,000
STOCKHOLDERS' EQUITY		
Preferred Stock, 5.5% cumulative—par value $23 per share, callable at $25 per share; authorized 100,000 shares in each class; Class A—issued and outstanding 98,420 shares	**2,263,000**	2,263,000
Class B—issued and outstanding 98,425 shares	**2,264,000**	2,264,000
Common Stock—par value $5 per share: Authorized 3,500,000 shares; issued 2,373,000 shares, including shares in the treasury	**11,864,000**	11,865,000
Capital surplus	**78,000**	78,000
Retained earnings—Note G	**38,981,000**	34,147,000
	55,451,000	50,617,000
Less cost of 136,671 shares of Common Stock in the treasury	**1,970,000**	2,970,000
TOTAL STOCKHOLDERS' EQUITY	**53,481,000**	48,647,000
	$109,326,000	$112,039,000

NOTE B—Discontinuance of Sugar Processing Operations

The company announced in November 1978 that its sugar factories and terminals were for sale and, in January 1979, that it would close those sugar facilities for which it was unable to find buyers. In February 1979, the company adopted a plan for the sale or other disposal of the company's sugar facilities.

A substantial part of the sugar inventory associated with the discontinuance was sold during the year ended February 29, 1980 in accordance with the company's normal terms and prices. The remaining sugar inventory was sold during the year ended February 28, 1981 in the same manner. Since March 1979 the company has proceeded with its plan to sell or salvage sugar processing assets related to the discontinuance.

In accordance with Opinion No. 30 of the Accounting Principles Board of the American Institute of Certified Public Accountants, the recognition of the gain on disposal has been deferred until actually realized. Accordingly, the gain from the disposal of discontinued sugar processing assets over the last two years is shown in the accompanying Statements of Operations within the year ended February 28, 1981. Details of the gain are as follows:

Revenues	$134,888,000
Costs and expenses, including provision for estimated additional phase-out costs of $2,600,000	93,913,000
	40,975,000
Write-off of unsold assets	37,816,000
Gain on disposal before income taxes	3,159,000
Income taxes, including investment tax credit recapture of $1,244,000	2,357,000
Gain on disposal	$ 802,000

The above costs and expenses include sugar inventories valued at LIFO cost which was $48,804,000 less than FIFO cost. Certain assets with a net book value of approximately $2,630,000 were sold to another corporation in which a director of the company is a principal officer. For the year ended February 28, 1979, discontinued sugar processing operations had revenues of approximately $134,000,000 and $8,900,000 in tax benefits from losses for discontinued operations.

Management is continuing to sell or salvage the remaining sugar processing assets at as favorable a return to the company as is practical. Management is unable to predict when all of the remaining assets will be sold.

NOTE D—Inventories

Inventories are comprised of the following:

	February 28 1981	February 28 1980
Potatoes and farm products	$20,542,000	$10,676,000
Livestock, operating materials and supplies and other inventories	3,430,000	3,269,000
Sugar and related sugar products	900,000	1,585,000
	$24,872,000	$15,530,000

Inventories when valued at FIFO cost exceed the LIFO cost method by $3,104,000 at February 28, 1981 and $2,651,000 at February 29, 1980.

NOTE I—INCOME TAXES

The provision for income taxes is comprised of the following:

	Year Ended		
	February 28 1981	February 29 1980	February 28 1979
Current (benefit)	$(1,850,000)	$(1,750,000)	$ 400,000
Investment tax credits	(1,988,000)	(1,250,000)	(200,000)
	(3,838,000)	(3,000,000)	200,000
Deferred	1,430,000	100,000	500,000
	$(2,408,000)	$(2,900,000)	$ 700,000

The sources and related deferred tax expense resulting from timing differences in recognition of revenue and expense for income tax and financial reporting purposes are as follows:

	Year Ended		
	February 28 1981	February 29 1980	February 28 1979
Accelerated depreciation	$ 881,000	$ 85,000	$ 361,000
Capitalized interest	309,000		
All others	240,000	15,000	139,000
	$ 1,430,000	$ 100,000	$ 500,000

The differences between the provision for income taxes and the amount computed by applying the federal statutory income tax rate are as follows:

	Year Ended		
	February 28 1981	February 29 1980	February 28 1979
Computed "expected" tax (46% in 1981 and 1980, and 48% in 1979) on earnings (loss)	$ 862,000	$(1,637,000)	$ 728,000
Increases (decreases) in taxes resulting from:			
Investment tax credit	(1,988,000)	(1,250,000)	(200,000)
Tax rate differential, primarily capital gains	(1,171,000)		
Allowance for real estate revaluation	(167,000)		
State income taxes, net of federal benefit	28,000	(60,000)	140,000
All others	28,000	47,000	32,000
	$(2,408,000)	$(2,900,000)	$ 700,000

The provision for income taxes has been calculated in conjunction with income taxes applicable to discontinued operations (Note B). Income tax benefits or charges have been classified in accordance with the classification (as to continuing or discontinued operations) of the transaction which gives rise to such benefit or charge.

3.1. NCR CORPORATION

Purchase, rental, and disposal of property and equipment.
(Straightforward: 45 minutes)

NCR Corporation develops, manufactures, markets, installs, and services business information-processing systems for selected worldwide markets. The company offers a broad range of hardware and software. For instance, NCR's computers range from small business systems to powerful general-purpose processors and are supported by an array of terminals, office automation products, peripherals, data communications networks, and an extensive library of software products.

Study the 1980–81 Statement of Assets (from Consolidated Financial Position), Statement of Changes in Consolidated Financial Position, and Note 3, "Other (Income) Expenses," to the 1980–81 statements. Note 1, "Summary of Accounting Policies," states the following:

> Gain or loss realized on disposition of properties is included in income. Depreciation is computed over estimated useful lives primarily on the straight-line basis. Rental equipment and parts are depreciated at rates of 20% to 25% per annum.

In answering the questions below, assume that depreciation on rental equipment is calculated by multiplying the year-end acquisition cost of rental equipment by 20 percent.

1. Determine the acquisition cost of property, plant, and equipment disposed of (sold or scrapped) in 1981. Determine the cost of rental equipment and parts disposed of in 1981.

2. Assuming that all rental equipment and parts were disposed of at their book value (acquisition cost less accumulated depreciation) and that rental equipment was depreciated as indicated above, determine the book value of rental equipment and parts sold in 1981.

3. Estimate the cash sales price of property, plant, and equipment sold during 1981. How would that estimate change if the applicable marginal corporate tax rate was lowered from 46 percent (at present) to 25 percent? Explain.

Consolidated Financial Position

Assets

	December 31	
	1981	1980
	(000 omitted)	
Current assets		
Cash and short-term investments.	**$ 182,448**	$ 119,063
Accounts receivable, net	**1,025,116**	1,009,807
Inventories:		
Finished	**618,712**	672,218
In-process and raw materials.	**265,249**	345,332
	883,961	1,017,550
Other current assets.	**80,735**	90,607
Total current assets	**2,172,260**	2,237,027
Rental equipment and parts	**876,519**	829,034
Less: Accumulated depreciation	**574,404**	551,593
	302,115	277,441
Property, plant and equipment		
Land	**32,759**	30,977
Buildings.	**411,431**	382,266
Machinery and equipment	**597,412**	540,873
	1,041,602	954,116
Less: Accumulated depreciation	**479,608**	436,701
	561,994	517,415
Excess of acquisition cost over net assets of businesses acquired, net of amortization	**132,168**	136,132
Other assets	**217,997**	198,440
Total assets.	**$3,386,534**	$3,366,455

Changes in Consolidated Financial Position

| | Year ended December 31 | | |
	1981	1980	1979
		(000 omitted)	
Cash provided by operations			
Net income.	$ 208,234	$ 254,686	$ 234,602
Items not requiring current outflow of cash:			
Depreciation	243,846	227,101	209,672
Net book value of rental equipment and			
other properties sold	48,863	35,468	49,879
Other	17,123	16,953	20,741
Current items*	141,042	(301,910)	(156,410)
Total provided by operations	659,108	232,298	358,484
Cash (used for) operations			
Additions to rental equipment and parts	(222,986)	(207,629)	(196,181)
Additions to property, plant and equipment	(138,976)	(163,677)	(125,413)
Excess of acquisition cost over net assets			
of businesses acquired	—	(24,312)	(118,086)
Total (used for) operations	(361,962)	(395,618)	(439,680)
Net cash provided by (used for) operations	297,146	(163,320)	(81,196)
Cash provided by (used for) financing and investment activities			
Notes payable and commercial paper	(114,207)	209,372	41,810
Current installments on long-term debt	(351)	8,206	(642)
Issuance of long-term debt	30,763	10,772	14,402
Retirement of long-term debt	(52,645)	(33,800)	(17,625)
Issuance of common stock and treasury stock	13,336	26,466	95,178
Purchase of treasury stock	(13,779)	(46)	(110,700)
Cash dividends declared	(58,923)	(52,936)	(42,353)
Non-current other assets	(37,955)	(33,904)	1,288
Net cash provided by (used for) financing and investment activities . . .	(233,761)	134,130	(18,642)
Increase (decrease) in cash and short-term investments	$ 63,385	$ (29,190)	$ (99,838)
***Current items**			
Note receivable	$ —	$ —	$ 173,505
Accounts receivable, net	(15,309)	(55,532)	(287,014)
Inventories	133,589	(268,992)	(106,038)
Other current assets	9,872	5,345	(46,508)
Payables and other current liabilities	4,441	7,896	62,346
Customers' deposits and deferred service revenue	8,449	9,373	47,299
Total current items	$141,042	$(301,910)	$(156,410)

III.   PROPERTY, PLANT, AND EQUIPMENT

Note 3 — Other (Income) Expenses, Net. The composition of other (income) expense was as follows:

| | Year Ended December 31 | | |
	1981	1980	1979
		(000 omitted)	
Interest income (including financing income on accounts receivable)	$(50,460)	$(40,157)	$(46,722)
Dividend income	(3,700)	(3,142)	(2,482)
Foreign exchange (gain) loss, net	(14,118)	(5,905)	3,465
(Gain) on disposal of fixed assets .	(6,446)	(3,264)	(6,474)
(Gain) on disposal of marketable securities	—	—	(9,933)
Other	(18,787)	(16,119)	(10,497)
	$(93,511)	$(68,587)	$(72,643)

3.2. STAUFFER CHEMICAL COMPANY

Plant and other asset write-down, and disposal of plant.
(Moderate: 45 minutes)

Stauffer Chemical Company and its subsidiaries manufacture and sell chemicals and chemical-related products serving a broad variety of end-use markets. The largest markets are agriculture, building and construction, food systems, petroleum products and refining, packaging, transportation, consumer goods, textiles, and water treatment.

Study Stauffer's 1978–80 Statement of Consolidated Earnings, the assets section of its 1979–80 Consolidated Balance Sheet, the 1978–80 Statement of Changes in Consolidated Financial Position, and a note relating to facility disposals and asset write-downs.

1. Why is the Gain on Facility Disposals—Net subtracted out in the Statement of Changes in Financial Position when, in fact, the company made a substantial gain of facility disposals in 1980?

2. a. Prepare journal entries to record the facility disposals and asset write-downs that occurred during December 1980. Assume that the transaction took place on December 1, 1980.

   b. Prepare a journal entry, dated December 31, 1980, that would record the cash collected on the receivable (between date of disposal and year-end).

3. Current Assets Related to Facility Disposals increased by $155,897,000 during 1980. To what items does this number relate? Reconcile numerically.

STATEMENT OF CONSOLIDATED EARNINGS

Stauffer Chemical Company
and Subsidiaries

Year ended December 31	1980	1979	1978
	(Dollars in thousands, except per-share amounts)		
Revenues			
Net Sales	$1,695,219	$1,526,160	$1,328,114
Interest and Dividends	13,154	10,227	12,044
Total Revenues	**1,708,373**	**1,536,387**	**1,340,158**
Cost and Expenses			
Cost of Goods Sold	1,265,977	1,106,658	926,381
Selling, General and Administrative	190,957	161,866	135,883
Research and Development	44,351	36,963	33,562
Interest	41,791	31,839	37,923
Other Expense (Income) — Net	3,957	(3,730)	6,432
Minority Interest	23,136	16,555	10,206
Gain on Facility Disposals — Net	(10,815)		
Total Cost and Expenses	**1,559,354**	**1,350,151**	**1,150,387**
Earnings before Provision for Income Taxes	**149,019**	**186,236**	**189,771**
Provision for Income Taxes	**25,700**	**61,075**	**72,810**
Earnings from Consolidated Operations	**123,319**	**125,161**	**116,961**
Equity in Earnings of Associated Companies	**13,256**	**10,800**	**9,054**
Net Earnings	**$ 136,575**	**$ 135,961**	**$ 126,015**
Earnings per Common Share	**$ 3.11**	**$ 3.10**	**$ 2.88**

CONSOLIDATED BALANCE SHEET

Stauffer Chemical Company
and Subsidiaries

ASSETS	1980	1979
December 31	(Dollars in thousands)	
Current Assets		
Cash	$ 20,868	$ 24,712
Marketable Securities	54,085	31,191
Receivables:		
Trade — Net of Allowance for Doubtful Receivables: 1980 — $3,884; 1979 — $2,963	295,111	266,726
Notes and Other	66,692	41,836
Inventories:		
Finished Products and Work in Progress	219,359	226,195
Raw Materials and Supplies	85,828	92,548
Prepaid Expenses	18,208	15,489
Receivable from Facility Disposals	132,808	
Assets held for Disposal	23,089	
Total Current Assets	**916,048**	**698,697**
Property, Plant and Equipment		
Land	26,281	27,011
Buildings	184,588	186,130
Machinery and Equipment	1,472,428	1,417,536
Mineral Deposits	8,433	10,790
Property, Plant and Equipment — at Cost	**1,691,730**	**1,641,467**
Less: Accumulated Depreciation	618,834	600,925
Property, Plant and Equipment — Net	**1,072,896**	**1,040,542**
Investments and Other Assets		
Investments and Advances — Associated Companies	46,972	40,819
Intangibles Arising from Business Acquisitions	27,123	29,368
Other Assets	48,525	66,808
Total Investments and Other Assets	**122,620**	**136,995**
Total	**$2,111,564**	**$1,876,234**

III. PROPERTY, PLANT, AND EQUIPMENT

STATEMENT OF CHANGES IN CONSOLIDATED FINANCIAL POSITION

Stauffer Chemical Company
and Subsidiaries

Year ended December 31	1980	1979	1978
		(Dollars in thousands)	
Source of Working Capital			
Operations:			
Net Earnings	$136,575	$135,961	$126,015
Depreciation	110,756	93,064	78,340
Deferred Income Taxes	16,114	37,816	23,689
Gain on Facility Disposals — Net	(10,815)		
Other — Net	26,413	18,645	4,616
Provided from Operations	**279,043**	**285,486**	**232,660**
Funds Provided from Facility Disposals	109,969		
Long-term Debt Issued	21,040	9,475	9,736
Common Stock Issued	491	979	1,353
Other Property Disposals	6,108	6,125	5,474
Total Source	**416,651**	**302,065**	**249,223**
Application of Working Capital			
Capital Expenditures	246,454	239,303	201,196
Dividends Paid	51,598	47,132	42,660
Reduction of Long-term Debt	11,340	34,444	10,867
Acquisition — Net Non-current Assets			18,715
Other — Net	(9,073)	16,677	7,431
Total Application	**300,319**	**337,556**	**280,869**
Increase (Decrease) in Working Capital	**$116,332**	**$ (35,491)**	**$ (31,646)**
Change in Working Capital by Component			
Cash and Marketable Securities	$ 19,050	$ (33,104)	$ (7,777)
Receivables	53,241	48,056	48,300
Inventories	(13,556)	40,430	44,614
Prepaid Expenses	2,719	1,055	1,517
Current Assets Related to Facility Disposals	155,897		
Notes Payable	(65,119)	(60,858)	(112,451)
Accounts Payable	(23,878)	(19,751)	(7,470)
Income Taxes Payable	6,993	(2,778)	15,501
Other Current Liabilities	(4,908)	(8,541)	(13,880)
Accrued Shutdown Expenses	(14,107)		
Increase (Decrease) in Working Capital	**$116,332**	**$ (35,491)**	**$ (31,646)**

NOTES TO FINANCIAL STATEMENTS

FACILITY DISPOSALS AND ASSET WRITE-DOWNS

In December, 1980, the Company sold a major portion of its Fertilizer and Mining Division, comprised of phosphate rock reserves in Utah and associated mining and fertilizer manufacturing operations, and its Chemical Systems Division business. Also, the Company recorded asset write-downs (primarily plant and inventories) and estimated shutdown expenses (plant closing costs and 1981 operating losses) for other operations and properties, principally plastics resins, food ingredient products, and a phosphate rock-processing plant, which do not fit long-range plans. These assets (estimated net realizable value of $23,089,000) are currently shut down or the subject of negotiations for sale and are expected to be disposed of by the end of 1981.

Components of the net gain recorded in the fourth quarter of 1980 are summarized below:

	(In thousands)
Gain on facility disposals	$110,991
Write-down of assets to estimated net realizable value	(86,069)
Accrued shutdown expenses	(14,107)
Gain on facility disposals — net	**10,815**
Income tax credits	4,017
After-tax gain ($.34 per share)	**$ 14,832**

The current receivable due the company at December 31, 1980, from the facilities sold is $132,808,000, of which substantially all has been collected.

3.3. GOODYEAR TIRE AND RUBBER COMPANY, INC.

Depreciation accounting for property, plant, and equipment. (Straightforward: 45 minutes)

Goodyear is the world's largest manufacturer of tires and rubber products. The company operates over three thousand facilities around the world for the sale and distribution of its products. Goodyear also owns seven rubber plantations, a resort hotel, and a 12,260-acre farm for research, and it operates a uranium enrichment plant.

Study the Consolidated Statement of Income, the Consolidated Balance Sheet, the Consolidated Statement of Changes in Financial Position, and a relevant section from notes to the financial statements for the Goodyear Tire & Rubber Company for the year 1980 (with 1978 and 1979 comparative data where applicable). (Note: Certain items on the 1980 Consolidated Statement of Changes in Financial Position have been left blank on purpose.)

State the dollar amounts of:

1. a. Depreciation expense for 1980.

   b. Purchases of properties and plants during 1980, excluding capitalized interest.

2. a. Accumulated depreciation relating to properties and plants disposed of during 1980.

   b. Original acquisition cost of properties and plants disposed of during 1980, inclusive of capitalized interest.

3. a. Long-term debt additions (that is, fill in the space designated by the question mark in the 1980 column of the Consolidated Statement of Changes in Financial Position).

   b. Actual cash paid for long-term debt.

Consolidated Statement of Income
The Goodyear Tire & Rubber Company and Subsidiaries

(Dollars in thousands, except per share)	Year ended December 31,		
	1980	1979	1978
Net Sales.	$8,444,015	$8,238,676	$7,489,102
Other Income.	54,102	92,427	46,019
	8,498,117	8,331,103	7,535,121
Cost and Expenses:			
Cost of goods sold.	6,654,066	6,569,675	5,786,317
Selling, administrative and general expense.	1,263,913	1,193,327	1,103,103
Interest and amortization of debt discount and expense.	226,847	204,030	181,635
Plant closures and sale of facilities.	(16,764)	60,594	8,366
Foreign currency translation loss.	7,429	40,075	53,346
Minority interest in net income of foreign subsidiaries.	11,089	6,457	8,682
	8,146,580	8,074,158	7,141,449
Income before income taxes and extraordinary credit.	351,537	256,945	393,672
United States and foreign taxes on income.	144,826	110,761	167,545
Income before extraordinary credit.	206,711	146,184	226,127
Extraordinary credit — tax benefit of loss carryovers.	23,978	—	—
Net Income for the Year.	$ 230,689	$ 146,184	$ 226,127
Per Share:			
Income before extraordinary credit.	$2.85	$2.02	$3.12
Extraordinary credit.	.33	—	—
Net Income.	$3.18	$2.02	$3.12

III.   PROPERTY, PLANT, AND EQUIPMENT

Consolidated Balance Sheet
The Goodyear Tire & Rubber Company and Subsidiaries

	December 31, 1980	1979
ASSETS		
Current Assets:		
Cash and short term securities.	$ 67,823	$ 72,004
Accounts and notes receivable.	1,144,043	1,216,830
Inventories.	1,582,213	1,536,095
Prepaid expenses.	62,052	50,071
Total Current Assets.	2,856,131	2,875,000
Other Assets:		
Investments in and receivables from nonconsolidated subsidiaries and affiliates, at equity.	164,567	147,724
Long term accounts and notes receivable.	32,179	23,004
Investments and miscellaneous assets, at cost.	18,283	23,111
Deferred charges.	19,290	18,499
	234,319	212,338
Properties and Plants.	2,277,851	2,283,901
	$5,368,301	$5,371,239
LIABILITIES AND SHAREHOLDERS' EQUITY		
Current Liabilities:		
Accounts payable — trade.	$ 523,873	$ 492,060
Accrued payrolls and other compensation.	234,018	199,793
Other current liabilities.	155,453	165,359
United States and foreign taxes:		
Current.	170,353	145,272
Deferred.	113,229	114,810
Notes payable to banks and overdrafts.	147,109	182,871
Long term debt due within one year.	35,642	40,405
Total Current Liabilities.	1,379,677	1,340,570
Long Term Debt.	1,063,353	1,272,205
Long Term Capital Lease Obligations.	177,287	189,931
Other Long Term Liabilities.	176,607	158,493
Deferred Income Taxes.	202,997	192,173
Minority Equity in Foreign Subsidiary Companies.	65,880	54,517
Shareholders' Equity:		
Common stock, no par value:		
Authorized, 100,000,000 shares		
Outstanding shares, 71,761,086 (71,680,906 in 1979) after deducting 1,494,614 treasury shares (1,574,794 in 1979).	57,807	57,726
Capital surplus.	225,062	223,406
Retained earnings.	2,019,631	1,882,218
Total Shareholders' Equity.	2,302,500	2,163,350
	$5,368,301	$5,371,239

Consolidated Statement
of Changes in Financial Position
The Goodyear Tire & Rubber Company and Subsidiaries

(Dollars in thousands)		Year Ended December 31,	
	1980	1979	1978
Source of Working Capital:			
Income before extraordinary credit..........................	$ 206,711	$ 146,184	$ 226,127
Items not affecting working capital:			
Depreciation......................................		227,350	214,022
Deferred taxes.....................................	10,824	24,394	4,365
Plant closures.....................................	(5,312)	39,601	—
Other items.......................................	(6,921)	(10,263)	(5,343)
		281,082	213,044
Total from operations before extraordinary credit............	435,654	427,266	439,171
Extraordinary credit—tax benefit of loss carryovers..........	23,978	—	—
Total from operations.............................	459,632	427,266	439,171
Long term debt additions...............................		236,298	465,154
Long term capital lease obligation additions................	1,432	3,879	56,867
Common stock issued under employees' stock option			
and incentive profit sharing plans....................	1,737	2,136	1,151
Property and plant dispositions........................	24,300	29,452	10,000
Other items.	19,729	—	16,957
		699,031	989,300
Application of Working Capital:			
Property and plant expenditures........................	248,602	360,063	411,388
Long term debt reductions............................	406,536	182,475	213,940
Long term capital lease obligation reductions...............	14,076	13,988	15,499
Cash dividends.....................................	93,276	93,129	92,973
Other items.		10,757	—
		660,412	733,800
Increase (Decrease) in Working Capital.	$	$ 38,619	$ 255,500
Changes in Working Capital:			
Cash and short term securities..........................	$ (4,181)	$ (34,150)	$ 28,027
Accounts and notes receivable..........................	(72,787)	(4,475)	233,697
Inventories..	46,118	36,443	84,415
Prepaid expenses....................................	11,981	(4,331)	262
Accounts payable and accrued expenses..................	(56,132)	(66,379)	(129,853)
United States and foreign taxes.........................	(23,500)	56,448	25,603
Notes payable to banks and overdrafts....................	35,762	26,201	34,365
Long term debt due within one year.....................	4,763	28,862	(21,016)
Increase (Decrease) in Working Capital.	(57,976)	38,619	255,500
Working Capital at Beginning of Year.	1,534,430	1,495,811	1,240,311
Working Capital at End of Year.	$1,476,454	$1,534,430	$1,495,811

III.   PROPERTY, PLANT, AND EQUIPMENT

Notes to Financial Statements

Properties, Plants and Depreciation

(In thousands)	1980	1979
Land and improvements.	$ 207,201	$ 193,043
Buildings.	1,003,035	989,826
Machinery and equipment.	3,381,630	3,223,359
Construction in progress.	178,611	252,441
Properties and plants, at cost.	4,770,477	4,658,669
Less accumulated depreciation.	2,492,626	2,374,768
	$2,277,851	$2,283,901

Capital expenditures for expansion, modernization and replacement amounted to $248,602,000 (including $12,943,000 capitalized interest) in 1980 compared with $360,063,000 (including $18,904,000 capitalized interest) in 1979 and $411,388,000 in 1978.

3.4. CAMPBELL SOUP COMPANY—II

Plant assets, gains/losses on retirement, amortization
of intangibles. (Moderate: 60 minutes)

Study Campbell's 1979–81 Consolidated Statements of Changes in Financial Position and notes from the financial statements on Other Assets and Plant Assets. (*Note:* The numbers in this case should not be used in Case 1.4, Campbell Soup Company—I. Treat the cases as independent. All numbers are in thousands of dollars.)

1. Estimate the historical cost of Plant Assets sold during 1981.

2. Estimate the accumulated depreciation relating to Plant Assets sold during 1981.

3. Estimate what the loss of retirement (i.e., loss on "sale") would have been had Campbell's actually "sold" its Plant Assets for zero dollars in 1981. State the loss on a pretax basis.

4. Estimate the historical cost of Other Assets sold (or otherwise disposed of or retired) in 1981.

5. Assuming Other Assets sold at book value (acquisition cost less accumulated depreciation to date), what apparently was the gain or loss on Plant Assets actually sold during 1981?

6. Assume that the intangibles are being amortized on a straight-line basis over thirty years. Approximately when (i.e., in what month) were Goodwill and Other Intangibles of $48,480 ($133,950 − $85,470) acquired?

Consolidated Statements of Changes in Financial Position

	1981	1980	1979
		(000 omitted)	
Additions			
Net earnings	$129,717	$121,655	$132,744
Items not requiring the use of working capital			
Depreciation	75,118	67,958	60,360
Amortization of intangibles	4,300	1,758	3,067
Deferred income taxes	5,692	3,534	5,747
Other	789	1,677	64
Working capital from operations	215,616	196,582	201,982
Plant and other assets sold	13,268	13,806	4,170
Conversion to equity of advance to foreign supplier		20,000	
Treasury stock issued (23,219 shares—1981; 25,213 shares—1980; 90,078 shares—1979), at cost	693	827	2,766
Long-term debt incurred	36,114	109,855	5,337
Other liabilities incurred	13,421		
Additions to working capital	279,112	341,070	214,255
Deductions			
Plant assets purchased	135,402	97,391	108,132
Plant assets acquired	19,873	58,405	51,471
Dividends	66,298	61,479	57,304
Advance to foreign supplier			20,000
Goodwill and other assets	49,470	69,503	3,520
Treasury stock purchased (702,200 shares—1981; 79,600 shares—1980; 953,748 shares—1979)	21,754	2,405	32,849
Reduction in long-term debt	23,406	8,274	12,969
Other	291	172	194
Deductions from working capital	316,494	297,629	286,439
Increase (decrease) in working capital	$ (37,382)	$ 43,441	$ (72,184)
Increase (decrease) in working capital			
Cash and temporary investments	$ (18,059)	$ 53,515	$ (97,742)
Accounts receivable	11,555	32,692	32,469
Inventories	(16,819)	86,883	53,954
Prepaid expenses	6,821	7,800	9,530
Notes payable	3,877	(79,289)	(26,608)
Payable to suppliers and others	(16,411)	(37,276)	(9,608)
Dividend payable		14,503	(971)
Accrued liabilities	(8,346)	(35,387)	(33,208)
	$ (37,382)	$ 43,441	$ (72,184)

The accompanying Summary of Significant Accounting Policies and Notes are an integral part of the financial statements.

Campbell Soup Company—II

Other Assets, At Cost

	1981	1980
Intangibles		
Cost of investments over net assets of purchased companies	$ 128,233	$ 79,774
Other intangibles	5,717	5,696
	133,950	85,470
Accumulated amortization	(13,001)	(8,510)
	120,949	76,960
Other	1,564	755
	$ 122,513	$ 77,715

Plant Assets, At Cost

	1981	1980
Land	$ 68,617	$ 61,175
Buildings	430,834	413,074
Machinery and equipment	783,126	729,034
Projects in progress	86,086	45,452
	1,368,663	1,248,735
Accumulated depreciation	613,643	560,730
	$ 755,020	$ 688,005

Depreciation provided in costs and expenses was $75,118 in 1981, $67,958 in 1980 and $60,360 in 1979.

Approximately $96,000 is required to complete projects in progress at August 2, 1981.

III. PROPERTY, PLANT, AND EQUIPMENT

3.5. PORTLAND GENERAL ELECTRIC COMPANY AND SUBSIDIARIES

Interest capitalization, accounting for allowance of funds used during construction. (Difficult: 60 minutes)

Serving more than one million people, Portland General Electric (PGE) is Oregon's largest supplier of electricity. PGE serves the needs of fifty-four incorporated cities and 40 percent of the state's population in a compact 3,350-square-mile area.

Study PGE's Consolidated Statements of Income for 1975–79, Consolidated Statements of Changes in Financial Position for 1975–79, the assets section of the 1978–79 Balance Sheet, portions of Note 1 to the 1979 financial statements, and Note 2 to the statements on income tax expense. An extract from a paper by R. M. Bowen of the University of Washington is included also to provide some background to, and an explanation of, the concept of Allowance for Funds Used during Construction (AFDC).

1. For 1978 and 1979, provide journal entries that record outlays for interest costs (exclude Other Interest and Amortization and non-cash amounts credited to income for Allowance for Funds Used during Construction). Ignore tax effects.

2. If PGE had not capitalized interest (i.e., credited Allowance for Funds Used during Construction to income) in years 1975–79, what would Net Income before Taxes on Income have been for those years?

3. Bowen hypothesizes that investors value AFDC credits differently from equal amounts of normal or regular operating earnings. As an investor or analyst attempting to assess PGE as an investment opportunity, how would you treat such credits in your calculations (for example, in a valuation equation)?

4. In the 1975–79 Consolidated Statements of Changes in Financial Position, why does PGE subtract out only one of the two AFDC credits that appear in the Statements of Income? Explain.

Consolidated Statements of Income

For the Years Ended December 31	1979	1978	1977	1976	1975
			(Thousands of Dollars)		
Operating Revenues (Note 1)	$349,981	$303,678	$253,073	$217,787	$179,942
Operating Expenses					
Purchased power	75,111	76,911	40,619	31,028	41,821
Production	69,522	23,794	30,239	15,093	9,087
Transmission and distribution	12,805	11,672	9,829	8,859	8,824
Administrative and other	38,728	33,914	29,248	23,639	18,514
Maintenance and repairs	18,418	13,313	12,895	8,897	7,194
Depreciation (Note 1)	33,642	31,587	28,159	22,112	13,890
Taxes other than income taxes	24,166	24,280	23,951	20,972	16,957
Taxes on income (Notes 1 and 2)	12,300	4,968	5,006	4,510	1,493
	284,692	220,439	179,946	135,110	117,780
Operating Income	65,289	83,239	73,127	82,677	62,162
Other Income					
Allowance for equity funds used during construction (Note 1)	27,445	9,058	5,089	4,360	6,317
Other income and deductions	1,270	5,325	541	988	(641)
	28,715	14,383	5,630	5,348	5,676
Interest Charges					
Interest on long-term debt	70,326	58,206	48,528	40,711	28,519
Interest on short-term borrowings	9,096	8,973	4,794	5,447	9,211
Other interest and amortization	1,030	1,183	846	899	347
Allowance for borrowed funds used during construction (Note 1)	(32,570)	(19,524)	(12,399)	(11,053)	(16,242)
	47,882	48,838	41,769	36,004	21,835
Income before cumulative effect of change in accounting policy	46,122	48,784	36,988	52,021	46,003
Cumulative effect to January 1, 1978 of accruing estimated unbilled revenues—less income taxes of $8,503 (Note 1)	—	7,845	—	—	—
Net Income	$ 46,122	$ 56,629	$ 36,988	$ 52,021	$ 46,003
Preferred Dividend Requirement	13,830	14,175	13,657	11,812	9,818
Common Stock					
Income available	$ 32,292	$ 42,454	$ 23,331	$ 40,209	$ 36,185
Average shares outstanding	30,403,911	24,709,977	21,414,344	17,687,431	14,333,333
Earnings per share					
Before cumulative effect of change in accounting policy	$1.06	$1.40	$1.09	$2.27	$2.52
Cumulative effect to January 1, 1978 of accruing estimated unbilled revenues—net	—	.32	—	—	—
Earnings per share	$1.06	$1.72	$1.09	$2.27	$2.52
Dividends declared per share	$1.70	$1.70	$1.70	$1.64	$1.58

Consolidated Statements of Retained Earnings

For the Years Ended December 31	1979	1978	1977	1976	1975
			(Thousands of Dollars)		
Balance at Beginning of Year	$ 94,918	$ 94,978	$108,146	$ 97,901	$ 84,626
Net Income	46,122	56,629	36,988	52,021	46,003
	141,040	151,607	145,134	149,922	130,629
Deduct					
Dividends declared					
Common stock	53,130	42,514	36,408	29,964	22,910
Preferred stock	13,830	14,175	13,748	11,812	9,818
	66,960	56,689	50,156	41,776	32,728
Balance at End of Year	$ 74,080	$ 94,918	$ 94,978	$108,146	$ 97,901

Consolidated Statements of Changes in Financial Position

For the Years Ended December 31	1979	1978	1977	1976	1975
			(Thousands of Dollars)		
Source of Funds					
Current operations					
Income before cumulative effect of change in accounting policy	$ 46,122	$ 48,784	$ 36,988	$ 52,021	$ 46,003
Non-cash charges (credits) to income					
Depreciation and amortization	46,840	35,008	39,548	24,708	13,890
Deferred income taxes—net	11,293	1,018	7,683	8,167	5,129
Reserve transferred to revenue	—	—	—	—	(1,989)
Allowance for equity funds used during construction	(27,445)	(9,058)	(5,089)	(4,360)	(6,317)
Other—net	2,799	3,038	(214)	138	134
	79,609	78,790	78,916	80,674	56,850
Cumulative effect of change in accounting policy (Note 1)	—	7,845	—	—	—
Funds provided internally	79,609	86,635	78,916	80,674	56,850
Proceeds from external financing					
Long-term debt	102,672	116,795	157,978	120,104	122,861
Preferred stock	—	—	27,000	27,375	30,000
Common stock	93,834	68,459	62,532	65,774	29,770
Short-term borrowings—net	59,000	26,000	(25,650)	(57,284)	32,143
Sale/leaseback of assets (Note 7)	20,246	50,310	—	—	—
	$355,361	$348,199	$300,776	$236,643	$271,624

	1979	1978	1977	1976	1975
Application of Funds					
Gross utility construction	$254,289	$278,265	$201,896	$191,475	$182,513
Reimbursement for prior years' construction expenditures	—	—	—	(18,940)	—
Allowance for equity funds used during construction	(27,445)	(9,058)	(5,089)	(4,360)	(6,317)
	226,844	269,207	196,807	168,175	176,196
Headquarters complex construction	—	—	9,259	21,342	18,982
Dividends declared	66,960	56,689	50,156	41,776	32,728
Retirement of long-term debt and preferred stock	45,119	45,666	54,156	4,480	40,124
Miscellaneous—net	13,984	8,459	(11)	2,812	1,219
Increase (decrease) in working capital excluding current maturities, sinking funds and short-term borrowings					
Cash	522	(681)	(2,966)	(3,675)	6
Receivables	4,684	7,457	(3,981)	5,802	7,404
Estimated unbilled revenues	1,572	20,209	—	—	—
Materials and supplies	24,525	(5,776)	7,209	(13,308)	7,309
Accounts payable and accruals	(41,516)	(50,810)	(13,171)	7,886	(13,824)
Other—net	12,667	(2,221)	3,318	1,353	1,480
	$355,361	$348,199	$300,776	$236,643	$271,624

III. PROPERTY, PLANT, AND EQUIPMENT

Consolidated Balance Sheets

Assets

At December 31	1979	1978
	(Thousands of Dollars)	
Electric Utility Plant—Original Cost		
In service		
Production	$ 597,917	$ 580,710
Transmission	134,495	133,310
Distribution	385,104	354,289
General	58,975	49,858
	1,176,491	1,118,167
Accumulated depreciation (Note 1)	(203,572)	(173,097)
	972,919	945,070
Construction work in progress (Note 6)	617,300	463,274
Nuclear fuel, less accumulated amortization		
of $29,476 and $16,278 (Note 1)	68,578	74,518
	1,658,797	1,482,862
Other Property and Investments	20,955	12,300
Current Assets		
Cash	4,909	4,387
Receivables		
Customer accounts	28,120	22,477
Other accounts and notes	4,625	5,886
Reserve for uncollectible accounts	(234)	(536)
Estimated unbilled revenues (Note 1)	21,781	20,209
Materials and supplies, at average cost		
Fuel oil	28,591	5,668
Other	13,187	11,585
Property taxes applicable to subsequent periods	9,697	9,402
Prepayments	7,394	2,342
Deferred power costs (Note 1)	7,320	—
	125,390	81,420
Deferred Charges	16,186	11,456
	$1,821,328	$1,588,038

Notes to Financial Statements

NOTE 1. **SUMMARY OF ACCOUNTING POLICIES**

Allowance for Funds Used During Construction (ADC)— ADC represents the net cost for the period of construction of borrowed funds used for construction purposes and a reasonable rate on other funds used. ADC is capitalized as part of the cost of utility plant and is credited to income but does not represent current cash earnings. The allowance for borrowed funds used during construction is calculated on a pre-tax basis. ADC is not capitalized for income tax purposes.

Effective January 1, 1977 the Federal Energy Regulatory Commission (FERC) established a formula to determine the maximum allowable ADC rate and ordered that the allowance for borrowed funds used during construction be credited to interest charges and that the allowance for other (equity) funds used during construction be credited to other income. A 7% ADC rate was used on all construction expenditures until November 15, 1977 when the maximum rate allowed under the FERC order was adopted for certain construction projects. Effective January 1, 1979 the maximum rate (11.5% for 1979) was adopted for all construction expenditures.

NOTE 2. **INCOME TAX EXPENSE**

The following table shows the detail of taxes on income and the items used in computing the differences between the statutory Federal income tax rate and the Company's effective rate.

	1979	1978	1977	1976	1975
			(Thousands of Dollars)		
Utility					
Currently payable	$ 143	$ (25)	$ (1,045)	$ (1,727)	$ (3,637)
Deferred income taxes					
Capitalized interest	7,943	3,342	4,433	4,013	6,529
Liberalized depreciation	3,361	1,354	2,409	2,787	630
Deferred power costs	1,810	—	—	—	—
Other	(855)	400	(457)	(541)	(540)
Investment tax credit adjustments	(102)	(103)	(334)	(22)	(1,489)
Total utility	12,300	4,968	5,006	4,510	1,493
Nonutility					
Currently payable	265	(8)	(379)	(42)	316
Deferred income taxes	1,153	(3,103)	1,632	1,930	—
Total nonutility	1,418	(3,111)	1,253	1,888	316
	13,718	1,857	6,259	6,398	1,809
Cumulative effect of accounting change					
Deferred income taxes	—	8,503	—	—	—
Total income tax expense	$13,718	$10,360	$ 6,259	$ 6,398	$ 1,809
Computed tax based on statutory Federal income tax rates applied to income before income taxes and cumulative effect of accounting change	$27,526	$24,307	$20,758	$28,041	$22,950
Less reductions in taxes resulting from Flow-through items					
Excess tax over book depreciation	6,019	12,921	7,319	15,447	13,263
Items capitalized for books and expensed for tax	—	2,210	2,007	2,308	2,503
Allowance for equity funds used during construction	12,699	6,612	4,274	3,649	4,698
Other	(4,910)	707	899	239	677
	$13,718	$ 1,857	$ 6,259	$ 6,398	$ 1,809
Company's effective rate	22.9%	3.7%	14.5%	11.0%	3.8%

The Company has a Federal income tax net operating loss carryforward of approximately $41,000,000 expiring principally in 1985 and 1986. Deferred taxes will be recorded to the extent that the loss carryforward is realized in the future.

It is anticipated that cash outlays for income taxes will not exceed income tax expense during each of the next three years.

I. BACKGROUND, CONTROVERSY AND HYPOTHESES *

A. Background

Early in the history of electricity and gas service, an issue of equity arose over who should pay for expansion—current consumers or future consumers. Since most expansion was into new territories and current consumers received few direct benefits, the prevailing logic absolved current consumers from subsidizing construction expenditures. To achieve this goal, Construction Work in Progress (CWIP) was excluded from the rate base and thus current prices reflected only the plant in service.[1] Debt and equity dollars devoted to construction were "compensated" by capitalizing imputed interest on construction expenditures. An interest capitalization rate was applied to the balance in CWIP and this amount was added to the asset account. The credit side of the entry resulted in an increase in a nonoperating income account, Allowance for Funds Used During Construction (AFC).[2]

In recent years, these AFC credits have become an increasingly significant portion of reported income for many utilities (see Table 1—right-hand panel). The growth in this phenomenon is due to at least three factors: increased construction budgets, inflation, and the longer duration of the projects. These can be attributed, in part, to the construction of nuclear power plants beginning in the late 1960s.

B. The Controversy

As AFC credites have grown, the market value of equity relative to the book value of equity has declined (see Table 1—left-hand panel).[3] Many industry observers (e.g., accountants, businessmen, consultants, economists, financial analysts, and regulators) have made a causal link between the decline in market values and the rise in AFC earnings. General disagreement exists as to the propriety of the interest capitalization technique and the value inherent in each dollar of AFC earnings. The opinions of industry observers can be divided into three groups: (1) those who believe AFC credits to be worthless; (2) those who believe AFC credits are as good as operating earnings; and (3) those in the middle who believe AFC credits are of "lower quality" than operating earnings.

The first group is reflected in two Business Week articles entitled, "A Case of Phantom Profits?" [1974] and " 'Psychedelic Accounting' " [1974]. The first article labels AFC credits as "phantom earnings" and reports on those who totally discount this regulatory procedure. The latter article quotes financial analysts who describe the AFC accounting technique as "truly psychedelic" and subtract AFC (among other items) from reported earnings to arrive at "actual earnings." These opinions represent one

---

[1] See the appendix for a brief description of the regulatory process (and terminology).

[2] Prior to 1971, the title was "Interest During Construction" and the account appeared as an offset to interest expense on the income statement. From 1977 onward, AFC was split into debt and equity components.

[3] To alleviate these problems it has been proposed (and adopted by some regulatory commissions) that construction work in progress (CWIP) be included in the rate base. This would eliminate the necessity for capitalization of interest by compensating funds devoted to construction in current rates billed to customers. Van Susteren [1977, p. 4] reports that 12 states allow CWIP in the rate base. Those who advocate a switch to direct inclusion of CWIP in the rate base include: Dixon [1970, p. 4], Walker [1970, p. 23], Bolster [1971, p. 28], Morris [1971, p. 28], Hyde, [1977, p. 16], Mattutat [1977, p. 37], and Nash [1978, p. 17].

Bowen [1979] provides necessary and sufficient conditions (in a restricted setting) for shareholder indifference between the "AFC" and "direct inclusion of CWIP in the rate base" techniques.

From Robert M. Bowen, "Valuation of Earnings Components in the Electric Utility Industry," Accounting Review, January 1981.

TABLE 1

DESCRIPTIVE STATISTICS ON EQUITY VALUES AND AFC EARNINGS IN THE ELECTRIC UTILITY INDUSTRY

	(V/B)*						(AFC/NI)**				
Year	Ave.	Std. Dev.	Min.	Max.	N	Ave.	Std. Dev.	Min.	Max.	N
62	2.15	.56	1.27	3.92	107	.04	.04	.00	.30	107
63	2.19	.57	1.28	4.06	107	.04	.04	.00	.26	107
64	2.33	.62	1.25	4.39	107	.04	.04	.00	.20	107
65	2.18	.58	1.13	4.05	107	.04	.04	.00	.16	107
66	1.86	.54	.91	3.53	107	.05	.04	.00	.20	107
67	1.65	.46	.86	3.17	107	.07	.05	.00	.26	107
68	1.70	.38	.90	2.85	107	.10	.07	.00	.54	107
69	1.31	.34	.73	2.57	107	.12	.10	.00	.53	107
70	1.35	.36	.71	2.65	107	.17	.13	.00	.61	107
71	1.25	.29	.74	2.39	107	.21	.18	.00	1.06	107
72	1.19	.29	.76	2.40	107	.24	.18	.00	.88	107
73	.87	.18	.59	1.41	107	.31	.38	.01	3.56	107
74	.60	.17	.24	1.24	107	.35	.31	.00	2.22	107
75	.79	.17	.41	1.42	105	.30	.21	.00	.90	107

* (V/B) = Market Value of Equity/Book Value of Equity.
** (AFC/NI) = Allowance for Funds Used During Construction/Net Income Available for Common.
N = Number of firms in the statistics.
Source: Annual Utility COMPUSTAT Tape.

extreme—that capitalization of interest on CWIP has no economic value to the firm's owners.

The group at the other extreme, those who believe AFC credits are as good as operating earnings, is possibly the fewest in number. Albert C. Barkwill, a chartered financial analyst and Investment Vice President of the Lehman Corporation, summarized his position in a paper delivered to the New York Society of Security Analysts:

My conclusion is that interest during construction earnings are as good as operating earnings. Aside from giving the procedure a better title, I would do nothing to change it. It records the construction profit at the proper time and then collects it, in cash, from the proper customers at the proper time. To repeat, let's leave well enough alone [1970].

The implication here is clear—a dollar of AFC credits should be viewed as equivalent to a dollar of operating earnings.

Not surprisingly, the largest group

seems to hold an intermediate position. An excerpt from testimony given before the Florida Public Utilities Commission by Richard Walker, Managing Partner—Regulated Industries of Arthur Andersen & Co., provides an example:

Investors apparently do not value a dollar of earnings from the allowance for funds charged to construction as much as they do a dollar of earnings from operations for, in this sense, they view it as being of lesser quality than cash flow earnings [1973].

Similar viewpoints have been expressed by Value Line Investment Survey [1969], Walker [1970; 1971], Benose [1973], Peter [1973], Hyde [1975], Pomerantz and Suelflow [1975], Johnson [1977], and Fitzpatrick and Stitzel [1978].

Much of the reasoning that AFC credits are "lower quality earnings" rests on the disparity between the timing of cash inflows and outflows. Cash outflows to meet interest payments on debt and dividends on equity are immediate and certain. Cash inflows "earned" during construction are postponed until the plant goes into service and are spread over its depreciable life. Thus, while AFC credits are of positive economic value, they are believed to be more risky than operating earnings.

The economic factors causing this phenomenon likely stem from increased uncertainty over the receipt of future cash flows represented by AFC credits. The firm's "regulatory climate" combined with concerns over future inflation, demand, and technology contribute to the level of this uncertainty. In this study, market expectations are impounded in the regression coefficients of the valuation models. These regression coefficients will be interpreted as aggregate market multipliers applied to earnings in determining equity value.

The regulatory process can only indirectly alter these earnings multipliers. By adjusting the allowed rate of return (on plant in service) and/or the interest capitalization rate (on CWIP), regulators can (to the extent demand for power is inelastic) prevent value from changing in spite of smaller coefficients.[4] This ad-justment could also increase the coefficients if regulatory actions are perceived to be a signal about an improved "regulatory climate." Value is therefore a function of (1) the market-perceived risk inherent in a dollar of interest capitalization, and (2) the regulation-determined interest capitalization rate.

For example, suppose the earnings multiplier on AFC credits has been decreasing over time because of a perception of increased probabilities that future cash inflows resulting from current construction will fail to materialize. One way by which regulators can attempt to ensure that value does not drop is to increase the interest capitalization rate on CWIP where the additional increment to CWIP is sufficient to offset the decline in the valuation multiplier. Inadequately risk-adjusted rates will cause a decrement in equity value.

[4] From the commission's perspective, strong factors might argue against a price increase. For example, higher power costs might influence businesses to locate in regions with less expensive power. In an attempt to prevent, say, the loss of jobs in the region, the regulatory authority might explicitly choose to forego preservation of equity value.

4.1. AMERICAN BROADCASTING COMPANIES, INC.

Television rights and copyright amortization.
(Straightforward: 30 minutes)

ABC, Inc., is a diversified communications and entertainment corporation. ABC's broadcast operations include the ABC Television Network, five owned television stations, the ABC Radio Network, and seven owned AM radio stations. The company also has interests in the publishing, recreation, and motion picture industries.

On December 15, 1980, the *Wall Street Journal* reported: "ABC is changing the method by which it accounts for prime-time programming in a way that will enhance its earnings for the fourth quarter (of 1980) and for all of next year.... In effect, the company will absorb a smaller proportion of programming costs when a show is originally broadcast than previously, while a higher proportion of costs will be charged against reruns [in future years]."

Study the assets section of ABC's Consolidated Balance Sheet for 1980 and Note M, "Program Amortization," of ABC's notes to consolidated financial statements. Net earnings (after provision for income tax expense) for 1979 and 1980 were $159,310,000 and $146,304,000, respectively.

1. Restate 1980 Net Earnings on a basis consistent with the methods used in calculating 1979 Net Earnings. Calculate the percentage change in Net Earnings from 1979 to 1980 as reported and *as if* consistent methods of accounting for prime-time programming costs had been used. (Ignore the fact that 1979 earnings are for 52 weeks and 1980 earnings are for 53 weeks.)

2. Assuming that a 40 percent tax rate is applicable to pretax net income, restate the current asset account balance for Television Program Rights, Production Costs, and Advances less Amortization on a basis consistent with the methods used in 1979 (i.e.,

assuming amortization rates for prime-time programming costs were not modified.)

3. Provide a journal entry to recognize the change in rate of amortization in the 1980 balance sheet.

4. Why would ABC's management choose to adopt this new accounting policy? Is it in the best interests of ABC's stockholders? Explain briefly.

Consolidated Balance Sheets
(Dollars in thousands)

Assets	Jan. 3, 1981	Dec. 29, 1979	Dec. 30, 1978
Current assets:			
Cash	$ 26,265	$ 16,798	$ 29,989
Marketable securities (including certificates of deposit of $44,170 in 1980, $84,275 in 1979 and $150,684 in 1978), at cost, which approximates market	121,176	196,195	220,802
Receivables, less allowances of $23,829 in 1980, $22,409 in 1979 and $29,134 in 1978	297,343	271,853	231,346
Television program rights, production costs and advances less amortization (notes A, L and M)	265,656	212,161	207,402
Inventory of merchandise and supplies, at the lower of cost (principally on the first-in first-out basis) or market	21,816	21,708	18,232
Prepaid expenses (note F)	74,942	58,280	53,481
Total current assets	807,198	776,995	761,252
Property and equipment, at cost (notes A and K):			
Land and improvements	29,994	28,504	23,940
Buildings and improvements	199,601	150,969	119,966
Operating equipment	281,931	234,399	172,689
Leasehold and leasehold improvements	34,393	29,094	26,073
	545,919	442,966	342,668
Less—accumulated depreciation and amortization	168,131	142,898	124,492
Property and equipment—net	377,788	300,068	218,176
Other assets:			
Intangibles, at cost, less amortization (notes A and B)	77,726	80,512	57,726
Television program rights, non-current (notes A and L)	88,732	58,540	19,768
Deferred charges (note E)	15,142	16,085	10,118
Other (notes A and F)	44,290	42,125	34,100
Total other assets	225,890	197,262	121,712
Total assets	$1,410,876	$1,274,325	$1,101,140

Note M: Program Amortization

Based on a Company study completed in the fourth quarter of 1980 of the relationships between program revenues and costs, amortization rates for prime-time programming were modified. In order to more closely match revenues and costs for programming during prime time, amortization rates on the original broadcast were reduced and the rates on subsequent broadcasts of a program were increased. This modification of amortization rates for prime-time programming increased net earnings by $8,928,000 or $.32 per share for the year 1980.

4.2. EDUCATIONAL DEVELOPMENT CORPORATION

Production costs, capitalization, and amortization.
(Moderate: 60 minutes)

The Educational Development Corporation (EDC) is a publisher engaged in the business of developing, producing, and marketing materials and systems for use by elementary and secondary schools. Substantially all sales are made to schools, which are usually state or local government agencies.

Study EDC's 1979–80 Balance Sheet, Statement of Income (Loss), and Notes 1 and 4 to the financial statements.

1. Why did Other Assets increase from 1979 to 1980? Provide journal entries to explain the increase from $33,742 to $398,462.

2. Using information in part 1 as well as in the financial statements, estimate when in 1979–80 the acquisition actually occurred.

3. Calculate 1980 net income (loss) before provision (credit) for income taxes and extraordinary item assuming that EDC had adopted the following accounting treatments for product acquisition costs. Each case should be treated independently. The accounting method for tax purposes remains unchanged as the reporting policy is changed.

   a. Amortization is computed on a sum-of-year's-digits method using an estimated useful life of five years.

   b. Amortization is computed on an effective-interest basis. Assume that the acquisition price of the testing program is the present value of an annuity of forty equal quarterly installments discounted at 3 percent per quarter. Each installment is received at the end of the quarter. In other words, the economic life of the testing program is ten years—twice the period over which the program is now being depreciated.

4. Evaluate the appropriateness of EDC's existing policy with respect to product acquisition costs.

educational development corporation

BALANCE SHEET
February 29, 1980 and February 28, 1979

	1980	1979
ASSETS		
Current assets:		
Cash	$ 89,163	$ 29,427
Time certificates of deposit	950,000	1,600,000
Refundable income taxes (Note 5)	113,652	42,000
Accounts receivable (less allowances for doubtful accounts and returns: 1980, $50,000; 1979, $116,707)	937,409	973,584
Notes receivable	7,289	187,050
Inventories (Note 2)	1,450,349	1,041,206
Prepaid expenses	56,027	134,688
Deferred income tax benefits (Note 5)	243,731	14,841
Total current assets	3,847,620	4,022,796
Notes receivable	166,550	273,839
Property, plant and equipment, at cost (less accumulated depreciation: 1980, $568,985; 1979, $460,382) (Notes 3 and 6)	1,002,698	962,368
Other assets (Note 4)	398,462	33,742
	$5,415,330	$5,292,745
LIABILITIES AND SHAREHOLDERS' EQUITY		
Current liabilities:		
Current maturities of long-term debt	$ 34,773	$ 16,760
Accounts payable	362,372	294,799
Accrued salaries and bonuses	44,246	42,284
Accrued test scoring	352,652	305,139
Income taxes payable (Note 5)	219,774	131,385
Other liabilities and accruals	66,998	68,982
Total current liabilities	1,080,815	859,349
Long-term debt (less current maturities) (Note 6)	272,197	205,821
Commitments (Note 7)		
Shareholders' equity (Note 8):		
Common stock, par value of $.20 per share (authorized 3,000,000 shares; issued 2,104,120 shares)	420,824	420,824
Capital in excess of par value	4,308,321	4,308,321
Retained earnings	18,843	152,581
	4,747,988	4,881,726
Less common shares held in treasury at cost (1980 — 420,422 shares; 1979 — 394,970 shares)	685,670	654,151
Total shareholders' equity	4,062,318	4,227,575
	$5,415,330	$5,292,745

Certain reclassifications of the figures as of February 28, 1979, not affecting net income, have been made to conform with the presentation for the current year.

IV.   INTANGIBLES AND CAPITALIZED EXPENSES

STATEMENT OF INCOME (LOSS)
Years ended February 29, 1980 and February 28, 1979

	1980	1979
Revenues:		
Sales and royalties (Note 9)	**$4,533,855**	$4,639,196
Interest and other income	**212,984**	212,839
	4,746,839	4,852,035
Costs and expenses (Note 3):		
Publication costs	**1,672,911**	1,495,987
Research and development costs	**657,594**	443,847
Marketing expense	**2,188,610**	1,882,600
General and administrative expense	**490,417**	429,280
Interest expense	**20,045**	18,120
	5,029,577	4,269,834
Income (Loss) before provision (credit) for		
income taxes and extraordinary item	**(282,738)**	582,201
Provision (Credit) for income taxes (Note 5)	**(118,540)**	285,000
Income (Loss) before extraordinary item	**(164,198)**	297,201
Extraordinary item — realization of tax benefit not		
previously recorded (Note 5)	**30,460**	—
Net income (loss)	**$ (133,738)**	$ 297,201
Earnings (Loss) per share:		
Income (Loss) before extraordinary item	**$(.10)**	$.17
Extraordinary item (Note 5)	**.02**	—
Net income (loss)	**$(.08)**	$.17
Average common shares and common		
share equivalents outstanding	**1,696,177**	1,759,277

Educational Development Corporation

NOTES TO FINANCIAL STATEMENTS

Years Ended February 29, 1980 and February 28, 1979

1. Summary of Significant Accounting Policies

(d) *Product acquisition costs* — Amortization is computed on the straight-line method using an estimated useful life of five years.

4. Other Assets

Other assets at February 29, 1980 and February 28, 1979 consist of the following:

	1980	1979
Product acquisition costs (less		
accumulated amortization of $60,003)	$340,017	—
Other	58,445	33,742
	$398,462	$33,742

Product acquisition costs are outlays to acquire title to a testing program the Company has marketed in the past under an agreement with the author wherein the Company paid royalties to the author as sales were made.

4.3. LOCKHEED CORPORATION—I*

Capitalization of nonrecurring production costs on the TriStar project, matching concepts, and deferred revenues. (Moderate: 45 minutes)

The assets section of the 12/31/72 and 12/30/73 Balance Sheets and the Earnings Statements for 1972–73 for Lockheed are related to this case. Excerpts from Note 2 pertaining to the TriStar accounting are given below:

> **Note 2:** All of the development costs and the normal production cost on the TriStar Jet Transport have been included in inventory except for General and Administrative expenses which are charged to Income in the year incurred. These G & A expenses amounted to $70 million in 1973 and $81 million in 1972. Customer advances are accounted for as liabilities until the aircrafts to which they relate have been delivered. Since the cumulative development costs to date have been substantial, it is estimated that 300 aircraft will have to be delivered to make the total program profitable. Since 56 aircraft have been delivered to date (all during 1972 and 1973), the Company does not expect that a final determination of recoverability of Inventoried Cost can be made until a later date. Zero gross profit was recorded on the $730 million of sales in 1973 and $302 million of sales in 1972 (for deliveries in those years) and no gross profit will be recorded on deliveries until uncertainties are reduced. The customer advances applicable to deliveries were about $180 million for deliveries in 1973 and $90 million for 1972 deliveries.

1. How much of the cost of inventories for each year (12/31/72 and 12/30/73) were related to the TriStar Jet Transport?

2. Give the journal entries for 1972 and 1973 which would be associated with the TriStar deliveries and the General and Administrative Costs for those years. Assume that the General and Administrative Costs were paid in cash.

---

*Prepared by Robert K. Jaedicke.

3. What do you think of Lockheed's treatment of costs and expenses associated with the TriStar program?

Lockheed Consolidated Balance Sheet

	DECEMBER 30, 1973	DECEMBER 31, 1972
ASSETS		
CURRENT ASSETS:		
Cash (including $7,288,000 restricted at December 30, 1973) (Note 5)	$ **60,664,000**	$ 88,964,000
Short term securities	**15,449,000**	——
Accounts receivable—U.S. Government (Note 1)	**121,272,000**	139,211,000
Other accounts receivable	**48,755,000**	35,692,000
Inventories (including TriStar Inventories of $1,160,000,000 in 1973 and $959,000,000 in 1972) (Note 2)	**1,291,806,000**	1,065,755,000
Prepaid expenses and deposits	**25,257,000**	31,537,000
Total current assets	**1,563,203,000**	1,361,159,000
INVESTMENTS, at lower of cost or estimated realizable value	**1,727,000**	1,447,000
PROPERTY, PLANT AND EQUIPMENT, at cost, partially pledged as security for long term debt (Note 5):		
Land	**29,708,000**	24,918,000
Buildings, structures, and leasehold improvements	**282,565,000**	271,745,000
Machinery and equipment	**395,558,000**	364,947,000
	707,831,000	661,610,000
Less accumulated depreciation and amortization	**429,149,000**	393,823,000
	278,682,000	267,787,000
OTHER NONCURRENT ASSETS (net of allowance for doubtful notes receivable of $3,200,000 at December 30, 1973)	**10,913,000**	1,833,000
	$1,854,525,000	$1,632,226,000

Lockheed Consolidated Earnings and Retained Earnings

	YEAR ENDED	
	DECEMBER 30, 1973	DECEMBER 31, 1972
Sales (Notes 2 and 8)	$2,756,791,000	$2,472,732,000
Costs and expenses (Note 2)	2,674,686,000	2,404,235,000
(a) Program profits	82,105,000	68,497,000
Interest and other income	6,845,000	6,698,000
	88,950,000	75,195,000
Interest expense	69,329,000	47,461,000
Earnings before income taxes and extraordinary gain	19,621,000	27,734,000
Provision for income taxes (Note 3)	5,540,000	14,700,000
Earnings before extraordinary gain (Notes 2 and 10)	14,081,000	13,034,000
Gain on disposition of land and idle facilities, less applicable deferred federal income tax of $2,520,000 in 1973 and $2,930,000 in 1972	2,731,000	3,177,000
Net earnings for the year based on the assumptions of a 300 airplane TriStar program (Notes 2 and 10)	16,812,000	16,211,000
Retained earnings at beginning of year	176,015,000	159,804,000
Retained earnings at end of year (Notes 2, 5, and 10)	$ 192,827,000	$ 176,015,000
Earnings per share of capital stock based on the assumptions of a 300 airplane TriStar program (Note 7):		
Earnings before extraordinary gain	$1.24	$1.15
Gain on disposition of land and idle facilities	.24	.28
Net earnings	$1.48	$1.43

(a) TriStar and Other Program profit or (loss), expressed in millions:

	1973			1972		
	TriStar	Other	Total	TriStar	Other	Total
Sales	$730	$2,027	$2,757	$302	$2,171	$2,473
Costs and expenses	800	1,875	2,675	383	2,021	2,404
Program profit (loss)	$ (70)	$ 152	$ 82	$ (80)	$ 150	$ 69

IV. INTANGIBLES AND CAPITALIZED EXPENSES

4.4. LOCKHEED CORPORATION—II

Reclassification of TriStar, nonrecurring production costs.

(Moderate: 60 minutes)

The assets sections of the 12/28/75 and 12/29/74 (Reclassified) Balance Sheets for Lockheed Corporation are related to this case. An excerpt from Note 2 which refers to the L-1011 TriStar Program is given below. Also included is the 12/29/74 Statement of Assets *prior to reclassification.* (The *12/30/73 statements prior to reclassification accompany case 4.3.)*

Note 2: L-1011 TriStar Program

Sales prices of TriStar aircraft and spare parts delivered during the first three quarters of 1975 exceeded their production costs by $34.8 million and, since this gross profit was not recognized in earnings, it served to reduce the carrying amount of initial planning and tooling costs and of prior years' unrecovered production start-up costs of delivered aircraft. Although management believes gross profit on future TriStar deliveries will be sufficient to recover the remainder of such costs, estimates of the extent and timing of their recovery have become less reliable because of the increased uncertainties referred to above. In recognition thereof, the Company changed its method of accounting for the TriStar, commencing with the fourth quarter of 1975, to amortize such costs to earnings ratably through 1985 ($12.5 million in the fourth quarter of 1975), so long as studies continue to indicate they are recoverable (see "Uncertainties"). If future assessments indicate that any such amortized costs would not be recoverable, the Company would be required to charge to earnings immediately the portion of any such costs determined to be nonrecoverable.

1. Provide a journal entry dated January 1974 which reflects the write-down of inventories made in the 1974 Consolidated Balance Sheet regarding 1973 comparative data.

2. Provide a journal entry dated January 1975 to record the reclassification made in the 1975 Balance Sheet.

3. Give the journal entries made (a) September 30, 1975 and (b) De-

cember 28, 1975 to record the reduction in the carrying amount of "initial planning and tooling costs and of prior year's unrecovered start-up costs of delivered aircraft."

IV. INTANGIBLES AND CAPITALIZED EXPENSES

CONSOLIDATED BALANCE SHEET

Lockheed

	(Dollars in Millions)	
	December 28 1975	December 29 1974 (Reclassified— Note 2)
ASSETS		
CURRENT ASSETS:		
Cash and equivalents (Note 3)	$ **52.7**	$ 96.8
Restricted cash (Note 3)	**5.6**	25.4
Accounts receivable (Note 4)	**209.8**	174.9
Inventories (including TriStar inventories of $204.3 in 1975 and $185.3 in 1974) (Notes 2, 5, and 8)	**387.5**	342.7
Future tax benefits (including $18.7 of deferred tax charges in 1975) (Note 6)	**61.7**	39.7
Prepaid expenses and deposits	**49.1**	48.4
Total current assets	**766.4**	727.9
PROPERTY, PLANT, AND EQUIPMENT, at cost (Note 8):		
Land	**29.6**	29.7
Buildings, structures, and leasehold improvements	**288.4**	282.0
Machinery and equipment	**414.6**	397.4
	732.6	709.1
Less accumulated depreciation and amortization	**476.6**	451.2
Net property, plant, and equipment	**256.0**	257.9
NONCURRENT ASSETS AND DEFERRED CHARGES:		
Future tax benefit, long-term portion (Note 6)	**9.1**	64.6
TriStar initial planning and tooling and unrecoverd production start-up costs (Note 2)	**502.5**	549.8
Other noncurrent assets (net of allowance of $4.2 for doubtful notes receivable) (Note 3)	**39.4**	33.9
	$1,573.4	$1,634.1

CONSOLIDATED BALANCE SHEET

Lockheed

	(Dollars in Millions)	
	December 29 1974	December 30 1973
		(Restated— Note 2)

ASSETS

CURRENT ASSETS:

Cash and equivalents (including $25.4 restricted at December 29, 1974) (Note 3)	$ 122.2	$ 76.1
Accounts receivable—U.S. Government (Note 4)	129.8	121.3
Other accounts receivable	45.1	48.7
Inventories (including TriStar inventories of $735.1 at December 29, 1974 and $702.8 at December 30, 1973) (Note 5)	892.5	834.6
Current portion of future tax benefit (Note 6)	39.7	——
Prepaid expenses and deposits	48.4	25.3
Total current assets	1,277.7	1,106.0

PROPERTY, PLANT, AND EQUIPMENT:

at cost (Note 8):

Land	29.7	29.7
Buildings, structures, and leasehold improvements	282.0	282.5
Machinery and equipment	397.4	395.6
Less accumulated depreciation and amortization	451.2	429.1
	257.9	278.7

FUTURE TAX BENEFIT, long-term portion (Note 6)	64.6	104.3
OTHER NONCURRENT ASSETS (net of allowance of $4.2 at December 29, 1974 and $3.2 at December 30, 1973 for doubtful notes receivable) (Note 3)	33.9	12.6
	$1,634.1	$1,501.6

IV. INTANGIBLES AND CAPITALIZED EXPENSES

4.5. LOCKHEED CORPORATION—III

Abandonment of TriStar program, effects on profit and financial position. (Moderate: 45 minutes)

Study Lockheed's 1978-1980 Consolidated Statement of Earnings, 1979-1980 Consolidated Balance Sheet, 1978-1980 Consolidated Statement of Changes in Financial Position, and note on the L-1011 TriStar program.

1. Assess the effect on current profits and financial position if Lockheed were to completely abandon the L-1011 TriStar program (except for current orders that should be filled sometime in 1984). More specifically, recast the 1980 financial statements as if the TriStar program had been terminated on December 28, 1980. Assume that the amounts available as unamortized costs have no effect on present or future tax liabilities.

2. Assume that you hold 500 shares of Lockheed's common stock. If you knew, secretly, that Lockheed was about to abandon its TriStar program, would you buy more of the stock or sell your existing holdings? (*Note:* Such a transaction would be considered illegal if it were based on "insider information.")

Consolidated Statement of Earnings

Dollars in millions except per-share data	Year Ended		
	December 28, 1980	December 30, 1979	December 31, 1978
Sales	$5,395.7	$4,057.6	$3,485.0
Costs and expenses	5,252.2	3,935.0	3,345.0
Program profits*	143.5	122.6	140.0
Other income (deductions)—net	(.1)	6.6	9.8
Interest expense	(106.1)	(72.1)	(48.6
Earnings from continuing operations before income taxes	37.3	57.1	101.2
Provision for income taxes	9.7	20.6	46.2
Earnings from continuing operations	27.6	36.5	55.0
Operations sold net of applicable income taxes:			
Net gain from sale			18.8
Net loss from operations			(8.9
Extraordinary tax benefits from carryforward of operating losses and foreign tax credits		20.0	
Net earnings	27.6	56.5	64.9
Preferred stock dividend requirement and provision for redemption value	(5.2)	(5.8)	(5.8
Net earnings applicable to Common Stock	$ 22.4	$ 50.7	$ 59.1
Earnings per share of Common Stock:			
Primary:			
Continuing operations	$ 1.53	$ 2.16	$ 3.51
Net earnings	1.53	3.56	4.21
Fully diluted:			
Continuing operations	1.50	2.01	3.20
Net earnings	1.50	3.22	3.81

*See note on the "L-1011 TriStar Program," page 38.

See accompanying notes.

IV. INTANGIBLES AND CAPITALIZED EXPENSES

Dollars in millions	*December 28, 1980*	*December 30, 1979*
Assets		
Current assets:		
Cash	$ 44.2	$ 70.5
Accounts receivable	518.5	435.0
Inventories	1,031.6	798.5
Deferred tax charges	32.8	27.5
Prepaid expenses	55.5	71.5
Total current assets	1,682.6	1,403.0
Property, plant, and equipment, at cost:		
Land	24.7	24.6
Buildings, structures, and leasehold improvements	380.7	349.2
Machinery and equipment	639.6	533.3
	1,045.0	907.1
Less accumulated depreciation and amortization	618.4	574.7
Net property, plant, and equipment	426.6	332.4
Noncurrent assets and deferred charges:		
TriStar initial planning and tooling and unrecovered production start-up costs	280.2	335.8
Investment-Lockheed Finance Corporation	42.2	25.5
Other noncurrent assets	10.9	16.2
	$2,442.5	$2,112.9
Liabilities and Shareholders' Equity		
Current liabilities:		
Accounts payable	$ 434.6	$ 331.9
Salaries and wages	187.0	160.9
Income taxes	29.8	35.0
Customers' advances in excess of related costs	157.6	200.2
Retirement plan contribution	66.6	104.4
Other liabilities	349.8	265.2
Total current liabilities	1,225.4	1,097.6
Deferred income tax—long-term	52.7	54.9
Long-term senior debt	713.6	526.2
4-1/4% Convertible Subordinated Debentures (Due March 1, 1992)	101.1	101.1
Commitments and contingencies		
Redeemable $9.50 Senior Preferred Stock	43.5	50.6
Common Stock, $1 par value	11.9	11.8
Additional capital	91.9	90.4
Retained earnings	202.4	180.3
	$2,442.5	$2,112.9

See accompanying notes.

Dollars in millions	Year Ended		
	December 28, 1980	December 30, 1979	December 31, 1978
Source:			
Continuing Operations:			
Earnings from continuing operations	$ 27.6	$ 36.5	$ 55.0
Add charges against earnings not involving working capital:			
Depreciation and amortization of plant and equipment	58.1	43.5	40.6
Amortization of TriStar initial planning and tooling and unrecovered production start-up costs	55.6	54.2	50.0
(Decrease) increase in deferred income tax	(2.2)	(14.8)	59.3
Other	1.6	2.2	2.0
Working capital from continuing operations	140.7	121.6	206.9
Total working capital from operations sold			39.8
Long-term borrowings and capital leases	187.4	236.9	
Other	12.4	24.7	5.0
	340.5	383.2	251.7
Application:			
Additions to property, plant, and equipment	155.1	138.1	53.7
Reduction of long-term debt			145.6
Additions to TriStar Dash 500 initial planning and tooling		12.4	12.4
Redemption of $9.50 Senior Preferred Stock	8.1		
Other	25.5	15.0	20.7
	188.7	165.5	232.4
Increase in working capital	$151.8	$217.7	$ 19.3
Change in components of working capital:			
Increases (decreases) in current assets:			
Cash	$ (26.3)	$ 12.3	$(161.0)
Accounts receivable	83.5	103.3	96.7
Inventories	233.1	279.7	177.1
Deferred tax charges	5.3	(2.8)	30.3
Prepaid expenses	(16.0)	(8.6)	27.1
Total increase in current assets	279.6	383.9	170.2
Increases (decreases) in current liabilities:			
Accounts payable	102.7	81.7	60.3
Customers' advances in excess of related costs	(42.6)	(.6)	4.7
Accrued expenses and other liabilities	67.7	85.1	85.9
Total increase in current liabilities	127.8	166.2	150.9
Increase in working capital	$151.8	$217.7	$ 19.3

See accompanying notes.

L-1011 TriStar Program

The Consolidated Financial Statements include significant inventories and deferred charges related to the L-1011 TriStar program as discussed below:

Inventories — L-1011 TriStar inventories are stated at the lower of the production cost of aircraft in process of manufacture or estimated net realizable value. Estimated net realizable value is based on projections of costs to complete, selling prices, and other factors, such as production rates. Therefore, such realizable value cannot be determined with precision and is subject to revision as later information affecting such projections becomes available.

L-1011 TriStar inventories, substantially all of which are covered by firm orders, were as follows (in millions of dollars):

	December 28, 1980	December 30, 1979
Work in process	$ 736	$637
Materials and spare parts	168	107
Advances to subcontractors	98	71
Gross inventories	1,002	815
Less customer advances	367	327
Net inventories	$ 635	$488

L-1011 TriStar Deferred Charges and Related Uncertainties — Deferred initial planning and tooling costs on the basic L-1011 and Dash 500 TriStar models and unrecovered production start-up costs related to the basic L-1011 TriStar model are stated at cost net of amortization. The cost is being amortized through 1985 on a straight-line basis.

Management believes that production and deliveries of L-1011 TriStars will extend at least into the late 1980s and that, based on currently projected sales and manufacturing costs, the gross profit on future L-1011 TriStar deliveries will be sufficient to recover the unamortized planning and tooling and unrecovered start-up costs as of December 28, 1980. Such recovery, however, is dependent upon the number of aircraft ultimately sold, continuity and rate of production, and actual selling prices and costs. While projected sales and manufacturing costs take into account factors such as expected sales price level increases and anticipated production costs, all such factors are subject to variations, and many of them are beyond Lockheed's control. Consequently, these factors cannot be quantified with precision, and these estimates are subject to periodic revisions. If future assessments indicate that any such unamortized costs would not be recoverable, Lockheed would be required to charge to earnings immediately any such costs determined to be unrecoverable.

TriStar Operating Results — The following summarizes L-1011 TriStar operating results, which include sales of aircraft, spare parts, and other related services, and in 1979, the sale of used aircraft (in millions of dollars):

Year Ended	December 28, 1980	December 30, 1979	December 31, 1978
Net sales	$ 950.9	$ 526.3	$ 294.3
Cost of sales	1,005.3	569.1	276.7
Standby production costs			12.7
Amortization of deferred charges	55.6	54.2	50.0
Development costs	8.6	20.0	16.7
General and administrative expenses	80.8	71.4	57.0
	1,150.3	714.7	413.1
Program loss	$ (199.4)	$(188.4)	$(118.8)

Included in cost of sales are provisions for excess production costs, both incurred and anticipated, of $80 million in 1980 and $67 million in 1979.

4.6. BOEING COMPANY AND SUBSIDIARIES

Research and development, capitalization, and amortization. (Moderate: 45 minutes)

The Boeing Company operates the following principal business divisions: Boeing Commercial Aircraft Company, Boeing Aerospace, Boeing Vertol Company, Boeing Military Airplane Company, Boeing Engineering and Construction Company, Boeing Computer Services, and Boeing Marine Systems.

Study Boeing's 1978–80 Consolidated Statements of Net Earnings and Retained Earnings, 1979–80 Consolidated Statements of Financial Position, and Notes 1 and 10 to the consolidated financial statements.

1. Explain Boeing's accounting treatment of research and development costs. Provide journal entries for the years 1978–80 to record Boeing's (assumed) cash expenditures in each of those years.

2. Assume that the FASB is reconsidering FASB *Statement No. 2* and may allow deferral of R & D costs of up to three years on either a straight-line or a sum-of-years'-digits basis. Recalculate 1980 net earnings before and after taxes under the alternative deferral method. Assume, for purposes of answering this question, that the tax rate is $414.6/$1,015.1 percent and that R & D expenditures in any given year are made on January 1.

3. If allowable, would you advise Boeing to make such a switch in accounting method? Discuss the pros and cons of a decision to report R & D expenditures on a deferral basis.

CONSOLIDATED STATEMENTS OF NET EARNINGS AND RETAINED EARNINGS

(In millions except per share data)	Year ended December 31		
	1980	1979	1978
Sales	$9,426.2	$8,131.0	$5,463.0
Other income	359.9	325.0	184.8
	9,786.1	8,456.0	5,647.8
Costs and expenses	8,759.9	7,572.9	5,056.1
Interest and debt expense	11.1	7.6	7.7
	8,771.0	7,580.5	5,063.8
Earnings before taxes	1,015.1	875.5	584.0
Federal taxes on income	414.6	370.1	261.1
Net earnings	600.5	505.4	322.9
Retained earnings, January 1	1,185.9	923.7	684.0
Amount transferred to common stock in connection with 3-for-2 stock split ($5 per share par value for new shares)	(162.6)	(108.4)	
Cash dividends paid: 1980—$1.40 per share; 1979—$1.40 per share; 1978—$.87 per share	(134.9)	(134.8)	(83.2)
Retained earnings, December 31	$1,488.9	$1,185.9	$ 923.7
Net earnings per share	$6.23	$5.25	$3.36

Per share data restated for the 1980 and 1979 3-for-2 stock splits.

CONSOLIDATED STATEMENTS OF FINANCIAL POSITION

(In millions)	December 31	
	1980	1979
ASSETS		
Current assets:		
Cash and certificates of deposit	$1,074.4	$1,985.6
Short-term investments, at cost, which approximates market	540.9	314.3
Accounts receivable	466.7	508.3
Current portion of long-term customer financing	33.6	30.1
Inventories	5,029.5	3,077.4
Less applicable advances and progress payments	(3,044.9)	(2,290.6)
Total current assets	4,100.2	3,625.1
Long-term customer financing	277.4	208.0
Property, plant and equipment, at cost	2,723.0	2,083.2
Less accumulated depreciation	(1,218.4)	(1,052.6)
Investments and other assets	49.1	33.5
	$5,931.3	$4,897.2
LIABILITIES AND STOCKHOLDERS' EQUITY		
Current liabilities:		
Accounts payable and accrued liabilities	$2,015.2	$1,590.5
Advances and progress billings in excess of related costs	428.7	534.2
Federal taxes on income ($430.5 deferred in 1980 and $472.4 deferred in 1979)	670.7	612.4
Current portion of long-term debt	13.9	13.8
Total current liabilities	3,128.5	2,750.9
Deferred taxes on income	260.3	126.4
Deferred investment credit	151.5	91.7
Long-term debt	76.2	80.7
Stockholders' equity	2,314.8	1,847.5
	$5,931.3	$4,897.2

IV.   INTANGIBLES AND CAPITALIZED EXPENSES

NOTES TO CONSOLIDATED FINANCIAL STATEMENTS

Years Ended December 31, 1980, 1979 and 1978
(Dollars in millions except per share data)

Note 1 • SUMMARY OF SIGNIFICANT ACCOUNTING POLICIES:

RESEARCH AND DEVELOPMENT, GENERAL AND ADMINISTRATIVE EXPENSES. Research and development (including basic engineering and planning costs on commercial programs) and general and administrative expenses are charged directly to earnings as incurred except to the extent estimated to be recoverable under contracts.

Note 10 • RESEARCH, DEVELOPMENT, GENERAL AND ADMINISTRATIVE EXPENSES:

Expenses charged directly to earnings as incurred include—

| | Year ended December 31, | | |
	1980	1979	1978
Research and development	$767.5	$525.2	$276.1
General and administrative	285.5	219.6	166.6

5.1. BORDEN, INC.

Constant-dollar and current-cost adjustments per FASB
*Statement No. 33, "Financial Reporting and Changing
Prices." (Moderate: 45 minutes)*

In an effort to produce financial information that discloses the effects of
inflation, the Financial Accounting Standards Board issued *FASB
Statement No. 33*, "Financial Reporting and Changing Prices," requir-
ing companies to explain the effect of inflationary factors on operations
using two different methods to adjust historical financial statements for
the effects of changing prices. One of these methods, *current cost*, ad-
justs the basic historical statements for price changes of specific assets.

Supplementary information on both a current-cost and a constant-
dollar basis for 1979 and 1980 is included here. For the purpose of
answering these questions, *ignore* the second column of data, namely,
sales, expenses, and income adjusted for general inflation. Use the accompanying balance sheet data also.

1. Reconcile Income from Continuing Operations on a historical basis, $147,863,000, with Income from Continuing Operations on a
   current-cost basis $35,135,000. What, specifically, does the differ-
   ence represent?

2. Assuming that the primary statements are to be converted to a
   current-cost basis, prepare a journal entry that would increase inventory and net property, plant, and equipment to their respective
   1980 current-cost values. Prepare a similar, second journal entry
   to convert the 1979 balance sheet to a current-cost basis.

3. Calculate the combined increase in current cost of inventories
   (sold or unsold) and *net* property, plant, and equipment that occurred during the twelve months ending December 31, 1980.
   (*Hint:* You may wish to use the relationship: Unrealized holding

gains [beginning of year] + Increase in current cost of assets held during the year − Gains realized through sale or use of assets during the year = Unrealized holding gains [end of year].)

4. Should the combined increase in the current cost of assets during 1980 (i.e., the amount calculated in part 3) be added to 1980 Income from Continuing Operations of $35,135,000 in order to obtain a more comprehensive picture of the firm's economic performance during 1980? In other words, is Borden, Inc., "better off" by this amount? Explain briefly.

Consolidated Balance Sheets

BORDEN, INC.
(*In thousands except share and per share data*)

	December 31	
ASSETS	**1980**	1979*
Current Assets:		
Cash (including time and certificates of deposit		
of $181,512 and $18,241, respectively)	$ **264,171**	$ 104,122
Accounts receivable (less allowance for doubtful		
accounts—$10,006 and $10,100, respectively)	**499,547**	490,387
Inventories:		
Finished and in process goods	**338,271**	358,211
Raw materials and supplies	**167,746**	183,862
Other current assets	**86,697**	43,244
	1,356,432	1,179,826
INVESTMENTS AND OTHER ASSETS:		
Investments in and advances to affiliated companies		
(at cost plus equity in undistributed income)	**44,429**	42,620
Miscellaneous investments and receivables		
(at cost or less)	**33,100**	16,118
Other assets	**26,040**	25,076
	103,569	83,814
PROPERTY AND EQUIPMENT:		
Land	**45,915**	61,678
Buildings	**337,915**	337,465
Machinery and equipment	**1,328,103**	1,288,217
	1,711,933	1,687,360
Less accumulated depreciation	**(721,612)**	(697,214)
	990,321	990,146
INTANGIBLES:		
Intangibles resulting from business acquisitions	**192,972**	208,974
	$2,643,294	$2,462,760

* Reclassified to conform with 1980 presentation.

STATEMENT OF INCOME FROM CONTINUING OPERATIONS ADJUSTED FOR CHANGING PRICES

(In thousands except per share data)		Year Ended December 31, 1980	
	As Reported in the Primary Statements	Adjusted for General Inflation (Constant Dollar)	Adjusted for Changes in Specific Prices (Curent Costs)
Net sales	**$4,595,795**	$4,595,795	$4,595,795
Cost of goods sold (excluding related depreciation expense)	**3,673,507**	3,731,653	3,710,616
Other operating expenses (excluding related depreciation expense	**521,238**	521,238	521,238
Depreciation expense	**100,322**	165,946	175,941
Interest expense	**57,565**	57,565	57,565
Earnings before income taxes	**243,163**	119,393	130,435
Income taxes	**95,300**	95,300	95,300
Income from continuing operations	**$ 147,863**	24,093	35,135
Gain on net monetary items		72,908	72,908
Earnings, net of general inflationary effects		$ 97,001	$ 108,043
Increase in current cost of inventories and property plant and equipment Less effect of increase in general price level			$ *
Excess of increase in specific prices over the increase in the general price level			$ 73,718
Net income per common share	**$ 4.79**	$. 78	$ 1.14
Gain on net monetary items		2.36	2.36
Earnings, net of general inflationary effects		$ 3.14	$ 3.50
Effective tax rate	**39.2%**	79.8%	73.1%

At December 31, 1980 the current cost of inventory was $515,149 and the current cost of net property and equipment was $1,867,674.

*This relates to question 3.

STATEMENT OF INCOME FROM CONTINUING OPERATIONS ADJUSTED FOR CHANGING PRICES

(In thousands except per share data)	As Reported in the Primary Statements	Year Ended December 31, 1979 Adjusted for General Inflation (Con- stant Dollar)	Adjusted for Changes in Specific Prices (Current Costs)
Net sales	**$4,312,533**	$4,312,533	$4,312,533
Cost of goods sold (excluding related depreciation expense)	**3,456,366**	3,506,240	3,477,111
Other operating expense (excluding related depreciation expense)	**480,466**	480,466	480,466
Depreciation expense	**100,777**	157,312	163,238
Interest expense	**55,009**	55,009	55,009
Earnings before income taxes	**219,915**	113,506	136,709
Income taxes	**85,900**	85,900	85,900
Income from continuing operations	**$ 134,015**	27,606	50,809
Gain on net monetary items		73,437	$ 73,437
Earnings, net of general inflationary effects		$ 101,043	$ 124,246
Increase in current cost of inventories and property plant and equipment			$
Less effect of increase in general price level			———
Excess of increase in specific prices over the increase in the general price level			$ 56,847
Net income per common share	**$ 4.31**	$ .89	$ 1.63
Gain on net monetary items		2.36	2.36
Earnings, net of general inflationary effects		$ 3.25	$ 3.99
Effective tax rate	**39.1%**	75.7%	62.8%

At December 31, 1979 the current cost of inventory was $553,761 and the current cost of net property and equipment was $1,848,572.

5.2. THE ROUSE COMPANY AND SUBSIDIARIES

Current-exit valuation, restatement of historical costs.
(Moderate: 45 minutes)

The Rouse Company operates fifty-three retail centers containing nearly 34 million square feet of retail space. Approximately 19 million square feet of this space is occupied by 114 of America's leading department stores, and the remaining 15 million square feet is leased to over 5,000 small merchants. The company is the owner/developer of thirty-four of these retail centers, while nineteen were acquired with financial partners or are operated for other owners under shared-growth management agreements.

Study Rouse's 1980–81 Balance Sheets on a cost and current-value basis and Notes 1a and 1b to the 1979–81 financial statements.

1. Provide a journal entry that would convert the 1981 historical-cost balance sheet to a current-exit-value basis, assuming that the decision to convert from historical-cost to current-value accounting was made on December 31, 1981. Provide a similar journal entry that would convert the 1980 historical-cost balance sheet to a current-exit-value basis assuming that the decision to convert was made on December 31, 1980.

2. Reconcile *changes* in the revaluation equity account. Explain the nature of the changes in value of properties (net) and present value of potential income taxes—i.e., why did the accounts increase or decrease during 1981?

3. How do current interest rates affect the various components of the company's Revaluation Equity account?

Consolidated Cost Basis and Current Value Basis Balance Sheets

December 31, 1981 and 1980
(in thousands)

	1981		1980	
	Current Value Basis (note 1)	Cost Basis	Current Value Basis (note 1)	Cost Basis
Assets				
Property and receivables under finance leases (notes 3, 4, 5, 8 and 14):				
Operating properties:				
Current value	$733,429		$648,890	
Property and deferred costs of projects		$480,636		$446,390
Less accumulated depreciation and amortization		78,983		71,828
		401,653		374,562
Receivables under finance leases		5,673		5,773
Current value of interests in retail centers managed under contract	11,000		5,280	
	744,429	407,326	654,170	380,335
Development operations:				
Construction and development in progress	19,845	19,845	45,364	45,364
Pre-construction costs	3,949	3,949	2,739	2,739
	23,794	23,794	48,103	48,103
Less development reserve	1,493	1,493	741	741
	22,301	22,301	47,362	47,362
Mortgage banking operations—receivables (notes 6 and 8)	16,942	16,854	24,968	24,909
Other property, net (note 14)	31,282	23,146	29,658	22,321
Other assets and deferred charges	18,287	18,287	16,887	16,887
Accounts and notes receivable (note 7)	35,797	35,797	30,093	30,093
Cash and temporary investments	29,140	29,140	6,331	6,331
Total	$898,178	$552,851	$809,469	$528,238

The accompanying notes are an integral part of these statements.

	1981		1980	
	Current Value Basis (note 1)	Cost Basis	Current Value Basis (note 1)	Cost Basis
Liabilities				
Debt (notes 3 and 8):				
Debt not carrying a Parent Company guarantee of repayment:				
Property debt	$333,834	$333,834	$295,021	$295,021
Mortgage banking notes payable	7,360	7,360	21,344	21,344
	341,194	341,194	316,365	316,365
Parent Company debt and debt carrying a Parent Company guarantee of repayment:				
Property debt	58,805	58,805	94,225	94,225
Other debt	16,582	17,368	7,023	7,023
Term loan notes payable	4,729	5,000	9,323	10,000
Senior subordinated notes payable	4,272	4,418	5,618	5,857
	84,388	85,591	116,189	117,105
Total debt	425,582	426,785	432,554	433,470
Obligations under capital leases (note 14)	5,929	8,203	5,957	7,681
Accounts payable and accrued expenses	36,650	36,650	33,966	33,966
Deferred credits and other liabilities	6,974	6,974	16,724	16,724
Commitments and contingencies (notes 6, 14 and 15)				
Deferred income taxes (note 10)	21,325	13,006	38,825	10,246
Redeemable $6 Cumulative Preferred stock of $100 par value per share (note 12)	1,397	1,397	1,576	1,576
Common stock and other shareholders' equity (notes 8 and 13)				
Common stock of 1¢ par value per share	159	159	146	146
Additional paid-in capital	59,770	59,770	22,896	22,896
Retained earnings	325	325	1,866	1,866
Revaluation equity (note 1)	340,485		255,292	
	400,739	60,254	280,200	24,908
Less common stock held in treasury, at cost	418	418	333	333
Total common stock and other shareholders' equity	400,321	59,836	279,867	24,575
Total	$898,178	$552,851	$809,469	$528,238

V. ALTERNATIVE VALUATION MODELS

Notes to Consolidated Financial Statements

(1) Current value basis financial statements

(a) Current value reporting

The current value of the Company's assets, primarily its operating properties, substantially exceeds the net book value of the assets as reflected in the cost basis financial statements prepared in accordance with generally accepted accounting principles. Such current value is shown in the current value basis financial statements which management believes reflect more realistically the Company's financial position and changes in shareholders' equity.

As more fully explained below, the current values of the Company's operating properties and the Company's interest in retail centers managed under contract represent management's estimates of the worth of these assets to the Company as investment properties—properties held for the long-term benefit of operating cash flows.

These estimates do not necessarily represent the sales values of these assets at the date of valuation and the total of these values should not be considered the liquidation value of these properties. In addition, current values are not presented for properties under development, as explained in "Bases of valuation" below, intangible assets and certain liabilities of the Company. Accordingly, the aggregate current value basis shareholders' equity does not represent the liquidation value of the Company, nor the fair market value of the net assets or the Company as a whole.

The Company's financial position on a current value basis as of December 31, 1981 and 1980 is reported on pages 16 and 17 as supplementary information alongside the cost basis balance sheets. The current value and cost bases are shown for each asset category and the aggregate increment of current value over net book value—$340,485,000 at December 31, 1981 and $255,292,000 at December 31, 1980—has been reflected in shareholders' equity as "revaluation equity." The changes in revaluation equity during the years ended December 31, 1981, 1980 and 1979 are reported in the statements of changes in revaluation equity on page 21.

As reflected in their report, Peat, Marwick, Mitchell & Co., the Company's auditors, have examined and reported on the current value basis financial statements. Further, Landauer Associates, Inc. (Landauer), independent real estate consultants, have examined and reported on management's estimates of the current values of the Company's operating properties and the Company's interest in retail centers managed under contract. These reports are contained on pages 22 and 23.

(b) Bases of valuation

The following describes the bases of management's estimates of current values:

- The current value of the Company's operating property assets has been defined as the value of each property's equity interest (i.e., the present value of its projected net cash flow after deducting principal and interest payments on the debt specifically related to the property) plus the outstanding balance of related debt. The current value of the Company's interest in retail centers managed under contract has been defined as the lower of the present value of incentive fees which will be earned based on projections of net cash flow of the respective retail centers or payments which will be received in the event the management contracts are terminated. The projections of net cash flow are based on an evaluation of the history and future of each property and include for each retail center:

  —a market study covering basic demographic and market volume projections plus competitive alignment and market share expectations for a six or seven year period;

  —tenant-by-tenant analyses of lease terms and sales performance and rentals during the projection period; and

  —analyses of projections of operating revenues and expenses over the projection period (including those portions of expenses passed on to tenants under lease agreements) plus financing costs—principal and interest payments and lender participations.

  The resulting values recognize the considerable differences between properties in terms of quality, age, outlook and risk.

  Landauer reviewed, analyzed and concurred with management's appraisal of the current value of the Company's operating properties and its interests in retail centers managed under contract and the present value of receivables under finance leases. The aggregate appraised values were $376,025,000 and $316,150,000 at December 31, 1981 and 1980, respectively. Concurrence, as used by Landauer, is defined as a variation of less than 10% from the probable value that might be estimated by Landauer in a full and complete appraisal.

- Construction and development in progress and pre-construction costs, net of the development reserve, are carried at the same values as in the cost basis financial statements—values which represent the lower of cost or net realizable value. While management believes that the properties under construction have values in excess of stated costs, management has taken the conservative position of not adjusting the cost basis by any value until the properties are opened and operating.

- Other property includes land held for sale, which is stated at estimated net realizable value, and the Company's headquarters building, which is valued at estimated current cost

- Mortgage banking notes receivable for which sale commitments have been pre-arranged are carried at the commitment price. The remaining notes are carried at aggregate market value.

- The liability for deferred income taxes on a current value basis is an estimate of the present value of related income tax payments which may be made over the remaining lives of the existing operating properties plus future, unnamed projects. Although the specific timing of related income tax payments cannot be determined, long-range projections of taxable income indicate such tax payments will begin in 2009 and extend beyond 2036. Such projections of taxable income include projects presently under development and future, unnamed development projects and reflect increased deductions for depreciation permitted under the Economic Recovery Tax Act of 1981. The inclusion of future, unnamed projects in the long-term projections reduced the estimated present value of potential tax payments by approximately $76,000,000 at December 31, 1981 and $31,560,000 at December 31, 1980.

  Long-term debt relating to the operating properties is carried at the same amount as in the cost basis balance sheet. Since the value of the Company's equity interest in each property is based on net cash flow after mortgage principal and interest payments, any difference between the current value and cost basis of this long-term mortgage debt is reflected in the value of the Company's interest in the operating property. The cost basis balances of mortgage banking notes payable and other property debt, primarily construction loans, represent the current value of this debt since interest rates thereon fluctuate with the prime interest rate.

  Term loan notes payable, senior subordinated notes payable, certain other debt and the obligation under the capital lease on the Company's headquarters building all carry interest rates which are substantially lower than current rates for similar liabilities. These obligations have been valued using estimated current market rates at December 31, 1981 and 1980.

- All other assets and liabilities are carried in the current value basis balance sheet at the lower of cost or net realizable value—the same stated value as in the cost basis balance sheet.

  The application of the foregoing methods for estimating current value, including the potential income tax payments, represents the best judgment of management based upon its evaluation of the current and future economy and anticipated investor rates of return at the time such estimates were made. Judgments regarding these factors are not subject to precise quantification or verification and may change from time to time as economic and market factors, and management's evaluation of them, change.

5.3. EXXON CORPORATION

Effects of restatement of historical cost to current values.
(Straightforward: 45 minutes)

The Exxon Corporation's principal business is energy, involving the exploration for and production of crude oil and natural gas, manufacture of petroleum products, and transportation and sale of crude oil, natural gas, and petroleum products. Exxon's business also involves exploration for and mining and sale of coal and uranium, and fabrication of nuclear fuel.

Study Exxon's 1979 Consolidated Balance Sheet and Statement of Income, and tables showing the effects of changing prices on Exxon's operations for 1979.

1. What were Exxon's realized holding gains (or realized cost savings) for 1979? In answering this question, compare the historical costs and the current (specific) costs columns only.

2. Estimate unrealized holding gains on inventories and property, plant, and equipment (valued using current [specific] prices) as of December 31, 1979. Approximately, how much of the unrealized gains at December 31, 1979 accrued (i.e., became realizable) in 1979?

3. Calculate the ratio of income from continuing operations to total assets on the historical-cost and the current (specific) cost basis. Which measure best gauges the company's rate of return on invested assets? Explain your answer in words.

Consolidated Balance Sheet

Assets	December 31, 1978	December 31, 1979
Current assets		
Cash, including time deposits of $1,360,181,000 and $1,755,758,000	$ 1,992,573,000	$ 2,515,964,000
Marketable securities	2,763,375,000	1,991,644,000
Notes and accounts receivable, less estimated doubtful amounts of $95,774,000 and $120,293,000	6,725,741,000	9,011,237,000
Inventories		
Crude oil, products and merchandise	3,726,938,000	4,789,936,000
Materials and supplies	570,030,000	690,758,000
Prepaid taxes and expenses	590,094,000	1,478,809,000
Total current assets	16,368,751,000	20,478,348,000
Investments and advances	1,533,078,000	1,474,601,000
Property, plant and equipment, at cost, less accumulated depreciation and depletion of $12,748,577,000 and $14,307,410,000 (Note 1)	22,805,824,000	26,292,952,000
Deferred charges and other assets	823,151,000	1,244,063,000
Total assets	41,530,804,000	**49,489,964,000**

Liabilities		
Current liabilities		
Notes and loans payable	1,400,735,000	1,867,924,000
Accounts payable and accrued liabilities	9,115,451,000	11,845,361,000
Income taxes payable	1,524,545,000	2,170,130,000
Total current liabilities	12,040,731,000	15,883,415,000
Long-term debt	3,749,241,000	4,258,018,000
Annuity and other reserves	1,099,722,000	1,413,881,000
Deferred income tax credits	3,436,848,000	4,385,082,000
Other deferred credits	95,264,000	104,925,000
Equity of minority shareholders in affiliated companies	880,400,000	892,692,000
Total liabilities	21,302,206,000	**26,938,013,000**
Shareholders' equity	20,228,598,000	**22,551,951,000**
Total liabilities and shareholders' equity	$41,530,804,000	**$49,489,964,000**

Consolidated Statement of Income

Revenue	1978	1979
Sales and other operating revenue, including excise taxes	$63,895,527,000	**$83,555,471,000**
Interest, earnings from equity interests and other revenue	990,512,000	1,253,577,000
	64,886,039,000	84,809,048,000
Costs and other deductions		
Crude oil and product purchases	31,407,903,000	40,831,456,000
Operating expenses	6,394,777,000	8,481,740,000
Selling, general and administrative expenses	3,639,772,000	4,291,395,000
Depreciation and depletion	1,677,882,000	2,027,064,000
Exploration expenses, including dry holes	775,220,000	1,052,134,000
Income, excise and other taxes	17,516,326,000	23,091,713,000
Interest expense	424,740,000	493,989,000
Foreign exchange loss (Note 3)	186,271,000	102,957,000
Income applicable to minority interests	100,148,000	141,357,000
	62,123,039,000	80,513,805,000
Net income	$ 2,763,000,000	**$ 4,295,243,000**
Per share	$6.20	$9.74

Income from continuing operations and other changes in shareholders' equity adjusted for changing prices

For the year ended December 31, 1979 (millions of dollars)   (millions of average 1979 dollars)

	As reported on page 25	Adjusted for	
		General inflation	Specific costs
Income from continuing operations			
Total revenue	$84,809	$84,809	$84,809
Costs and other deductions			
Crude oil and product purchases	40,831	40,831	40,831
Depreciation and depletion	2,027	3,270	3,932
Other	14,070	14,070	14,070
Interest expense	494	494	494
Income, excise and other taxes	23,092	23,092	23,092
Total costs and other deductions	$80,514	$81,757	$82,419
Income from continuing operations	**$ 4,295**	**$ 3,052**	**$ 2,390**
Gain from decline in the purchasing power of net amounts owed		998	998
Increase in current cost of inventories and property, plant and equipment during 1979			9,333
Less effect of increase in general price level during 1979			6,634
Excess of increase in specific prices over increase in the general price level			2,699
Net income	**$ 4,295**		
Adjusted net income		**$ 4,050**	
Net change in shareholders' equity from above	**$ 4,295**	**$ 4,050**	**$ 6,087**

Summarized balance sheet adjusted for changing prices

at December 31, 1979 (millions of dollars)   (millions of average 1979 dollars)

	As reported on page 24	Adjusted for	
		General inflation	Specific costs
Assets			
Inventories	$ 5,481	$ 7,585	$11,558
Property, plant and equipment	26,293	35,796	45,418
All other assets	17,716	16,892	16,892
Total assets	**49,490**	**60,273**	**73,868**
Total liabilities	26,938	25,599	25,599
Shareholders' equity	**$22,552**	**$34,674**	**$48,269**

V. ALTERNATIVE VALUATION MODELS

5.4. XEROX CORPORATION

Voluntary accounting change, foreign currency translation adjustments. (Difficult: 75 minutes)

Xerox Corporation manufactures and markets information products and systems with about 44 percent of its revenue outside the United States. Xerox's principal industry segment is reprographics, consisting of the development, manufacture, and marketing of xerographic copiers and duplicators, as well as electronic printing systems. Xerox also provides related services.

Study the Consolidated Balance Sheets for 1980–81 and 1979–80, Consolidated Statements of Income for 1979–81 and 1978–80, Consolidated Statement of Retained Earnings for 1979–81, and notes to 1981 consolidated financial statements on "Accounting Changes" and "Foreign Currency Translation."

1. Prepare a table that compares the 1980 Balance Sheet in the 1980 statements with the 1980 Balance Sheet in the 1981 statements. The comparative 1980 figures in the 1981 statements have been restated for accounting changes. Use the following format (an example is provided):

Account Title	1980 Restated	1980 Original	Effect on Stockholders' Equity
Inventories	$1,090.2M	$1,086.4M	$3.8M increase

2. Xerox's 1977, 1978, 1979, and 1980 net income numbers before accounting changes for foreign currency and vacation pay were $415M, $484M, $563M, and $619M, respectively.

a. Plot Xerox's 1977–81 net income assuming the accounting changes made in 1981 had not been made.

b. Now plot Xerox's 1977–81 net income after the accounting changes. Net income for 1977 and 1978 after such changes was $432M and $497M. Comment on Xerox's retrospective recognition of the accounting changes.

c. Suppose an investor wanted a measure of net income absent the effects of currency rate changes and exchange gains or losses. Compute Xerox's 1979–81 income without foreign currency gains or losses.

d. Was Xerox's profit performance in 1981 better or worse than its profit performance in 1980? Discuss briefly.

3. Reconcile the data on accounting changes in Consolidated Statement of Retained Earnings with the numbers provided in the Note on "Accounting Changes."

4. What is the most likely cause of the drop in cumulative translation adjustments from $98.8 million (credit) in 1980 to $150.1 million (debit) in 1981?

Consolidated Balance Sheets

Assets (Dollars in millions)	December 31	1981	1980
Current Assets			
Cash		$ **45.2**	$ 86.8
Bank time deposits, interest bearing		**234.0**	228.8
Marketable securities, at the lower of cost or market		**148.0**	207.3
Trade receivables (less allowance for doubtful receivables: 1981–$56.5; 1980–$59.1)		**1,245.3**	1,163.8
Receivable from Xerox Credit Corporation		**178.2**	196.3
Accrued revenues		**403.3**	376.8
Inventories, at the lower of average cost or market		**1,131.9**	1,090.2
Other current assets		**230.2**	210.0
Total current assets		**3,616.1**	3,560.0
Trade Receivables Due after One Year		**245.5**	199.4
Rental Equipment and Related Inventories			
At cost (less accumulated depreciation: 1981–$2,715.4; 1980–$2,878.6)		**1,905.1**	1,966.8
Land, Buildings and Equipment			
At cost (less accumulated depreciation: 1981–$1,126.7; 1980–$1,049.6)		**1,438.7**	1,410.4
Investments, at equity		**319.6**	226.6
Other Assets		**149.4**	150.6
Total Assets		**$7,674.4**	$7,513.8

Liabilities and Shareholders' Equity (Dollars in millions)	December 31	1981	1980
Current Liabilities			
Notes payable		$ **224.2**	$ 208.4
Current portion of long-term debt		**96.3**	80.0
Accounts payable		**340.2**	315.8
Salaries, profit sharing and other accruals		**909.9**	907.3
Income taxes		**346.5**	425.4
Other current liabilities		**163.7**	147.8
Total current liabilities		**2,080.8**	2,084.7
Long-Term Debt		**869.5**	898.3
Other Noncurrent Liabilities		**145.0**	133.0
Deferred Income Taxes		**247.0**	142.7
Deferred Investment Tax Credits		**108.9**	85.6
Outside Shareholders' Interests in Equity of Subsidiaries		**495.6**	539.5
Shareholders' Equity			
Common stock, $1 par value Authorized 100,000,000 shares		**84.3**	84.3
Class B stock, $1 par value Authorized 600,000 shares		**.2**	.2
Additional paid-in capital		**306.0**	304.9
Retained earnings		**3,500.1**	3,155.4
Cumulative translation adjustments		**(150.1)**	98.8
Total		**3,740.5**	3,643.6
Deduct Class B stock receivables and deferrals		**12.9**	13.6
Total shareholders' equity		**3,727.6**	3,630.0
Total Liabilities and Shareholders' Equity		**$7,674.4**	$7,513.8

V. ALTERNATIVE VALUATION MODELS

Consolidated Balance Sheets

Xerox Corporation and Subsidiaries

Assets (Dollars in millions) December 31	1980	1979
Current Assets		
Cash	$ 86.8	$ 42.2
Bank time deposits, interest bearing	228.8	267.7
Marketable securities, at the lower of cost or market	207.3	447.7
Trade receivables (less allowance for doubtful receivables: 1980–$59.1; 1979–$60.1)	1,163.8	1,120.4
Receivable from Xerox Credit Corporation	196.3	–
Accrued revenues	376.8	259.3
Inventories, at the lower of average cost or market	1,086.4	785.8
Other current assets	168.9	180.5
Total current assets	3,515.1	3,103.6
Trade Receivables Due after One Year	199.4	274.2
Rental Equipment and Related Inventories		
At cost (less accumulated depreciation: 1980–$2,770.1; 1979–$2,678.0)	1,922.3	1,736.4
Land, Buildings and Equipment		
At cost (less accumulated depreciation and amortization: 1980–$1,033.4; 1979–$880.3)	1,369.4	1,222.3
Investments, at equity		
Fuji Xerox Co., Ltd.	114.8	105.7
Xerox Credit Corporation	79.2	–
Total investments	194.0	105.7
Other Assets	149.0	111.4
Total Assets	$7,349.2	$6,553.6

Liabilities and Shareholders' Equity (Dollars in millions)	December 31	1980	1979
Current Liabilities			
Notes payable		$ 208.4	$ 96.3
Payments due within one year on long-term debt		80.0	40.2
Accounts payable		315.8	325.1
Salaries, profit sharing and other accruals		791.5	689.5
Income taxes		440.5	426.0
Other current liabilities		147.8	102.2
Total current liabilities		1,984.0	1,679.3
Long-Term Debt		898.3	913.0
Other Noncurrent Liabilities		133.0	127.9
Deferred Income Taxes		123.8	110.4
Deferred Investment Tax Credits		85.6	70.1
Outside Shareholders' Interests in Equity of Subsidiaries		499.8	431.5
Shareholders' Equity			
Common stock, $1 par value Authorized 100,000,000 shares		84.3	83.9
Class B stock, $1 par value Authorized 600,000 shares		.2	.2
Additional paid-in capital		304.9	286.8
Retained earnings		3,248.9	2,866.2
Total		3,638.3	3,237.1
Deduct Class B stock receivables and deferrals		13.6	15.7
Total shareholders' equity		3,624.7	3,221.4
Total Liabilities and Shareholders' Equity		$7,349.2	$6,553.6

Consolidated Statements of Income

(In millions, except per share data) Year Ended December 31	**1981**	1980	1979
Operating Revenues			
Rentals and services	**$5,279.6**	$5,151.6	$4,606.3
Sales	**3,411.4**	3,044.9	2,390.1
Total operating revenues	**8,691.0**	8,196.5	6,996.4
Costs and Expenses			
Cost of rentals and services	**2,269.5**	2,167.5	1,905.0
Cost of sales	**1,570.8**	1,435.6	1,075.1
Research and development expenses	**526.3**	435.8	378.1
Selling, administrative and general expenses	**3,095.0**	2,882.1	2,432.9
Total costs and expenses	**7,461.6**	6,921.0	5,791.1
Operating Income	**1,229.4**	1,275.5	1,205.3
Other Income (Deductions), Net (includes interest expense: 1981–$130.3; 1980–$115.2; 1979–$102.8)	**(49.5)**	3.6	1.7
Income before Income Taxes	**1,179.9**	1,279.1	1,207.0
Income Taxes	**454.4**	611.8	587.2
Income before Outside Shareholders' Interests	**725.5**	667.3	619.8
Outside Shareholders' Interests	**127.3**	102.4	104.8
Net Income	**$ 598.2**	$ 564.9	$ 515.0
Average Common Shares Outstanding	**84.5**	84.4	84.1
Net Income per Common Share	**$7.08**	$6.69	$6.12

Consolidated Statements of Income

Xerox Corporation and Subsidiaries

(In millions, except per share data) Year Ended December 31	1980	1979	1978
Operating Revenues			
Rentals and services	$5,151.6	$4,606.3	$4,130.5
Sales	3,044.9	2,390.1	1,887.5
Total operating revenues	8,196.5	6,996.4	6,018.0
Costs and Expenses			
Cost of rentals and services	2,117.9	1,862.3	1,691.6
Cost of sales	1,425.3	1,065.8	770.6
Research and development expenses	434.1	376.4	311.0
Selling, administrative and general expenses	2,866.7	2,419.6	2,089.0
Total costs and expenses	6,844.0	5,724.1	4,862.2
Operating Income	1,352.5	1,272.3	1,155.8
Other Income (Deductions), Net (includes interest expense: 1980–$115.2; 1979–$102.8; 1978–$125.4)	(1.4)	11.0	(64.6)
Income before Income Taxes	1,351.1	1,283.3	1,091.2
Income Taxes	604.5	592.0	528.0
Income before Outside Shareholders' Interests	746.6	691.3	563.2
Outside Shareholders' Interests	127.4	128.2	86.7
Income before Extraordinary Item	619.2	563.1	476.5
Extraordinary Income (Net of Income Taxes)	–	–	12.0
Net Income	$ 619.2	$ 563.1	$ 488.5
Average Common Shares Outstanding	84.4	84.1	84.1
Income per Common Share			
Income before Extraordinary Item	$7.33	$6.69	$5.67
Extraordinary Income	–	–	.14
Net Income per Common Share	$7.33	$6.69	$5.81

V. ALTERNATIVE VALUATION MODELS

Consolidated Statements of Common and Class B Shares, Additional Paid-In Capital and Retained Earnings

(Dollars in millions, except per share data) Year Ended December 31	**1981**	1980	1979
Retained Earnings			
Balance at beginning of year, as previously reported	**$3,248.9**	$2,866.2	$2,501.3
Add (deduct) adjustments for the cumulative effect on prior years of retroactively applying the new methods of accounting for			
Foreign currency translation	**(35.4)**	11.1	51.6
Vacation pay benefits	**(58.1)**	(50.3)	(42.7)
Balance at beginning of year, as adjusted	**3,155.4**	2,827.0	2,510.2
Net income	**598.2**	564.9	515.0
Total	**3,753.6**	3,391.9	3,025.2
Deduct cash dividends declared			
On common and Class B stocks (Per share: 1981–$3.00; 1980–$2.80; 1979–$2.40)	**(253.5)**	(236.5)	(195.5)
On capital stock of pooled company prior to acquisition	**—**	—	(2.7)
Total cash dividends	**(253.5)**	(236.5)	(198.2)
Balance at end of year	**$3,500.1**	$3,155.4	$2,827.0

Notes to Consolidated Financial Statements

Accounting Changes
Foreign Currency Translation
In December 1981, the Financial Accounting Standards Board (FASB) issued Statement No. 52, Foreign Currency Translation, which revised the existing accounting and reporting requirements for translation of foreign currency transactions and foreign currency financial statements. The Company has elected the early application of the Statement encouraged by the FASB. As permitted by the Statement, the financial statements for the four years prior to 1981 have been restated. The effects of this change in accounting on net income and net income per common share were (in millions, except per share data):

Increase (decrease)	Net Income	Per Share
1981	$ 26.2	$ .31
1980	(46.5)	(.55)
1979	(40.5)	(.48)

Vacation Pay
Effective January 1, 1981, the Company adopted Statement No. 43 of the FASB whereby the costs of employees' vacation pay benefits are accrued as they are earned. Financial statements for the four years prior to 1981 have been restated as required by the Statement, resulting in a decrease in retained earnings as of January 1, 1979 of $42.7 million, net of

$40.6 million of income taxes. The effects of this change in accounting on net income and net income per common share were (in millions, except per share data):

Increase (decrease)	Net Income	Per Share
1981	$(7.6)	$(.09)
1980	(7.8)	(.09)
1979	(7.6)	(.09)

Foreign Currency Translation
An analysis of the changes in cumulative translation adjustments for each of the years in the three year period ended December 31, 1981 follows:

(Dollars in millions)	1981	1980	1979
Cumulative translation adjustments at beginning of year	$ 98.8	$ 76.5	$119.3
Translation adjustments and intercompany foreign currency transactions	(376.7)	35.5	(64.7)
Outside shareholders' interests	127.8	(13.2)	21.9
Cumulative translation adjustments at end of year	$(150.1)	$ 98.8	$ 76.5

The consolidated statements of income include net aggregate exchange losses of $64.5 million, $16.7 million and $4.5 million in 1981, 1980 and 1979, respectively.

5.5. INTERNATIONAL BUSINESS MACHINES CORPORATION

Adoption of FASB Statement No. 52, "Foreign Currency *Translation," preliminary announcements of earnings, analyst confusion, mandatory accounting change.*
(Straightforward: 45 minutes)

The International Business Machines Corporation (IBM) operates in the fields of information-handling systems, equipment, and services. Its products include data-processing machines and systems, telecommunication systems and products, information distributors, office systems, typewriters, copiers, educational and testing materials, and related supplies and services.

Study IBM's 1980–82 Consolidated Statement of Earnings and Notes to Consolidated Financial Statements for 1982, "Accounting Change—Foreign Currency Translation" and "Non-U.S. Operations." Also included is an article from the *Wall Street Journal,* January 25, 1983, commenting on IBM's preliminary earnings announcement.

1. For the years 1980–82, calculate (a) the percentage of gross income from sales, rentals, and services derived from non-U.S. operations to total gross income and (b) the percentage of net earnings derived from non-U.S. operations to total net earnings.

2. Prepare a chart showing 1980–82 earnings per share compiled on the basis of (1) *FASB Statement No. 52,* adopted fourth quarter 1982, and (2) *FASB Statement No. 8,* the accounting measurement rule used by IBM prior to that date.

3. By how much would 1980–82 earnings from non-U.S. operations have changed had *Statement No. 52* not been adopted in late 1982?

4. Did 1981 earnings increase or decrease relative to 1980? Explain. Should IBM have voluntarily adopted *Statement No. 52* in fourth-quarter 1981, as was allowed by the provisions of that standard?

5. Comment on the stock price movements surrounding the release of IBM's preliminary earnings data (not the annual report, which was released in February). Do such movements violate the concept of market efficiency?

International Business Machines Corporation
and Subsidiary Companies

Consolidated Statement of Earnings
for the year ended December 31:

(Dollars in millions except per share amounts)	1982		1981*		1980*	
Gross Income:						
Sales	$ 16,815		$ 12,901		$ 10,919	
Rentals	11,121		10,839		10,869	
Services	6,428		5,330		4,425	
		$ 34,364		$ 29,070		$ 26,213
Cost of sales	6,682		5,162		4,238	
Cost of rentals	3,959		4,041		3,841	
Cost of services	3,047		2,534		2,187	
Selling, general and administrative expenses	9,578		8,583		8,094	
Research, development and engineering expenses	3,042		2,451		2,287	
Interest expense	454		407		273	
		26,762		23,178		20,920
		7,602		5,892		5,293
Other income, principally interest		328		368		430
Earnings before income taxes		7,930		6,260		5,723
Provision for U.S. Federal and						
non-U.S. income taxes		3,521		2,650		2,326
Net Earnings		$ 4,409		$ 3,610		$ 3,397
Per share		$ 7.39		$ 6.14		$ 5.82

Average number of shares outstanding:
1982–596,688,501
1981–587,803,373
1980–583,516,764

*Restated. See Accounting Change –
Foreign Currency Translation note

V. ALTERNATIVE VALUATION MODELS

The company adopted Statement of Financial Accounting Standards (SFAS) No. 52, "Foreign Currency Translation," in the fourth quarter of 1982, effective January 1, 1982. The consolidated financial statements for the years 1981 and 1980 have been restated to give effect to this change in accounting principle.

Non-U. S. subsidiaries which operate in a local currency environment account for approximately 85% of the company's non-U. S. gross income. In applying SFAS No. 52 to financial statements of these subsidiaries, assets and liabilities are translated to U. S. dollars at year-end exchange rates. Income and expense items are translated at average rates of exchange prevailing during the year. Translation adjustments are accumulated in a separate component of stockholders' equity.

The remaining 15% of the company's non-U. S. gross income is derived from subsidiaries and branches which operate in U. S. dollars or whose economic environment is highly inflationary. In accordance with SFAS No. 52, inventories and plant, rental machines and other property, applicable to these operations, are remeasured in U. S. dollars at approximate rates prevailing when acquired. Inventories charged to cost of sales and depreciation are remeasured at historical rates. Gains and losses which result from remeasurement are included in earnings.

The effects of this accounting change on net earnings and earnings per share are an increase of $449 million and $.75 in 1982, an increase of $302 million and $.51 in 1981 and a decrease of $165 million and $.28 in 1980.

Aggregate transaction gains (losses) included in earnings are $(7) million in 1982, $78 million in 1981 and $(18) million in 1980.

Non-U. S. Operations	(Dollars in millions)	1982	1981	1980
At end of year:				
Net assets employed				
Current assets		$ 6,299	$ 5,436	$ 5,531
Current liabilities		4,240	4,108	3,914
Working capital		2,059	1,328	1,617
Plant, rental machines and other property, net		6,740	7,152	7,006
Deferred charges and other assets		887	890	931
		9,686	9,370	9,554
Reserves for employees' indemnities and retirement plans		1,198	1,184	1,443
Long-term debt		480	496	437
		1,678	1,680	1,880
Net assets employed		$ 8,008	$ 7,690	$ 7,674
Number of employees		150,444	149,794	146,973
For the year:				
Gross income from sales, rentals and services		$ 15,336	$ 13,982	$ 13,787
Earnings before income taxes		$ 3,226	$ 2,664	$ 2,772
Provision for U. S. Federal and non-U. S. income taxes		1,577	1,123	1,035†
Net earnings		$ 1,649	$ 1,541	$ 1,737
Investment in plant, rental machines and other property		$ 2,682	$ 3,274	$ 3,367

†See Taxes

For the years 1982 and 1981, non-U. S. financial results were severely impacted by the strength of the U. S. dollar relative to the currencies of many countries around the world. The Management Discussion on page 29 refers to this effect in greater detail. The graphs on the following page further illustrate the decline in value, in relation to the dollar, of the five major foreign currencies in which IBM conducts most of its non-U. S. business.

Undistributed earnings of non-U. S. subsidiaries included in consolidated retained earnings amounted to $7,538 million at December 31, 1982, $6,565 million at December 31, 1981, and $5,943 million at December 31, 1980. These earnings are indefinitely reinvested in non-U. S. operations. Accordingly, no provision has been made for taxes that might be payable upon remittance of such earnings.

International Business Machines Corporation

135

IBM's Second Set of 1982 Earnings Statistics Brings a Sigh of Relief From Puzzled Analysts

By R. Foster Winans

Even a computer couldn't help Wall Street securities analysts untangle International Business Machines' fourth-quarter and 1982 earnings announcement late last week.

Friday, the stock sagged 3¼ in the confusion. There were fears that, when all the pieces were assembled correctly, the resulting picture would spell trouble.

On the face of it, IBM performed like a trouper in 1982. While a badly battered economy tried to struggle to its feet, the big computer maker's 1982 net income leaped 22% on an 18% jump in revenue. And the fourth quarter looked even rosier: Net rose 28% on a 23% increase in revenue.

But Wall Street was dismayed to find that a sizable chunk of the increase didn't come from the company's growth but from an accounting change in the way IBM reports its overseas operations. IBM rushed a second set of figures to analysts yesterday, and a collective sigh of relief gusted through the financial community.

Heard on the Street

Analysts say the second set of figures showed that even using the prior accounting standards the company would have done well in 1982. "The confusion on Friday was that we didn't have enough detail," says Barry Tarasoff, an analyst at Goldman, Sachs & Co. "Well, we got it today, and the fourth quarter looks fine."

IBM recovered yesterday from a morning low of 92¼ to close at 93⅝, off 1 in a dismal market, as analysts decided the stock had become "cheap."

IBM had been reporting its results under Financial Accounting Standards Board Rule No. 8, which requires companies operating overseas to carry the effect of foreign currencies vs. the dollar directly to the bottom line.

During 1982 the company switched to the board's new rule, No. 52, which minimizes both the negative and positive impacts of foreign currency exchange rates. With foreign currencies currently weak, the switch to FASB 52 makes the foreign operations of U.S. concerns look better than they did under FASB 8.

But analysts Friday wanted to strip away the minimizing effect of FASB 52 and look at the company's results under the old rule. What they found disturbed them.

"If you looked at the fourth-quarter results under FASB 8, net income grew 15.4% but revenue was up 23.1%," says Daniel Mandresh, an information processing analyst at Merrill Lynch, Pierce, Fenner & Smith Inc. "Because profits grew slower than revenue, it appeared that profit margins were eroding."

But Mr. Mandresh says that anyone who came to that conclusion Friday ignored an important aspect of FASB 8: The effective tax rate is higher than under FASB 52 because of accounting peculiarities. As a result, he calculates the company did better than original numbers suggested. "I figure pre-tax income in the fourth quarter rose about 24.5% vs. revenue growth of 23%," even under FASB 8, he says.

IBM, in an effort to clear up the confusion, issued a statement late yesterday saying that under the old accounting method, 1982 pre-tax earnings would have been 25.7% above 1981, and net income would have risen 19.7%. Under the new accounting rule, pre-tax earnings were up 26.7%, and net rose 22.1%, the company said.

"We believe 1982 represented a strong performance by IBM regardless of the method of accounting," said John R. Opel, president and chief executive.

Mr. Mandresh and others agree. Profit margins remain strong, and, at its current price, "the stock is a buy," he says.

Looking behind the numbers, analysts found even more to cheer about. "Sales were very strong in the fourth quarter," says Goldman's Mr. Tarasoff. He says the figures suggest continued strength in IBM's flagship line of large business computers and a high rate of conversion from computer leasing to outright sales.

IBM is encouraging its customers to buy instead of lease by raising leasing fees and cutting purchase prices. This is a positive move, Mr. Tarasoff says, because the company becomes less vulnerable to obsolete, leased equipment being returned when newer, more efficient models are brought to market.

Analysts estimate that the company sold 200,000 of its personal computers during 1982, up from 55,000 in 1981, when they were on the market less than six months. Dataquest Inc., a unit of A.C. Nielsen, the market-research concern, estimates that IBM will sell 300,000 in 1983.

Alex D. Stein, a Dataquest analyst, says he was surprised by the market's reaction to IBM's original earnings report. "The market's been very emotional, but I was surprised that people paid as much attention to it as they did."

Money managers mostly were unmoved by the debate. Martin D. Sass, president of M.D. Sass Investors, says the confusion left unchanged his feeling about the company and the 180,000 or so shares he owns.

"IBM is right on track," he says. "But the earnings came out in a skittish market, and people were itchy to take profits."

V. ALTERNATIVE VALUATION MODELS

5.6. WITCO CHEMICAL CORPORATION

Reserve recognition accounting, present value calculations.
(Difficult: 75 minutes)

The Witco Chemical Corporation produces a wide range of special-purpose chemical and petroleum products as well as engineered materials and parts for industrial and consumer use. Witco reported 1981 Income before Federal and Foreign Income Taxes of $68.4 million, including operating income from oil and gas activities of $9.2 million.

The accompanying supplemental financial data relating to oil and gas activities is reported in compliance with disclosure rules established by the Securities and Exchange Commission, called reserve recognition accounting (RRA).

1. Assume that future net revenues from proved developed and proved undeveloped oil and gas reserves will continue for only twenty years, and that the net revenues for the years 1985–2011 (i.e., the seventeen years following 1984) are expected to be constant.[1] What is the constant *annual* net revenue stream to be generated in each of years 1985, 1986, etc? (*Note:* The present value of proved reserves as of December 31, 1981, was $76,520,000, assuming a 10 percent discount rate.)

2. Assume that a subsidiary of Witco called Witco Oil and Gas Exploration Company has assets of cash $10,000,000 and oil and gas properties with end-of-1980 present value of $85,419,000. The subsidiary has no liabilities, contributed capital of $20,000,000, with the remainder of equity retained in the business as undistributed earnings.

---

[1]In actuality, the estimated future net revenues are not expected to be constant over periods 4–20. This means that the sum of the *constant* annual net revenue stream derived in part 1 will not equal the $112,732,000 value assigned to the 1985-plus future net revenues.

a. Prepare a journal entry that would establish a beginning-of-1981 balance sheet for Witco Oil and Gas.

b. Based on Witco's Summary of Oil and Gas Producing Activities, prepare a 1981 Statement of Income and end-of-1981 Balance Sheet for Witco Oil and Gas in accordance with reserve recognition accounting. Assume that all transactions with outside parties are for cash, except a federal taxes refund that the company receives on January 2, 1982. (Note: Additional development expenses of $4,282,000 are assumed paid in cash.)

3. Explain in words why the present value of proved oil and gas reserves *decreased* by $8,899,000 in 1981 when, in fact, the company discovered, extended, or added to it oil and gas quantities in 1981 by 4,336,000 barrels and 1,134 cubic feet, respectively.

Oil and Gas Producing Information

Valuation of Proved Reserves: The present value and summary of oil and gas producing activities have been prepared in accordance with the methodology prescribed by the Securities and Exchange Commission (SEC) called Reserve Recognition Accounting (RRA). Under RRA, an asset is recognized and earnings are recorded when oil and gas reserves are proved through exploration and development activities. Proved oil and gas reserves are the estimated quantities of crude oil and natural gas which geological and engineering data demonstrate with reasonable certainty to be recoverable in future years from known reservoirs under existing economic and operating conditions.

The RRA valuation of proved reserves is determined as follows:

(1) Estimates are made of quantities of proved reserves and the future periods during which they are expected to be produced based on year end economic conditions;

(2) The estimated future production of proved reserves is priced on the basis of year end prices;

(3) The resulting future gross revenue streams are reduced by estimated future costs to develop and to produce the proved reserves, based on year end cost estimates;

(4) The resulting future net revenue streams are reduced to present value amounts by applying a 10 percent discount factor.

As acknowledged by the SEC, this valuation procedure does not necessarily yield the best estimate of the fair market value of a company's oil and gas properties. An estimate of fair market value should also take into account, among other factors, a discount factor that reflects current economic conditions, the likelihood of future recoveries of oil and gas in excess of proved reserves and anticipated future prices of oil and gas along with related development and production costs.

Summary of Changes in Present Value of Estimated Future Net Revenues From Proved Oil and Gas Reserves

(thousands of dollars)	1981	1980	1979
Additions and revisions			
Revisions to reserves proved in prior years	$(32,337)	$ 9,951	$104,726
Revisions to reserves due to Windfall Profit Tax	26,559	(40,112)	—
Purchase of reserves in place (at acquisition cost)	—	—	353
Revisions to reserves purchased	—	—	1,758
Extensions, discoveries and other additions	4,886	1,765	2,674
Estimated future development costs incurred during the year	6,075	5,833	5,326
	5,183	(22,563)	114,837
Decreases for sales of oil and gas and value of transfers, net of lifting costs	(14,082)	(14,867)	(11,529)
Net increase (decrease)	(8,899)	(37,430)	103,308
Balance at beginning of year	85,419	122,849	19,541
Balance at end of year	$ 76,520	$ 85,419	$122,849

Summary of Oil and Gas Producing Activities Prepared on the Basis of Reserve Recognition Accounting

(thousands of dollars)	1981	1980	1979
Additions and revisions to proved reserves			
Revisions to reserves proved in prior years			
Increase (decrease) in prices	$ **(7,459)**	$ 3,571	$114,332
Interest factor — accretion of discount	**8,542**	12,285	1,954
Other	**(33,420)**	(5,905)	(11,560)
Total revisions to reserves proved in prior years	**(32,337)**	9,951	104,726
Revisions due to Windfall Profit Tax	**26,559**	(40,112)	—
Extensions, discoveries and other additions	**4,886**	1,765	2,674
Revisions to reserves purchased	**—**	—	1,758
Total additions and revisions to proved reserves	**(892)**	(28,396)	109,158
Development costs in excess of amounts previously estimated	**4,282**	1,251	438
Results of oil and gas producing activities on the basis of reserve recognition accounting before federal income taxes	**(5,174)**	(29,647)	108,720
Provision (benefit) for federal income taxes	**(1,372)**	(13,111)	51,149
Results of oil and gas producing activities on the basis of reserve recognition accounting	$ **(3,802)**	$(16,536)	$ 57,571
Operating income from oil and gas producing activities before federal income taxes based upon historical costs	$ **9,150**	$ 12,032	$ 9,010

Analysis of RRA Presentation: Results of oil and gas producing activities on the basis of reserve recognition accounting are arrived at by (i) additions to proved reserves from new field discoveries and extensions and revisions to the RRA valuation of reserves proved in prior years, and (ii) costs incurred in development activities.

Included in the revisions of reserves proved in prior years are the changes in valuation resulting from the use of the year end price. During the year 1981, the market value of crude oil declined affecting the RRA valuation by $7,459,000 while in previous years the year end market prices increased, thereby contributing $3,571,000 and $114,332,000 in 1980 and 1979, respectively.

Interest factor — accretion of discount, results from applying a discounted cash flow technique in the RRA valuation of proved reserves. The resulting increase is due to the production schedule of proved reserves being moved up one year on the discount table.

Also included in revisions to reserves proved in prior years — other are revisions to reserves estimates, changes in cost and changes in timing of production which all individually and collectively affect the RRA valuation. In 1981, downward revisions to previous years reserves estimates and increases in costs are the primary factors contributing to the change in this caption.

The favorable impact of Windfall Profit Tax is due to amendments to the 1980 Windfall Profit Tax Act as prescribed by The Economic Recovery Tax Act of 1981, which restored $26,559,000 of the 1980 reduction.

The caption extensions, discoveries and other additions represents proved reserves added through exploration and development activities. The increase in the current period is reflective of an expanded scope of exploration activity on previously unproven properties.

Development costs in excess of amounts previously estimated reflects the actual costs incurred during the year adjusted for development costs estimated in prior years.

The RRA provision for income taxes is based on the year end tax rates taking into account differences in the timing of recognizing RRA and taxable income and giving effect to investment tax credits. The effective tax rate as a percent of the results of oil and gas producing activities on the basis of RRA before federal income taxes was 27 percent, 44 percent, and 47 percent for the years 1981, 1980 and 1979, respectively.

V. ALTERNATIVE VALUATION MODELS

Other Considerations: The Company cautions against projecting future RRA results on the basis of individual past years. RRA seeks to reflect events relating to developments projected to occur, whereas under generally accepted accounting principles, the impact of such events is reported over many future years. A number of years may elapse between incurring costs and knowing the economic results of the expenditures. New information about reservoir characteristics may significantly change previous estimates of proved reserves and their valuation. For these and other reasons, a year is too short a period to evaluate the results of a development program. An analysis of the RRA information should not, therefore, give undue emphasis to the results of any particular year; rather, the RRA information should help explain and demonstrate the impact of major factors affecting the Company over a number of years.

As discussed above, the RRA valuation of proved reserves will be revised in the future on the basis of new information as it becomes available, as estimates of proved reserves are imprecise. The Company's production and its exploration and development programs will require the continued revisions of reserve estimates. Further, future RRA valuations of the Company's proved reserves will reflect prices and related costs in effect in the future.

RRA estimated future net revenues and operating income from· oil and gas producing activities have been reduced to reflect the Windfall Profit Tax. In calculating the amounts of such reductions the Company has applied the provisions applicable to independent producers, under which as a result of the 1981 amendment, (i) the tax rate until 1983 for most of the Company's production is 30% rather than 60% of the windfall profit amount on the first 1,000· barrels per day of production and (ii) such production beginning in 1983 is exempt. The Company believes it has good grounds for its position that it is an independent producer, but the factors controlling the determination are complex and no definitive interpretation has been promulgated by the Internal Revenue Service. The Company is currently involved in a proceeding seeking judicial affirmation of its status as an independent producer for 1975, and the outcome of that litigation is expected to affect its status for future years. Until the criteria for such status are established, estimates of future net revenues are subject to this additional uncertainty. The Company is hopeful that the issue will be resolved during calendar 1982 and believes that an adverse determination of its independent producer status would not have a material adverse effect on earnings for such year. However, such an adverse determination could, unless the Company subsequently qualifies as an independent producer, have a significant effect on RRA estimated future net revenues and operating income if the Windfall Profit Tax remains in effect without amendment and if the amount of the estimated windfall profit for future periods remains substantial.

Since December 31, 1981 the market value of crude oil has declined further. The impact of these price declines would have an adverse affect on RRA unless offset by future price increases. At present, management cannot assess the impact of the future market conditions on the price of crude oil.

The Company will review and adjust oil and gas reserves to reflect current conditions. The Company is not aware of any other event either favorable or unfavorable that occurred since December 31, 1981, that would cause a significant change in the Company's proved reserves.

All of these uncertainties should be considered in reviewing the RRA data.

Estimated Future Net Revenues from Proved Oil and Gas Reserves

(thousands of dollars)	Proved Developed And Undeveloped	Proved Developed
Year ended December 31		
1982 (1)	$ 8,544	$13,079
1983	14,261	13,928
1984	13,950	11,390
Remainder	112,732	50,876
Total	$149,487	$89,273

Present Value of Estimated Future Net Revenues
From Proved Oil and Gas Reserves at December 31

1979	$122,849	$71,459
1980	$ 85,419	$58,643
1981	$ 76,520	$59,093

(1) 1982 estimated future net revenues from proved developed oil and gas reserves are greater than the estimated future net revenues from proved developed and undeveloped oil and gas reserves because a significant amount of development costs have been projected.

6.1. MATTEL, INC., AND SUBSIDIARIES

Analysis of footnote on debt, market value vs. book value of debt. (Moderate: 60 minutes)

Mattel operates through five principal divisions—Mattel Toys, Mattel Electronics, Monogram Models, Circus World, and Western Publishing. Mattel Toys is the world's largest single toy manufacturer and has produced and sold the Barbie Doll for twenty-three years.

Study Note 3, "Long-Term Liabilities and Credit Lines," and the liabilities section of the 1982 Consolidated Statement of Financial Position.

1. Prove that the scheduled maturities of long-term loans for the 1983 fiscal year amount to $9,643. Assume that the principal payments on the 6¾ percent note in 1983 amount to approximately $76,000.

2. Calculate the present value of the 9½ percent notes, payable $1,400,000 annually from fiscal 1986 through 1998, with the balance payable in 1999. Assume that all payments, interest and principal, are made at the end of each fiscal year. Use a discount factor of 12 percent.

3. Interpret (in words) the difference between your answer in part 2 and the $20 million amount shown as a long-term loan (on January 30, 1982). How should stockholders be informed about such differences?

Note 3

Long-Term Liabilities and Credit Lines

Long-Term Loans — Long-term loans consist of the following:

(In thousands)	1982	1981
Bank term loans, payable fiscal 1984 through fiscal 1990	$ 73,400	$ 73,434
9½% secured term loan, payable $6,667,000 in fiscal 1983, balance in fiscal 1984	10,000	16,667
10% Malaysian term loan secured by land and building, payable fiscal 1985 through 1991	1,964	—
6¾% note secured by land and building, due through fiscal 1988	847	918
Unsecured debt of Western 9⅝% notes, payable $1,300,000 annually through fiscal 1995, balance in fiscal 1996	18,700	20,000
9½% notes, payable $1,400,000 annually fiscal 1986 through 1998, balance in fiscal 1999	20,000	20,000
8⅝% note, payable $600,000 annually through fiscal 1986, balance in fiscal 1987	7,000	7,600
5¾% note, payable $1,000,000 in fiscal 1983	1,000	2,000
	132,911	140,619
Less: Current portion	9,643	9,638
	$123,268	$130,981

The bank term loans were obtained in connection with the acquisition of Western and the Ice Shows (see Note 2). During fiscal 1982, the bank term loan agreement was amended to provide for repayment in twenty-four consecutive quarterly installments commencing April 30, 1983 and a reduction of interest rates to the bank prime rate plus ¾% during the first thirty-three months and a gradual increase in interest rates thereafter. The amendment also provides the Company with the option to fix interest rates for varying periods of time by conversion to Eurodollar borrowings tied to the London Inter-bank Rate.

The 9½% term loan of $10,000,000 is secured by certain tangible personal property of Circus World.

With respect to the bank term loans, the Company has agreed to meet various financial requirements including the maintenance of certain levels of tangible net worth and certain ratios of liabilities to tangible net worth and current assets to current liabilities.

Consolidated Statement of Financial Position

LIABILITIES AND SHAREHOLDERS' EQUITY (In thousands)

	January 30, 1982	January 31, 1981
Current Liabilities		
Notes payable to banks	$ 16,992	$ 23,967
Current portion of long-term liabilities	10,233	10,279
Accounts payable	72,772	54,380
Accrued liabilities	99,552	68,585
Income taxes payable	43,771	13,212
Total current liabilities	243,320	170,423
Long-Term Liabilities		
Long-term loans	123,268	130,981
Capitalized lease obligations	14,150	14,750
Subordinated debentures	9,825	9,898
Other long-term liabilities	12,657	12,518
Deferred Income Taxes	5,522	2,586
Minority Interest	2,862	2,038
Shareholders' Equity		
Preferred stock, $1 par value, 580,000 shares authorized; none outstanding	—	—
$25 Series A convertible preferred stock, $2.50 annual dividend, $1 par value, 2,420,000 shares authorized	2,417	2,417
Common stock, $1 par value, 50,000,000 shares authorized	16,531	16,464
Additional paid-in capital	91,422	91,066
Common stock warrants	4,453	4,455
Retained earnings	121,007	92,897
Total shareholders' equity	235,830	207,299
	$647,434	$550,493

Litigation, Contingencies and Commitments

6.2. COLT INDUSTRIES, INC. AND SUBSIDIARIES

Present value of leases, long-term debt.
(Moderate: 75 minutes)

Colt Industries conducts operations through divisions within five industry segments: industrial and power equipment, fluid control systems, specialty carbon and low-alloy steels, industrial seals and components, and shock mitigation systems.

Study Colt's Consolidated Statement of Earnings for 1978–80, Consolidated Balance Sheet for 1979–80, and Notes 1 and 3 to the 1980 financial statements.

1. State assets recorded under capital leases in 1979 and 1980; state liabilities recorded under capital leases in 1979 and 1980; explain the difference between the capital lease asset and liability values. Conjecture as to why that difference increased dramatically from 1979 to 1980.

2. The 1980 Consolidated Statement of Changes in Financial Position states that long-term debt provided funds of $36,631,000 during 1980. Estimate cash paid to decrease long-term debt during 1980. (Note: Colt defines funds to be equivalent to "working capital" in its Statement of Changes in Financial Position.)

3. Assume that long-term debt, including capital lease obligations, will be paid off in accordance with Note 3d and that the remaining annual payments of principal are spread equally over the years 1986–2000. Assume also that the weighted-average rate of interest paid on debt outstanding is 9 percent per annum. Calculate the present value of Colt's long-term debt given a discount factor of 12 percent per annum. To answer this question, construct a table showing the following columns: (1) year, (2) principal payment, (3) interest expense, (4) total cash flow, (5) discount factor, and (6) present value.

Consolidated Statement of Earnings

For the three years ended December 31, 1980

Colt Industries Inc and Subsidiaries

		(In thousands, except per share data)		
		1980	1979	1978
Revenue	Net sales	**$2,165,602**	$2,140,515	$1,807,882
Costs and Expenses	Cost of sales	**1,782,976**	1,728,194	1,446,844
	Selling and administrative	**206,159**	194,501	181,785
	Interest expense	**24,345**	29,620	29,804
	Interest income	**(16,414)**	(14,300)	(13,191)
	Total costs and expenses	**1,997,066**	1,938,015	1,645,242
Earnings	Earnings before income taxes	**168,536**	202,500	162,640
	Provision for income taxes (Note 2)	**70,785**	91,125	75,620
	Net earnings	**97,751**	111,375	87,020
	Dividends on preferred stock	**1,636**	2,255	3,282
	Net earnings applicable to common stock	**$ 96,115**	$ 109,120	$ 83,738
Earnings Per Share Data	Earnings per common share including common equivalent share (Note 1)	**$7.38**	$8.40	$6.66
	Earnings per common share assuming full dilution (Note 1)	**$7.04**	$7.86	$6.07
	Average number of shares (Note 1)— Common and common equivalent basis	**13,021**	12,992	12,565
	Fully diluted basis	**13,859**	14,152	14,304
	Cash dividends per common share	**$2.90**	$2.50	$2.03⅓

Colt Industries, Inc. and Subsidiaries

Consolidated Balance Sheet
December 31

Assets		(In thousands)	
		1980	1979
Current Assets	Cash, including certificates of deposit of $48,763 and $44,693	**$ 52,570**	$ 45,383
	Marketable securities, at cost (approximates market)	**81,681**	55,023
	Accounts and notes receivable—		
	Trade	**295,396**	277,120
	Other	**9,847**	12,193
		305,243	289,313
	Less allowance for doubtful accounts	**8,238**	6,785
		297,005	282,528
	Inventories (Notes 1 and 11)—		
	Finished goods	**86,928**	89,863
	Work in process and finished parts	**255,857**	230,661
	Raw materials and supplies	**110,200**	120,140
		452,985	440,664
	Deferred income taxes (Note 2)	**29,430**	20,620
	Other current assets	**11,246**	9,964
	Total current assets	**924,917**	854,182
Property, Plant, and Equipment, at Cost (Notes 1, 3, 10, and 11)	Land and improvements	**26,004**	24,733
	Buildings and equipment	**159,446**	150,536
	Machinery and equipment	**705,317**	670,702
	Leasehold improvements	**9,183**	7,159
	Construction in progress	**76,042**	32,093
		975,992	885,223
	Less accumulated depreciation and amortization	**538,849**	494,568
		437,143	390,655
Other Assets	Funds held by trustee for capital projects	**19,958**	—
	Notes receivable from officers and employees	**7,174**	6,770
	Other assets (Note 1)	**48,961**	50,012
		$1,438,153	$1,301,619

Liabilities and Shareholders' Equity		(In thousands of dollars, except par values)	
		1980	1979
Current Liabilities	Notes payable to banks (Note 3)	$ **17,196**	$ 15,763
	Current maturities of long-term debt (Note 3)	**13,231**	16,179
	Accounts payable	**172,036**	133,521
	Accrued expenses—		
	Salaries, wages, and employee benefits	**74,332**	64,742
	Taxes	**59,624**	60,778
	Interest	**4,985**	4,419
	Other	**43,441**	40,132
		182,382	170,071
	Total current liabilities	**384,845**	335,534
Noncurrent Liabilities	Long-term debt (Note 3)	**284,114**	264,450
	Deferred income taxes (Note 2)	**60,917**	52,034
	Minority interest in subsidiaries	**4,983**	4,269
	Other liabilities	**25,658**	23,740
	Commitments and contingencies (Note 10)		
Shareholders' Equity (Notes 3, 5, and 7)	Preferred stock— $1 par value, 2,077,189 and 2,246,023 shares authorized, 421,694 and 590,528 shares outstanding (involuntary liquidation value at December 31, 1980—$31,479)	**422**	590
	Common stock— $1 par value, 30,000,000 shares authorized, 13,269,650 and 13,209,875 shares issued	**13,270**	13,210
	Capital in excess of par value	**149,472**	160,700
	Retained earnings	**522,532**	463,979
		685,696	638,479
	Less cost of 209,525 and 420,021 shares of common stock in treasury	**8,060**	16,887
		677,636	621,592
		$1,438,153	$1,301,619

Notes to Financial Statements

December 31, 1980

1. Summary of Accounting Policies

Property and Depreciation—Depreciation and amortization of plant and equipment are provided generally by using the straight-line method, based on estimated useful lives of the assets which, in some instances, may be less than the lives allowed for tax purposes. For federal income tax purposes, most assets are depreciated using allowable accelerated methods and the Class Life Asset Depreciation Range System (ADR).

The ranges of estimated useful lives used in computing depreciation and amortization for financial reporting were as follows:

	Years
Land improvements	10-25
Buildings and equipment	10-50
Machinery and equipment	3-25
Leasehold improvements	Generally life of lease

The cost of special equipment and facilities purchased for specific contracts is amortized over a period not exceeding the lesser of the contract life or the estimated useful life of the asset.

Interest cost incurred during the period of construction of plant and equipment is capitalized as part of the cost of such plant and equipment.

Renewals and betterments are capitalized by additions to the related asset accounts, while repair and maintenance costs are charged against earnings. The company and its subsidiaries generally record retirements by removing the cost and accumulated depreciation from the asset and reserve accounts, reflecting any resulting gain or loss in earnings.

At December 31, 1980 and 1979, the company and certain of its subsidiaries had the following assets recorded under capital leases (in thousands):

	1980	1979
Land and improvements	$ 882	$ 683
Buildings and equipment	19,246	16,379
Machinery and equipment	27,683	26,383
Leasehold improvements	930	—
Construction in progress	4,964	—
	53,705	43,445
Less—Accumulated depreciation and amortization	20,050	24,986
	$33,655	$18,459

3. Long-Term Debt

	(In thousands)	
	1980	1979
Colt Industries Inc (a)—		
9¾% senior promissory notes due 1982-1996	$115,000	$115,000
8½% senior promissory notes due 1981-1992	39,998	43,332
6% notes repaid in 1980	—	2,000
7% pollution control bonds due 1998-2008	11,975	11,975
Capital lease obligations 4.3%-11.5% 1981-2010 (c)	50,084	16,524
	217,057	188,831
Subsidiaries—(*indicates average interest rates for 1980)		
First mortgage sinking fund bonds 5.3%-6⅞% due serially 1981-1992 (b)	38,745	44,403
8⅞% notes payable to insurance company in installments to 1990	19,000	21,000
Notes due 1981-1990—9.5%*	9,782	11,302
Capital lease obligations 4.6%-12% due 1981-2070 (c)	7,091	8,219
Other long-term debt due 1981-1992—8.7%*	5,670	6,874
	297,345	280,629
Less—Amounts due within one year	13,231	16,179
	$284,114	$264,450

a) The company's loan agreements include various covenants that require maintenance of working capital and limit the payment of dividends. Under the most restrictive of these covenants at December 31, 1980, working capital was $263,368,000 in excess of minimum requirements, and retained earnings available for dividends were $252,049,000. The company is in compliance with all covenants under its loan agreements.

b) At December 31, 1980, $38,745,000 of first mortgage bonds outstanding were secured by approximately $212,000,000 of assets, principally property, plant, and equipment.

c) The amounts payable under capital lease obligations are as follows (in thousands):

1981	$ 7,236
1982	6,267
1983	6,148
1984	6,048
1985	6,023
Remainder	159,934
Total minimum lease payments	191,656
Less—Amount representing interest	134,481
Present value of net minimum lease payments, included in long-term debt	$ 57,175

d) Minimum payments on long-term debt, including capital lease obligations, due within five years from December 31, 1980 are as follows (in thousands):

1981	$13,231
1982	19,576
1983	19,294
1984	21,168
1985	18,135

e) At December 31, 1980, the company had unused lines of credit aggregating $60,000,000 for short-term bank borrowings. The company has understandings with the banks regarding compensating balances for these unused lines of credit, but the aggregate amount of such compensating balances was not material at December 31, 1980.

6.3. TAX BREAK INVOLVING "ZERO-COUPON" BONDS

Introduction to accounting for zero-coupon bonds.
(Moderate: 60 minutes)

Read the accompanying article from the *Wall Street Journal*.

1. a. What is the harm in companies' being able to "... grossly overstate the true interest cost in an issue's early years"? Don't the same companies "grossly understate" the cost in later years? Construct a table showing the interest expense for the $100 zero-coupon bond given in the example in the article using the two methods described.

   b. Using the interest rates associated with the two methods in 1a, construct an additional table depicting interest expense for the $100 zero-coupon bond using the two methods described, assuming that a new five-year $100 zero-coupon bond is sold every year. Extend the analysis to seven years.

   c. Given your answers in 1a and 1b, which method allows for a bigger tax break?

2. Give the company's journal entries for both methods for the

   a. Initial issuance

   b. First year's interest expense

   c. Final payment and (interest expense)

3. On a traditional 15 percent bond, the after-tax cost is 8.1 percent according to the article. Can you reconcile the two rates? In other words, to what tax rate is the article referring? Make a simple-interest table using the tax break (straight-line) method. Use simple average interest to reconcile the two rates. Assume, if necessary, that the applicable tax rate is 46 percent.

4. As a consumer, how would you feel about having to pay taxes on interest you won't receive until maturity of your "zero" bond? What method would you like to use to account for your future gain?

Deduction in Danger

Tax Break Involving 'Zero-Coupon' Bonds Is Attacked by Treasury, Backed by Issuers

By Edward P. Foldessy and Jill Bettner
Staff Reporters of The Wall Street Journal

NEW YORK—Just when the Reagan administration is staking an economic rebound partly on lower interest rates, the Treasury wants to plug a tax loophole that has enabled companies to borrow billions of dollars cheaply.

The Treasury is seeking to halt revenue losses that are already threatening to run into hundreds of millions of dollars annually. But many observers are dismayed.

"It's the wrong move at the wrong time," warns Irwin Kellner, the chief economist at Manufacturers Hanover Trust Co. "It will keep short-term rates higher than otherwise would have been the case."

At issue is a tax break granted to companies issuing some of Wall Street's hottest-selling securities: "zero-coupon" bonds, which don't pay any annual interest, and other deeply discounted debt instruments, which pay very low rates. For investors, the deep discount from the face value of all these securities is appealing because they can "lock in" their total return. For companies, the extension of this guarantee allows borrowing at bargain rates.

Major Tax Break

The deep discount also supplies the corporate tax break. Companies can start writing off the discount as an interest expense right away, even though, in the case of "zeros," not a cent is paid out until the bonds mature, perhaps 30 years later. Moreover, through a quirk in the tax rules, companies can overstate these deductions for the "phantom" interest in the early years of a zero's life—and sharply reduce the financing costs.

The Treasury views the exaggerated deductions as an unintended "federal tax subsidy" and has asked Congress to limit them to companies' true interest expenses.

But loss of the tax break will hurt many companies, especially those awash in short-term debt. "It will significantly reduce the ability of corporations to raise long-term money," says Stuart A. Schweitzer, an economist at Morgan Guaranty Trust Co. "This will be a setback for the efforts to bolster corporate balance sheets."

If the Treasury proposal is enacted, adds H. Frederick Krimendahl II, a partner in Goldman, Sachs & Co., "it will be taking away one of the prime financing tools" of industry. And if long-term corporate financing consequently dwindles, "it will take the economy a long time to come back," he says.

Popular Among Investors

With the volatility in interest rates and bond prices, companies have had a hard time selling traditional long-term bonds to nervous investors. But they have sold plenty of deeply discounted issues, especially zeros. Almost 40%, or $4 billion, of all corporate bonds sold publicly in the U.S. so far this year have been zero-coupon or other deeply discounted securities, according to First Boston Corp. Such issues have been marketed even more aggressively abroad, although accurate tallies aren't available.

The fact that buyers of deeply discounted issues can lock in their total returns contrasts sharply with the uncertainty faced by buyers of traditional bonds, which force investors to reinvest the semiannual interest payments at whatever rates prevail at the time.

Because investors in zeros can predict their total returns, they are willing to accept lower interest rates than those on ordinary bonds. For example, when J.C. Penney Co. sold the first zero-coupon bonds publicly last year, they yielded investors 14.25%. Paull F. Hubbard, vice president and treasurer, estimates that a standard issue would have required a yield of 14.9%.

Calculating Yields

A zero's yield is determined by the discount from face value and years to maturity. On a five-year, zero-coupon note selling at $49.72 for each $100 face amount, for example, the investor's dollar return would be the $50.28 difference between his cost and the redemption value of $100 at maturity. The investor's yield to maturity works out to 14.476%, which, after semiannual compounding, results in an effective annual cost to the company of 15%.

It is how companies treat the discount that bothers the Treasury. Under current practices, corporations can deduct the phantom-interest expense in equal installments over an issue's life. In the above example, a company could deduct one-fifth of the discount, or about $10 each year.

But the Treasury contends that companies can thereby grossly overstate the true interest cost in an issue's early years. The Treasury wants the interest to be reported so as to reflect the fact that the company initially has the use of only a portion of the issue's face value.

In the first year, for instance, the company owes only the $49.72 that the investor paid. The interest cost at the 15% effective rate would be only $7.46, and that's the amount that the Treasury proposes as the tax deduction for that year. At the end of the first year, the company owes investors the $49.72 plus the $7.46 interest; on that total of $57.18, the next year's interest expense would be $8.58. That expense—and the tax deduction—would increase each year to $13.04 in the final year.

For most companies, "the economics of zeros clearly have been based largely on the tax benefits," says David Goodrich, a tax partner at Coopers & Lybrand.

Amount of Benefits

Some figures on the benefits are offered by Dexter Senft, a vice president of First Boston. He calculates a company's annual after-tax cost on a traditional 15% bond at 8.1%. But the cost drops to 7.6% on a 10-year, zero-coupon note and to 4.61% on a 30-year zero. Without the tax break, the after-tax cost on all three issues would be the same, 8.1%.

Even if Congress takes away this "overwhelming" tax advantage, Jon Rotenstreich, a managing director of Salomon Brothers Inc., doesn't "think the market is dead." Some companies will continue to sell zeros because investors accept a lower yield on them than on ordinary bonds. "From our perspective," says Alan J. Pabst, senior vice president and treasurer of Wells Fargo & Co., "we could look at zeros, depending on what rate we could issue them at."

However, Mr. Rotenstreich concedes that "the supply will slow," and Manufacturers Hanover's Mr. Kellner believes that "most companies are going to borrow in the short-term market" instead. He contends that such borrowings will keep upward pressure on short-term rates and thus compound the Federal Reserve's difficulties in controlling the money supply. He adds that the government "would be denying companies an opportunity to pick up long-term financing for capital spending and for paying off (existing) short-term debt. It's discouraging something they should be encouraging."

Timothy Howard, chief economist of the Federal National Mortgage Association, worries that the Treasury proposal would hurt companies' credit-worthiness by forcing them into even more short-term debt. "It's going to make already-strained financial positions even worse," he says.

Cautious Companies

Most analysts say companies will take a wait-and-see attitude on their financing plans until Congress acts on the proposal—which isn't expected to encounter much opposition on Capitol Hill.

If enacted, the tougher tax treatment will apply to all issues sold after the Treasury's May 3 announcement. The proposal, however, exempts securities that corporations were required to sell at a later date under written commitments in force May 3.

As a result, several companies scrambled to sign contracts with underwriters the day of the announcement. Among them were Caterpillar Tractor Co., Sears, Roebuck & Co. and Transamerica Financial Corp. The three companies sold a total of $750 million of deep-discount securities the following day.

Without the tax break, the risks that zero-coupon bonds impose on issuing companies may loom larger. Chief among those risks is the danger involved in a company locking itself into fixed interest costs. The vast majority of zeros can't be redeemed before maturity—unlike most traditional bonds, which companies often can prepay within five to 10 years. If interest rates fall sharply, companies that have issued zeros have given up the possibility of refinancing the debt at lower cost. "You lose some flexibility," J.C. Penney's Mr. Hubbard concedes.

Mortgaging the Future

Richard B. Hoey, chief economist for Bache Halsey Stuart Shields Inc., warns that long-term issues could be hazardous to a company's health. "Zero coupons out in the 20- to 30-year range represent a mortgaging of the future," he says. "Up until now, only the U.S. government felt it could take the risk of locking itself into issuing bonds that weren't callable."

He also notes that although interest rates have been rising for about 40 years, rates of 3% and 4% were common about 30 years ago. "Who's to say that interest rates won't be 3% to 4% 20 years from now? Who's smart enough to forecast inflation and interest rates a generation ahead of time?" he asks.

But for companies that have already sold zeros and any that might contemplate doing so in spite of the proposed tax change, much of the concern centers on companies' ability to repay those large, balloon maturities.

"As these things mature, one of them will catch a company short," one Wall Street analyst says. Adds another analyst, "As long as there's any economic advantage in issuing zeros, the fad will continue. The only thing that will kill it is if somebody defaults. But then watch what happens."

VI. DEBT

6.4. THE FIRESTONE TIRE AND RUBBER COMPANY

Contingent liabilities, actual liabilities, phasing-out operations, tire recall. (Straightforward: 30 minutes)

The Firestone Tire and Rubber Company's principal business is the development, production and marketing of tires for all types of vehicles both in the United States and abroad. Firestone also produces and markets thousands of other products, including rims and wheels for trucks, tractors, and earthmoving equipment; synthetic and natural rubber; polyurethane foam; vinyl resins and sheeting; metal and industrial rubber products; synthetic fibers; textiles and chemicals. With 130,000 acres of rubber estates on three continents, Firestone is the largest natural rubber producer in the tire industry.

Study Firestone's Statements of Income for 1978–79; Balance Sheets for 1978–79; Note 14, "Provision for Phase-out of Facilities"; Note 15, "Provision for Tire Recall and Related Costs"; and Note 16, "Contingent Liabilities," to the 1979 financial report. The "Report of Independent Certified Public Accountants" (Coopers & Lybrand) is also included.

1. a. Provide a journal entry dated April 1978 that would record the $110 million charge against income to cover costs of terminating bias tire production in various U.S. and non-U.S. facilities.

   b. Provide a journal entry dated October 1978 that would record the $234 million charge against income representing management's estimate of the cost of fulfilling the company's obligations under the National Highway Traffic Safety Administration (NHTSA) agreement and program for cash refunds.

   Ignore tax effects.

2. a. Provide journal entries to explain all changes in the Provision

for Phase-out of Facilities account during 1979. Assume that "Amounts Charged Thereto" were paid in cash on December 31, 1979.

b. Provide journal entries to explain all changes in the Provision for Tire Recall and Related Costs account during 1979. Assume that "Amounts Charged Thereto" were paid in cash on December 31, 1979.

Ignore tax effects.

3. What is the auditor's view with respect to the potential liability that may result from litigation now pending in various state and federal courts? What kind of assurance does Coopers & Lybrand give stockholders and investors that the statements as a whole are fairly presented?

The Firestone Tire & Rubber Company and Consolidated Subsidiaries

Statements of Income

	1979	1978
Net sales	$5,284.2	$4,878.1
Cost of goods sold	4,325.1	3,958.7
Selling, administrative and general expenses	709.3	669.5
Interest and debt expense (Notes 1, 6, 7 and 8)	104.1	100.6
Other income, net	(24.2)	(23.0)
Provision for phase-out of facilities (Note 14)	42.6	110.0
Provision for (credit from) tire recall and related costs (Note 15)	(46.9)	234.0
	5,110.0	5,049.8
Income (loss) before income taxes, minority interests and extraordinary credit	174.2	(171.7)
Domestic and foreign income taxes (Notes 1, 3, 6, 14 and 15)	86.2	(27.2)
Minority interests in income of subsidiary companies (Note 10)	10.3	3.8
Income (loss) before extraordinary credit	77.7	(148.3)
Extraordinary credit – tax carryforwards (Note 3)	35.2	–
Net income (loss)	$ 112.9	$ (148.3)
Per share of common stock*		
Income (loss) before extraordinary credit	$ 1.35	$ (2.58)
Extraordinary credit	.61	–
Net income (loss)	$ 1.96	$ (2.58)

*Based on average number of shares outstanding during the year.

The Firestone Tire & Rubber Company and Consolidated Subsidiaries

Balance Sheets

ASSETS

Dollars in millions, except per share amounts

	October 31 1979	1978
Current assets		
Cash	$ 27.8	$ 26.7
Time deposits and short-term investments (Note 4)	63.8	130.5
	91.6	157.2
Accounts and notes receivable, less allowance for doubtful accounts: 1979 – $8.8; 1978 – $9.8	864.6	959.8
Inventories (Notes 1 and 5)		
Raw materials and supplies	244.1	213.3
Work in process	82.6	73.2
Finished goods	527.9	531.6
	854.6	818.1
Prepaid expenses	15.0	13.0
Total current assets	1,825.8	1,948.1
Properties, plants and equipment, at cost (Note 9)		
Land and improvements	127.2	122.5
Buildings and building fixtures	668.5	637.3
Machinery and equipment	2,196.2	2,077.7
	2,991.9	2,837.5
Less accumulated depreciation (Note 1)	1,496.1	1,392.6
	1,495.8	1,444.9
Other assets		
Investments, at cost or equity (Note 6)	100.1	55.2
Miscellaneous assets	23.3	25.6
Deferred charges (Note 1)	12.1	12.6
	135.5	93.4
Total assets	$3,457.1	$3,486.4

VI. DEBT

LIABILITIES AND STOCKHOLDERS' EQUITY

	October 31	
	1979	1978
Current liabilities		
Short-term loans (Note 7)	$ 216.6	$ 215.5
Accounts payable, principally trade (Note 9)	301.9	300.8
Accrued compensation	165.2	141.3
Domestic and foreign taxes (Note 3)	128.6	128.0
Accrued liability for phase-out of facilities (Note 14)	70.1	14.2
Accrued liability for tire recall and related costs (Note 15)	56.4	227.2
Long-term debt due within one year	18.0	14.2
Other accrued liabilities	129.2	114.4
Total current liabilities	1,086.0	1,155.6
Accrued liability for phase-out of facilities —		
non-current (Note 14)	16.2	53.4
Long-term debt (Note 8)	613.0	616.1
Long-term capital lease obligations (Note 9)	62.9	68.0
Deferred income taxes (Notes 1 and 3)	123.6	94.8
Minority interests in subsidiary companies (Note 10)	89.6	90.7
Commitments and contingent liabilities (Notes 9 and 16)		
Stockholders' equity		
Serial preferred stock (cumulative), $1 par value, voting, authorized 10,000,000 shares, none issued		
Common stock, without par value, authorized 120,000,000 shares, shares issued: 1979 and 1978 — 60,090,127 (Notes 8 and 13)	62.6	62.6
Additional paid-in capital	194.6	194.7
Reinvested earnings	1,267.2	1,210.5
	1,524.4	1,467.8
Less common stock in treasury	58.6	60.0
Total stockholders' equity	1,465.8	1,407.8
Total liabilities and stockholders' equity	$3,457.1	$3,486.4

The Firestone Tire and Rubber Company

14. Provision for phase-out of facilities

In April, 1978, a charge of $110 million ($73 million after income taxes) was made against income to cover costs of terminating bias passenger tire production in Akron, Ohio and another domestic location and all tire production at plants in Calgary, Canada, and Switzerland. Costs of terminating bias passenger tire production in Los Angeles, California, announced in August, 1979, were included in the April, 1978 provision. In October, 1979, based on experience to date and anticipated future charges, the 1978 provision was reduced by $32.5 million ($19.1 million after income taxes).

In October, 1979, a charge of $75.1 million ($56.0 million after income taxes) was made against income to cover costs of discontinuing certain other foreign operations, including operating losses during the phase-out period. The charge includes the disposal of Australian facilities for manufacture and sale of tires and industrial products and the discontinuation of certain production and marketing operations in Europe.

Accordingly, the amount accrued and charged to income in 1979 for phase-out of facilities, net of the reduction in the 1978 provision, was $42.6 million ($36.9 million after income taxes).

The activity in the accrued liability for phase-out of facilities for 1979 and 1978, follows:

	1979	1978
Accrued liability at beginning of year	$ 67.6	$ —
Amount accrued during the year	42.6	110.0
Amounts charged thereto	(23.9)	(42.4)
Accrued liability at end of year	$ 86.3	$ 67.6

15. Provision for tire recall and related costs

In October, 1978, a provision for tire recall of $234.0 million ($147.4 million after income taxes) was charged against income. The provision represented management's estimate of the cost of fulfilling the Company's obligations under the agreement with the National Highway Traffic Safety Administration and the Company's program of cash refunds to those customers who had received an adjustment on tires that would otherwise have been subject to recall and free replacement.

In October, 1979, based on experience to date and anticipated future charges, the 1978 provision was reduced. Management also determined that the provision should be broadened to include $30.8 million of other related costs which were not considered for inclusion in the original provision. The net effect of the above was to reduce the provision by $46.9 million, for which no provision for income taxes was required because of the use of 1978 foreign tax credits of $20.8 million.

It should be recognized that the number of tires still to be returned and the other costs yet to be incurred may vary from management's estimates. Any additional adjustments required by such variance will be reflected in income in the future.

The activity in the accrued liability for tire recall and related costs for 1979 and 1978, follows:

	1979	1978
Accrued liability at beginning of year	$227.2	$ —
Amount accrued (reversed) during the year	(46.9)	234.0
Amounts charged thereto	(123.9)	(6.8)
Accrued liability at end of year	$ 56.4	$227.2

16. Contingent liabilities

Twelve purported consumer commercial class actions (one of which consolidates five previous actions) are presently pending against the Company in various state and federal courts. An additional case is pending which is not denominated as a class action but requests relief on behalf of all those similarly situated. In the purported class actions, the named plaintiffs are requesting, on behalf of claimed classes of consumers, six national in scope, five state-wide, and one city-wide, various forms of injunctive and monetary relief, including punitive damages, as a result of the Company's having manufactured and sold allegedly defective Steel Belted Radial 500 and other steel belted radial passenger tires.

The complaints in these cases define the classes of persons sought to be represented to include very broad and heterogeneous memberships with various kinds of potential claims under the National Traffic and Motor Vehicle Safety Act of 1966, the Magnuson-Moss Act, and under state warranty, consumer protection and other laws.

In all of the twelve actions the complaints pray for actual or compensatory damages such as recovery of the purchase price of the tires, or damages for injury to person or property, in amounts ranging from amounts to be determined at trial to over $2 billion. Ten of the complaints request punitive damages ranging to as much as $300 million on behalf of the class sought to be represented. Many of the complaints also include requests for equitable relief in the form of rescission of tire purchase transactions, recall and free replacement of the tires (see Note 15 for information with respect to tire recall), and other types of relief.

In addition to the class actions, there are several thousand individual claims pending against the Company for damages allegedly connected with steel belted radial passenger tires. Several hundred of these claims are the subject of pending litigation and in approximately two hundred cases the compensatory damages sought for wrongful death, personal injuries, or property damage are substantial. Punitive damages are sought in many of the cases.

The Company is also a defendant in approximately one hundred lawsuits that seek damages for personal injuries, wrongful death, or property damage arising from alleged malfunctions of multi-piece truck wheel components manufactured by the Company. Many of these cases seek substantial compensatory as well as punitive damages. Additionally, various other product liability lawsuits and other suits and claims are pending against the Company.

The Company is a defendant in a purported class action which seeks, among other things, recovery for losses by stockholders who purchased the Company's common stock between December 1975 and July 1978 by reason of the decline in market price for such stock alleged to result from the Company's alleged failure to make proper disclosure of, among other things, the steel belted radial passenger tire situation.

In March, 1979, the United States brought an action seeking recovery against the Company in the amount of approximately $62 million by reason of alleged illegal gold trading activity in Switzerland.

Following a federal grand jury investigation into the Company's income taxes, the Company entered into a plea agreement in July 1979 under which the Company pleaded guilty to two counts charging the inclusion in its taxable income for 1972 and 1973 amounts that had been generated in prior years; the court imposed a total fine of ten thousand dollars on the Company by reason of its plea. A civil tax audit by the Internal Revenue Service is currently in progress covering some of the same matters investigated by the grand jury as well as other matters. The government may assess substantial tax, interest and penalties in connection with the matters under investigation.

The Securities and Exchange Commission is conducting an investigation of the adequacy of the Company's disclosures in earlier years concerning the Steel Belted Radial 500 tire, and the Company is included in an industry-wide investigation by the National Highway Traffic Safety Administration regarding truck multipiece wheels and rims.

The Company has various other contingent liabilities, some of which are for substantial amounts, arising out of suits, investigations and claims related to other aspects of the conduct of its business and based upon various legal theories.

Increased uncertainties have developed during the past year with regard to some of the contingencies identified in this note. Because of the existing uncertainties, the eventual outcome of these contingencies cannot be predicted, and the ultimate liability with respect to them cannot be reasonably estimated. Since the minimum potential liability for a substantial portion of the claims and suits described in this note cannot be reasonably estimated, no liability for them has been recorded in the financial statements. Management believes, however, that the disposition of these contingencies could well be very costly. Although the Company's management, including its General Counsel, believes it is unlikely that the ultimate outcome of these contingencies will have a material adverse effect on the Company's consolidated financial position, such a consequence is possible if substantial punitive or other damages are awarded in one or more of the cases involved.

Report of Independent Certified Public Accountants

To the Stockholders and Board of Directors,
The Firestone Tire & Rubber Company:

We have examined the balance sheets of The Firestone Tire & Rubber Company and consolidated subsidiaries at October 31, 1979 and 1978, and the related statements of income, stockholders' equity, and changes in financial position for the years then ended. Our examinations were made in accordance with generally accepted auditing standards and, accordingly, included such tests of the accounting records and such other auditing procedures as we considered necessary in the circumstances.

As set forth in Note 16 to the financial statements, the Company is a party to various legal and other actions. These actions claim substantial amounts as a result of alleged tire defects and other matters. The ultimate liability resulting from these matters cannot be reasonably estimated. In our report dated December 18, 1978, our opinion on the financial statements for the year ended October 31, 1978, was unqualified. However, due to the increased uncertainties that developed during the year ended October 31, 1979, with respect to these matters, our present opinion on the financial statements for the year ended October 31, 1978, as presented herein, is different from that expressed in our previous report.

In our opinion, subject to the effects on the financial statements of adjustments that might have been required had the outcome of the matters referred to in the preceding paragraph been known, the financial statements referred to above present fairly the financial position of The Firestone Tire & Rubber Company and consolidated subsidiaries at October 31, 1979 and 1978, and the results of their operations and the changes in their financial position for the years then ended, in conformity with generally accepted accounting principles applied on a consistent basis.

Coopers & Lybrand

Cleveland, Ohio
December 12, 1979

6.5. WELLS FARGO AND COMPANY

Debt-for-equity swap, impact of the book "gain"
on earnings. (Straightforward: 30 minutes)

Wells Fargo is a diversified banking and financial services firm, head-quartered in San Francisco. Its banking and financial operations provide retail, corporate, and commercial services in the United States (principally California) and abroad.

Study Wells Fargo's 1979–81 Consolidated Statement of Changes in Financial Position, 1979–81 Consolidated Statement of Stockholders' Equity, and a portion of Note 9 to the financial statements, "Intermediate-Term and Long-Term Debt."

1. Prepare a journal entry that would record the exchanges of common stock for long-term debt that occurred during 1981 [combine the September and October events into one entry]. An adjustment of $914,000 to the deferred tax account relating to the exchange of stock for debt also occurred during 1981.

2. Comment on the trend in reported income from 1979 to 1981. Comment also on the chairman/president's statement that "in 1981, earnings [income before securities transactions] were $125.9 million, or $5.41 per share, compared with $121.7 million, or $5.32 per share, in 1980, *the only year in the past 15 that earnings declined.*" (Emphasis added)

Consolidated Statement of Changes in Financial Position

(In thousands)	Year ended December 31, 1981 Financial resources		Year ended December 31, 1980 Financial resources		Year ended December 31, 1979 Financial Resources	
	Provided from	Used for	Provided from	Used for	Provided from	Used for
Net income	$ 123,988	$ —	$ 121,864	$ —	$ 123,416	$ —
Non-cash items included in net income:						
Provision for loan losses	58,012		71,043		62,949	
Provision for deferred income taxes	4,177		25,739		35,483	
Provision for depreciation and amortization	32,507		25,485		19,965	
Gain on exchange of equity for debt		11,731				
Equity adjustment from foreign currency translation		2,404				
Cash dividends declared		45,026		43,914		39,023
Conversion of 3¼% convertible capital notes	1,465		269		2,321	
Common stock issued—other, net of repurchases	6,452		1,259		4,779	
Exchange of stock for debt	22,884					
Operations and equity	249,485	59,161	245,659	43,914	248,913	39,023
Interest-bearing deposits	579,457		913,784		25,587	
Net loans		1,025,219	1,304,648			2,255,719
Lease financing		163,804	117,503			184,777
Investment securities	461,598		10,853		142,471	
Funds sold	214,150			220,550	93,400	
Trading account securities	12,884			46,318	30,345	
Earning assets	1,268,089	1,189,023	10,853	2,602,803	291,803	2,440,496
Total deposits	646,459		376,453		1,012,344	
Total borrowings		1,020,073	1,858,898		482,448	
Intermediate-term and long-term debt	385,407		257,893		135,239	
Deposits and borrowings	1,031,866	1,020,073	2,493,244		1,630,031	
Cash and due from banks		15,442	78,597		336,708	
Net additions to premises and equipment		96,721		74,987		43,565
Other assets		110,362		75,394		37,435
Other liabilities		60,219		24,491	32,320	
Other, net	1,561			6,764	20,744	
Other	1,561	282,744	78,597	181,636	389,772	81,000
Total	$2,551,001	$2,551,001	$2,828,353	$2,828,353	$2,560,519	$2,560,519

Consolidated Statement of Stockholders' Equity

(In thousands)	Common stock	Additional paid-in capital	Retained earnings	Foreign currency translation	Total stockholders' equity
Balance December 31, 1978	$112,715	$239,546	$390,341	$ —	$742,602
Net income—1979			123,416		123,416
Conversion of convertible notes	393	1,928			2,321
Stock issued to employee benefit plans and other	904	3,963	(88)		4,779
Cash dividends declared			(39,023)		(39,023)
Net increase	1,297	5,891	84,305		91,493
Balance December 31, 1979	114,012	245,437	474,646		834,095
Net income—1980			121,864		121,864
Conversion of convertible notes	46	223			269
Stock issued to employee benefit plans and other	1,535	5,877			7,412
Stock repurchased	(1,201)	(4,952)			(6,153)
Cash dividends declared			(43,914)		(43,914)
Net increase	380	1,148	77,950		79,478
Balance December 31, 1980	114,392	246,585	552,596		913,573
Restatement of foreign currency translation (net of income tax benefit of $21)				(60)	(60)
Balance January 1, 1981	114,392	246,585	552,596	(60)	913,513
Net income—1981			123,988		123,988
Conversion of convertible notes	253	1,212			1,465
Stock issued to employee benefit plans and other	2,194	9,748			11,942
Exchange of stock for debt	4,486	18,398			22,884
Stock repurchased	(874)	(4,616)			(5,490)
Cash dividends declared			(45,026)		(45,026)
Equity adjustment from foreign currency translation (net of income tax benefit of $801)				(2,344)	(2,344)
Net increase	6,059	24,742	78,962	(2,344)	107,419
Balance December 31, 1981	**$120,451**	**$271,327**	**$631,558**	**$(2,404)**	**$1,020,932**

9. Intermediate-term & long-term debt

Intermediate-term debt has an original maturity of more than one year and not more than ten years. Long-term debt has an original maturity of ten years or more.

On September 30, 1981, the Company exchanged 538,480 shares of common stock for $20,000,000 aggregate principal amount of its long-term debt: $14,860,000 8.60% debentures plus $5,140,000 8⅝% notes described below. On October 27, 1981, the Company exchanged 358,767 common shares for $13,701,000 aggregate principal amount of its long-term debt: $7,360,000 8⅝% notes plus $4,010,000 7⅞% debentures plus $2,331,000 8.60% debentures. The gains resulting from these exchanges are included in 1981 other income.

7.1.   HELENE CURTIS INDUSTRIES, INC.

Change in accounting for leases, specific year and cumulative effects. (Straightforward: 45 minutes)

Helene Curtis manufactures beauty and hair-care products such as shampoos, conditioners, professional salon products, and equipment. A smaller segment of the company's operation includes the production of sealing and adhesive products such as sealants, caulking, glazing compounds, and strips for the automotive and architectural industries.

Study the comparative Consolidated Balance Sheets for 1980–81 and 1978–79 (1978 as restated); Note 11—"Leases"—to the financial statements; and the Consolidated Statement of Earnings and Retained Earnings for the years ended February 28, 1979–81 and 1978–79. Notes 11 to the 1978–79 and the 1977–78 financial statements are also included.

1. Complete the following table. (Current portion of lease obligation as of February 29, 1980, is $250,000.)

Year Ended February 28	Capital Leases (net of accumulated depreciation)	Obligations Under Capital Leases (current & long-term)
1978		
1979		
1980		
1981		

2. Refer to the 1978–79 Consolidated Statement of Earnings and Retained Earnings. What do the amounts for "Retroactive effect on prior years of change in method of accounting for leases (Note 11)" represent? In your answer state whether the amounts are cumulative or specific-year effects of the accounting change.

165

3. If the leases entered into prior to January 1, 1977, had not been capitalized—i.e., they had been accounted for as operating leases—by how much would Consolidated Net Earnings before income taxes for 1980 and 1981 change? In other words, restate 1980, 1981 Consolidated Net Earnings before taxes as if the operating lease method had been used. Ignore tax effects in your restatement.

4. What changes in investment and financing policy (in particular, leasing policy) would you recommend as a result of the mandated changes in accounting policy, namely, *FASB Statement No. 13,* "Accounting for Leases," and the SEC ruling to require retroactive application of *Statement No. 13* for leases entered into prior to January 1, 1977?

Consolidated Balance Sheets

February 28 or 29 Dollar amounts in thousands	1981	1980
Assets		
Current Assets:		
Cash, including time deposits of $988 (1981) and $337 (1980)	$ 2,576	$ 1,881
Receivables, less allowance for doubtful accounts of $1,268 (1981) and $865 (1980)	39,512	30,041
Inventories	22,505	18,239
Prepaid expenses	2,133	1,862
Total Current Assets	66,726	52,023
Property, Plant and Equipment		
Land	326	1,245
Buildings and improvements	2,387	2,292
Machinery and equipment	13,044	11,057
Capitalized leases	8,053	6,028
	23,810	20,622
Accumulated depreciation	(8,259)	(7,365)
Net property, plant and equipment	15,551	13,257
Other assets	1,739	1,119
Total Assets	**$84,016**	$66,399
Liabilities and Shareholders' Equity		
Current Liabilities:		
Short-term bank loans	$ 5,569	$ 400
Accounts payable	14,587	12,640
Income taxes	3,992	1,600
Advertising and promotion	3,691	2,975
Accrued expenses	7,244	5,283
Total Current Liabilities	35,083	22,898
Obligations under capital leases	5,828	4,245
Long-term bank loan	5,000	5,000
Accrued retirement benefits	2,524	1,906
Deferred income	—	208
Shareholders' Equity:		
Common shares, issued 2,248,035 (1981) and 2,208,285 (1980)	2,248	2,208
Capital in excess of par value	5,669	5,669
Retained earnings	30,935	26,400
	38,852	34,277
Less 374,917 (1981) and 260,718 (1980) treasury shares, at cost	3,271	2,135
Total Shareholders' Equity	35,581	32,142
Total Liabilities and Shareholders' Equity	**$84,016**	$66,399

February 28,	1979	1978
ASSETS		(as restated, Note 11)
Current Assets:		
Cash, including time deposits of $335,000 (1979) and		
$275,000 (1978) (Note 3)	$ 1,620,000	$ 1,889,000
Receivables, less allowance for doubtful accounts		
of $575,000 (1979) and $619,000 (1978)	29,986,000	28,750,000
Inventories (Notes 1 and 2)	15,635,000	15,783,000
Prepaid expenses	2,233,000	1,820,000
Total Current Assets	49,474,000	48,242,000
Property, Plant and Equipment (Notes 1 and 11):		
Land	1,169,000	1,170,000
Buildings and improvements	2,186,000	1,752,000
Machinery and equipment	9,108,000	7,876,000
Capitalized leases	6,028,000	5,954,000
	18,491,000	16,752,000
Accumulated depreciation	(6,581,000)	(5,703,000)
Net property, plant and equipment	11,910,000	11,049,000
Other assets	1,248,000	1,088,000
Total Assets	$62,632,000	$60,379,000
LIABILITIES AND SHAREHOLDERS' EQUITY		
Current Liabilities:		
Short-term bank loans (Note 3)	$ 5,161,000	$ 4,336,000
Accounts payable	11,611,000	11,382,000
Income taxes	722,000	1,503,000
Accrued expenses	7,954,000	8,112,000
Total Current Liabilities	25,448,000	25,333,000
Obligations under capital leases (Note 11)	4,361,000	4,449,000
Accrued retirement benefits (Notes 1 and 6)	1,869,000	1,344,000
Deferred income	428,000	
Shareholders' Equity:		
Common shares (Note 5)	2,193,000	2,184,000
Capital in excess of par value	5,636,000	5,609,000
Retained earnings	23,938,000	21,875,000
	31,767,000	29,668,000
Less 142,618 (1979) and 47,017 (1978) treasury shares, at cost	1,241,000	415,000
Total Shareholders' Equity	30,526,000	29,253,000
Total Liabilities and Shareholders' Equity	$62,632,000	$60,379,000

VII. LEASES AND PENSIONS

Consolidated Statements of Earnings and Retained Earnings

Years ended February 28 or 29
Dollar amounts in thousands, except per share data

	1981	1980	1979
Net Sales and Other Revenues	$163,097	$144,238	$130,938
Cost and Expenses:			
Cost of goods sold	90,757	82,335	74,785
Advertising, promotional, selling and administrative	63,308	56,884	51,824
Unusual item	—	—	1,194
	154,065	139,219	127,803
Earnings before income taxes	9,032	5,019	3,135
Provision for income taxes	4,497	2,557	1,277
Earnings Before Extraordinary Credit	4,535	2,462	1,858
Extraordinary credit—tax benefit from prior years' losses	—	—	205
Net Earnings	4,535	2,462	2,063
Retained Earnings, Beginning of Year	26,400	23,938	21,875
Retained Earnings, End of Year	$ 30,935	$ 26,400	$ 23,938
Per common share:			
Earnings before extraordinary credit	$2.34	$1.22	$.88
Extraordinary credit	—	—	.09
Net earnings	$2.34	$1.22	$.97
Weighted average number of shares outstanding	1,940,803	2,014,071	2,119,997

CONSOLIDATED STATEMENTS OF EARNINGS AND RETAINED EARNINGS

Years ended February 28,	1979	1978
		(as restated, Note 11)
Net Sales and Other Revenues (Note 1)	$130,938,000	$123,991,000
Costs and Expenses:		
Cost of goods sold	74,785,000	69,036,000
Advertising, promotional, selling and administrative expenses	51,824,000	46,777,000
Unusual items (Note 10)	1,194,000	3,094,000
	127,803,000	118,907,000
	3,135,000	5,084,000
Provision for income taxes (Notes 1 and 7)	1,277,000	1,350,000
Earnings Before Extraordinary Credit	1,858,000	3,734,000
Extraordinary credit—tax benefit arising from prior years' losses	205,000	136,000
Net Earnings	2,063,000	3,870,000
Retained Earnings, Beginning of Year:		
As previously reported	22,113,000	18,151,000
Retroactive effect on prior years of		
change in method of accounting for leases (Note 11)	(238,000)	(146,000)
As adjusted	21,875,000	18,005,000
Retained Earnings, End of Year	$ 23,938,000	$ 21,875,000
Per common share (Note 8):		
Earnings before extraordinary credit	$.88	$1.75
Extraordinary credit	.09	.06
Net earnings	$.97	$1.81

1981-1980

(11) Leases

At February 28, 1981 and February 29, 1980, leased property, plant and equipment under capital leases was comprised of:

	1981	1980
Land and buildings	$5,464	$5,464
Machinery and equipment	2,589	564
	8,053	6,028
Less accumulated depreciation	2,412	2,041
	$5,641	$3,987

Future minimum lease payments under capital leases at February 28, 1981 at interest rates from 4.7% to 13.2% were as follows:

Fiscal Year	
1982	$ 947
1983	936
1984	898
1985	862
1986	813
Thereafter	9,159
	13,615
Less estimated executory costs included in minimum lease payments	296
Net minimum lease payments	13,319
Less amount representing interest	7,161
Present value of net minimum lease payments	6,158
Less current portion included in accounts payable	330
Obligations under capital leases	$ 5,828

Rental expense under operating leases for the years ended February 28, 1981, February 29, 1980 and February 28, 1979 was $2,206, $1,640 and $1,442, respectively.

Future minimum lease payments under noncancellable operating leases at February 28, 1981 were as follows:

Fiscal Year	
1982	$ 798
1983	595
1984	393
1985	330
1986	256
Thereafter	1,034
	$3,406

1979-1978

(11) Leases

At February 28, 1979 the provisions of Financial Accounting Standards Board Statement No. 13—Accounting for Leases—were retroactively applied as required by the Securities and Exchange Commission. This required certain leases entered into prior to January 1, 1977, which were previously accounted for as operating leases, to be accounted for as capital leases. The effect of this change was a reduction in fiscal 1979 and fourth quarter net earnings of $42,000 (2¢ per common share).

The financial statements for fiscal 1978 have been restated for this accounting change which resulted in an increase in property, plant and equipment, net of $4,392,000, accounts payable of $181,000 and obligations under capital leases of $4,449,000 and a decrease in net earnings of $92,000 (4¢ per common share).

At February 28, 1979 and 1978, leased property, plant and equipment under capital leases was comprised of:

	1979	1978
Land and buildings	$5,464,000	$5,464,000
Machinery and equipment	564,000	490,000
	6,028,000	5,954,000
Less accumulated depreciation	1,799,000	1,562,000
	$4,229,000	$4,392,000

Future minimum lease payments under capital leases at February 28, 1979 were as follows:

Fiscal Year	
1980	$ 570,000
1981	549,000
1982	533,000
1983	520,000
1984	483,000
Thereafter	9,356,000
	12,011,000
Less estimated executory costs included in minimum lease payments	334,000
Net minimum lease payments	11,677,000
Less amount representing interest	7,127,000
Present value of net minimum lease payments	4,550,000
Less current portion included in accounts payable	189,000
Obligations under capital leases	$ 4,361,000

NOTE 11—Lease Commitments

The Company has various leases for real property and machinery and equipment. Many of these leases contain renewal options ranging from 5 to 25 years at pre-established amounts. In addition to rental payments, the majority of leases provide that the Company pay taxes, maintenance, insurance and certain other operating expenses applicable to the leased property.

Rental expense for 1978 and 1977 was comprised of:

	1978	1977
Rentals	$1,755,000	$1,752,000
Less sublease rentals	(129,000)	(209,000)
	$1,626,000	$1,543,000

Minimum commitments under all noncancellable leases at February 28, 1978 were as follows:

Fiscal Year	
1979	$ 755,000
1980	673,000
1981	602,000
1982	572,000
1983	499,000
Remainder	9,575,000
	$12,676,000

The aforementioned commitments do not include operating costs related to the leased property. At February 28, 1978, noncancellable sublease commitments were insignificant.

The Securities and Exchange Commission requires that the provisions of Financial Accounting Standards Board Statement No. 13—Accounting for Leases—be retroactively applied in the Company's fiscal 1979 financial statements for leases entered into prior to January 1, 1977. Had the consolidated financial statements been retroactively restated to conform to the Statement, the effect on reported net earnings for fiscal 1978 and 1977 would have been insignificant. In addition, the balance sheets would include the following items at February 28:

	1978	1977
Noncurrent assets:		
Leased property under capital leases, less accumulated amortization		
Current liabilities:		
Obligations under capital leases	$ 181,000	$ 165,000
Noncurrent liabilities:		
Obligations under capital leases	$4,449,000	$4,576,000

VII. LEASES AND PENSIONS

7.2. R. J. REYNOLDS INDUSTRIES, INC.—I

Accounting for leases, effects of operating vs. capital leases. (Moderate: 45 minutes)

R. J. Reynolds is a diversified, international corporation with major interests in domestic and international tobacco, processed foods, fresh fruit and beverages, containerized ocean shipping, energy, and packing. About one-third of the corporation's revenue is generated abroad.

Study the Consolidated Balance Sheets; Note 8, "Long-term Debt"; and Note 14, "Leases," of R. J. Reynolds Industries for 1980 (with comparative 1979).

Assume that all payments under leases are made on December 31 of each year, and that the lease payments for 1986 and thereafter are all made on December 31, 1990. (In other words, for purposes of present value calculations, lease payments *after* 1985 are all made on *one* date: December 31, 1990). Assume also that executory costs associated with Noncancelable Operating Leases are zero ($-0-). The relevant discount rate is 10 percent.

1. Complete the following table:

Year Ended December 31	Capital Leases (net of allowances for amortization)	Obligations Under Capital Leases (current and long-term)
1979		
1980		

2. **a.** If the capital leases had not been capitalized—that is, if they had been accounted for as operating leases from the very beginning—by how much would 1980 "Earnings Retained" change? Ignore any tax effects.

b. If the capital leases had not been capitalized—that is, they had been accounted for as operatng leases—by how much would 1980 "Earnings before Provision for Income Taxes" change? Ignore any tax effects.

3. Assume that the Financial Accounting Standards Board is now considering a requirement that *all* leases—capital leases and operating leases—be capitalized. Using the data in Note 14 and present value tables in your textbook, estimate the lease obligation for Noncancelable Operating Leases as of December 31, 1980. (Use the assumptions at the beginning of the question.)

Consolidated Balance Sheets

December 31

(Dollars in Millions)	1980	1979
ASSETS		
Current assets:		
Cash and short-term investments (Note 3)................................	$ **188.3**	$ 164.8
Accounts and notes receivable		
(less allowances of $40.2 and $27.4, respectively)........................	**1,019.6**	815.1
Inventories (Note 4)...	**2,371.8**	2,178.9
Prepaid expenses..	**61.8**	42.4
Total current assets	**3,641.5**	3,201.2
Property, plant and equipment — at cost (Notes 5 and 14)	**4,901.2**	4,111.3
Less allowances for depreciation, depletion and amortization	**1,636.5**	1,327.3
Net property, plant and equipment	**3,264.7**	2,784.0
Cost in excess of net assets of businesses acquired	**160.3**	162.0
Other assets and deferred charges	**288.8**	274.7
	$7,355.3	$6,421.9
LIABILITIES AND STOCKHOLDERS' EQUITY		
Current liabilities:		
Notes payable (Note 6)...	$ **514.3**	$ 395.3
Accounts payable and accrued accounts (Note 7)	**1,068.3**	883.0
Current maturities of long-term debt (Note 8)	**123.2**	87.0
Income taxes accrued..	**104.0**	119.3
Total current liabilities	**1,809.8**	1,484.6
Long-term debt (less current maturities) (Note 8)	**1,045.9**	988.9
Other noncurrent liabilities	**213.0**	183.5
Deferred income taxes..	**495.3**	411.4
Commitments and contingencies (Note 11)		
Series A Cumulative Preferred Stock (Note 12)	**342.1**	342.1
$2.25 Convertible Preferred Stock (Note 13)	**3.8**	13.6
Common stockholders' equity:		
Common Stock — net (Note 13)	**253.2**	244.8
Paid-in capital (Note 13)...	**213.5**	190.2
Earnings retained (Note 8)...	**2,978.7**	2,562.8
Total common stockholders' equity	**3,445.4**	2,997.8
	$7,355.3	$6,421.9

Note 8
Long-term Debt

	December 31, 1980		December 31, 1979	
	Due Within One Year	Due After One Year (e)	Due Within One Year	Due After One Year
Long-term debt consists of the following:				
8½% and 8¾% Ship Mortgage Bonds, payable in Dutch guilders, with semi-annual sinking fund payments through 1981 (a)	$ 8.9	$ —	$17.9	$ 8.9
7⅜% Debentures, due February 1, 2001, with annual sinking fund payments beginning in 1982 (reduced by $0.1 million of such debentures held by the Company on December 31, 1980 for future sinking fund requirements)	—	99.9	—	100.0
7⅞% Debentures, with annual sinking fund payments through 1994 (reduced by $4.9 million and $2.9 million of such debentures held by the Company on December 31, 1980 and 1979, respectively, for future sinking fund requirements)	0.1	65.0	2.1	70.0
8% Debentures, due January 15, 2007, with semi-annual sinking fund payments beginning in 1988	—	150.0	—	150.0
8.9% Notes, due October 1, 1996, with annual prepayments beginning in 1981 (b)	6.2	93.8	—	100.0
7½% Notes, due November 18, 1982, with equal annual sinking fund payments through 1982	32.0	32.0	32.0	64.0
7% Subordinated Debentures, due June 1, 1989. Annual sinking fund payments began in 1980 (reduced by $2.6 million and $1.7 million of such subordinated debentures held by the Company on December 31, 1980 and 1979, respectively, for future sinking fund requirements).	—	11.7	—	14.1
10¼% Notes, payable annually 1981 through 1990	5.0	45.0	—	50.0
10.45% Notes, due May 15, 1990	—	150.0	—	—
Revolving credit agreements with banks, due January 31, 1982, with interest at 102% of prime rate (c)	—	112.0	—	112.0
Exploration and development advances (d)	31.7	51.8	5.5	91.3
Capitalized lease obligations	11.1	96.2	11.5	79.6
Other indebtedness with various interest rates and maturities	28.2	138.5	18.0	149.0
	$123.2	$1,045.9	$87.0	$988.9

(a) During 1980, cash was substituted in lieu of vessels, containers and other marine equipment as collateral for the ship mortgage bonds. (See Note 3.)

(b) Under the terms of the Company's 8.9% Notes, dividend payments are generally limited to $150.0 million, plus net earnings after December 31, 1975. At December 31, 1980, $1.6 billion of earnings retained were unrestricted.

(c) The Company has revolving credit agreements with various banks expiring January 31, 1982 under which it may borrow up to $200.0 million. Under these agreements, the Company is obligated to pay a commitment fee of ½ of 1 percent on the unused balance. At December 31, 1980, these agreements support $112.0 million of commercial paper that has been classified as long-term debt based upon the Company's intention to continue that amount of debt in some form for more than one year.

(d) At December 31, 1980, the Company had $83.5 million of advances from certain gas pipeline companies (all of which were non-interest bearing) for the financing of exploration and development of various leases in the Gulf of Mexico in consideration for undertaking to execute gas purchase and sale agreements for future natural gas production.

(e) The payment schedule of debt due after one year is as follows: 1982 - $229.5; 1983 - $83.6; 1984 - $47.8; 1985 - $42.6; 1986 and later -$642.4.

VII. LEASES AND PENSIONS

Note 14
Leases

Most of the Company's leases are used in the transportation business, principally for vessels, truck terminals, port facilities and related equipment, and in the foods and beverages business, primarily for machinery, trucks, trailers and warehouses. Certain leases contain ordinary renewal options, although some container equipment leases provide for bargain renewal options extending over the economic life of the property. Some leases, principally those covering truck terminals and port facilities, contain escalation clauses based on the lessor's operating costs. Certain port facility and equipment leases call for contingent rentals based on usage. Many of the Company's leases are noncancelable operating leases relating to port facilities, trucks and trailers.

Property, plant and equipment accounts at December 31 include the following amounts for capital leases:

	1980	1979
Buildings and leasehold improvements	$ 15.0	$ 16.3
Machinery and equipment	26.3	30.0
Vessels, containers and other marine equipment (1)	90.4	59.0
	131.7	105.3
Less allowances for amortization (2)	30.5	24.7
	$101.2	$ 80.6

(1) Includes $67.2 million and $43.5 million for 1980 and 1979, respectively, attributable to certain leasing activities with less than 50 percent owned affiliates in the Company's transportation business.

(2) Lease amortization is included in depreciation expense.

At December 31, 1980, the Company was obligated to make future minimum lease payments as follows:

	Capital Leases	Non-cancelable Operating Leases	Total
1981	$ 22.4	$ 66.6	$ 89.0
1982	20.4	59.0	79.4
1983	17.2	50.6	67.8
1984	15.8	38.2	54.0
1985	14.4	34.5	48.9
Thereafter	114.4	342.8	457.2
Total minimum lease payments	204.6	$591.7	$796.3
Executory costs	(1.4)		
Amount representing interest.................	(95.9)		
Capitalized lease obligations (see Note 8)	$107.3		

Minimum future sublease rentals receivable under capital leases and noncancelable operating leases at December 31, 1980 amounted to $6.5 million and $8.6 million, respectively. Rental expense for all operating leases, cancelable and noncancelable, consisted of:

	1980	1979	1978
Minimum rentals	$183.1	$160.9	$107.0
Contingent rentals	32.5	25.3	0.6
Sublease rental income.....	(4.9)	(4.4)	(3.3)
	$210.7	$181.8	$104.3

7.3. K MART CORPORATION

Capital vs. operating leases, present value calculations.
(Moderate: 45 minutes)

K mart Corporation is the second-largest general merchandiser in sales volume (in the U.S.). The company is principally engaged in the distribution of a wide range of merchandise through the operation of a chain of discount department stores (K mart), variety stores (Kresge), and limited-line discount stores (Jupiter).

Study the 1981–82 Consolidated Balance Sheets and Note H, "Leases," to the financial statements.

1. Prepare journal entries to record the 1982 lease rental payment, 1982 depreciation (amortization) on leased property, and 1982 interest expense relating to lease obligations for *capital* leases only. (Use *minimum* lease payments, excluding executory costs.)

2. Assume that the taxing authority requires that capital lease rental payments be expensed for tax reporting; however, K mart records interest and depreciation relating to capital leases as expenses for reporting to stockholders. This difference in the reporting of leases for taxes and stockholders gives rise to deferred taxes. Provide a journal entry that would recognize the 1982 deferred taxes relating to capital lease expenses. Assume a 50 percent tax rate.

3. What amount is stated as the present value of minimum lease payments under capital leases as of January 28, 1981 and January 27, 1982? Estimate the present value of new lease obligations incurred during fiscal 1982. Assume that all lease payments and new acquisitions of leased assets took place on January 27, 1982.

4. By how much would retained earnings be affected if K mart were to restate all capital leases as operating leases as of January 27, 1982? In answering this question, consider the following footnote

on cumulative deferred taxes relating to capital leases, discussed in Note F:

The amounts shown in the balance sheets for deferred income taxes result principally from the difference between financial statement and income tax depreciation, reduced by the effect of accounting for certain leases as capital leases of $97.3 million at January 27, 1982. The net amount of current deferred taxes at January 27, 1982 ... relates principally to accrued employee benefits and uninsured claims. . . .

Consolidated Balance Sheets

(Thousands)	January 27,	January 28,
Assets	**1982**	**1981**
Current Assets:		
Cash (includes temporary investments of $48,216 in 1981		
and $139,874 in 1980)	$ 115,202	$ 212,987
Accounts receivable	89,878	79,783
Merchandise inventories	3,135,104	2,845,910
Operating supplies and prepaid expenses	73,378	58,651
Total current assets	3,413,562	3,197,331
Investments in and Advances to:		
Affiliated retail companies	210,725	137,992
Insurance operations	99,581	88,062
Other Assets and Deferred Charges	73,403	77,705
Property:		
Land	45,261	43,861
Buildings	177,063	172,743
Leasehold improvements	258,069	224,099
Furniture and fixtures	1,475,959	1,261,199
Construction in progress	58,742	44,087
	2,015,094	1,745,989
Less—Depreciation and amortization	760,175	654,895
Total property owned	1,254,919	1,091,094
Leased property under capital leases, less accumulated amortization		
of $629,144 and $563,904, respectively	1,620,814	1,510,278
Total property	2,875,733	2,601,372
	$6,673,004	$6,102,462

Liabilities and Stockholders' Equity	January 27, 1982	January 28, 1981
Current Liabilities:		
Long-term debt due within one year	$ 1,777	$ 1,845
Obligations under capital leases due within one year	62,322	57,153
Notes payable	168,154	
Accounts payable—trade	1,252,975	1,060,185
Accrued payrolls and other liabilities	269,995	269,472
Taxes other than income taxes	145,320	133,744
Dividends payable	29,754	28,377
Income taxes	52,895	120,068
Total current liabilities	1,983,192	1,670,844
Obligations under Capital Leases	1,751,961	1,618,143
Long-Term Debt	415,077	418,726
Deferred Income Taxes	67,180	51,577
Stockholders' Equity:		
Common stock	123,976	123,379
Capital in excess of par value	264,209	253,761
Income retained for use in the business	2,067,409	1,966,032
Total stockholders' equity	2,455,594	2,343,172
	$6,673,004	$6,102,462

(H) Leases

Description of Leasing Arrangements: The company conducts operations primarily in leased facilities. Store leases are generally for terms of 25 years with multiple five-year renewal options which allow the company the option to extend the life of the lease up to 50 years beyond the initial noncancellable term. Certain leases provide for additional rental payments based on sales volume in excess of a specified base. Also, certain leases provide for the payment by the lessee of executory costs (taxes, maintenance and insurance), and selling space has been sublet to other retailers in certain of the company's leased facilities.

Lease Commitments: Future minimum lease payments with respect to capital and operating leases are:

(Millions)	Minimum Lease Payments	
	Capital	Operating
Fiscal Year:		
1982	$ 306.9	$ 171.3
1983	303.7	168.8
1984	300.5	165.2
1985	296.6	161.8
1986	290.6	158.8
Later years	4,023.5	2,115.4
Total minimum lease payments	5,521.8	2,941.3
Less—minimum sublease rental income		(151.2)
Net minimum lease payments	5,521.8	$2,790.1
Less:		
Amount representing estimated executory costs	(1,514.0)	
Amount representing interest	(2,193.5)	
Present value of minimum lease payments, of which $62.3 million is due within one year	$ 1,814.3	

The company has guaranteed indebtedness related to certain leased properties financed by industrial revenue bonds. As of January 27, 1982 the total amount of such guaranteed indebtedness is $198.3 million, of which $89.6 million is included in capital lease obligations.

Rental Expense: A summary of operating lease rental expense, estimated executory costs of all leases and short-term rentals follows:

(Millions)	Fiscal Year Ended		
	January 27, 1982	January 28, 1981	January 30, 1980
Minimum rentals	$250.6	$217.2	$190.2
Rentals based on sales volume	33.3	27.9	25.6
Less—sublease rentals	(32.6)	(28.9)	(26.2)
Total	$251.3	$216.2	$189.6

Reconciliation of Capital Lease Information: Capital lease amortization and interest charged to operations are reconciled to minimum capital lease payments as follows:

(Millions)	Fiscal Year Ended		
	January 27, 1982	January 28, 1981	January 30, 1980
Amortization of leased property under capital leases	$ 88.9	$ 79.0	$ 72.2
Interest expense related to obligations under capital leases	160.7	135.0	120.3
Amounts charged to earnings	249.6	214.0	192.5
Related minimum lease payments (excluding executory costs)	(219.8)	(188.1)	(168.9)
Excess of amounts charged over related minimum lease payments	$ 29.8	$ 25.9	$ 23.6

The inclusion of capital leases of foreign operations reduced currency fluctuation gains by $.1 million in 1981, reduced currency fluctuation losses by $2.9 million in 1980 and increased currency fluctuation losses by $2.5 million in 1979. [See Note (I).]

7.4. GENERAL MOTORS

*Present value calculations, pension accounting, impact
of change in accounting estimate.
(Difficult: 45 minutes)*

Study General Motors' Statement of Consolidated Income for 1979–81; Consolidated Balance Sheet for 1980–81; Note 5 to the financial statements, "Pension Program"; and the Deloitte Haskins & Sells audit report.

In a *Forbes* article of May 10, 1982, Bernstein notes the following:

> Watch the Actuaries. With interest rates seemingly glued to the heavens, a number of firms have changed their assumptions about how much money their pension plans will earn for many years to come. By raising your interest rate assumptions, you can put vastly fewer dollars into the pension plan in a given year. Presto: higher earnings. (p. 78)

GM's pension fund is no different from that of other firms—i.e., it provides benefits for retired employees. How much to pay into the fund each year depends on the expected future retirement payments to be made—an obligation of the company. Pension fund costs are expensed periodically to update the expected future obligations of the company. Such periodic expenses are derived, in part, by discounting future employee benefits using assumed rates of return on pension fund assets.

1. Suppose a company expenses this year a lump-sum pension benefit to be paid in twenty years. Show the journal entry for an expected future payment of $100,000 if the company expects a rate of return on fund assets equal to (a) 6 percent and (b) 7 percent, compounded annually.

2. Using the present value (PV) formula $PV = F(1 + R)^{-N}$, which can be rewritten in log form as $\ln PV = \ln F - N \ln (1 + R)$, estimate the average future time period (N) that GM uses to determine its

future payments (F). Assume, for purposes of answering this question, that GM's future payments are a single amount F, not a series of future pension payments.[1]

3. Using the N estimate in part 2, what would pension expense have been in 1980 if GM had switched to the 7 percent discount rate in 1980? To answer this question, first calculate the assumed future payment (F) associated with the 1980 pension expense of $1,922.1 million. Given a 50 percent tax rate, determine the effect on 1980 net income.

4. Why should GM stop at 7 percent? Determine the impact on net income (assume a 50 percent tax rate) if the rate of return was increased from 6 percent to (a) 8 percent and (b) 10 percent.

5. Why doesn't the auditor's report alert stockholders to the change in accounting measurement rules?

---

[1]The pension expense amounts reported by GM are assumed to represent the actuarial value of pension obligations arising from labor services for the years 1980 and 1981. The analysis is simplified by assuming that instead of receiving a *series* of pension payments on retirement, the employee is given a *lump-sum* cash amount (denoted F). The analysis is also simplified in that GM's pension expense is most likely to include normal costs and sweetening effects. Alternately, we can view that lump-sum amount F as the actuarial value of pension payments as of the date of employee retirement. All amounts are estimates and averages, since GM must provide benefits for an entire spectrum of employees, retiring at different dates.

VII. LEASES AND PENSIONS

Statements of Consolidated Income

For The Years Ended December 31, 1981, 1980 and 1979
(Dollars in Millions Except Per Share Amounts)

	1981	1980	1979
Net Sales (Note 2)	$62,698.5	$57,728.5	$66,311.2
Costs and Expenses			
Cost of sales and other operating charges, exclusive of items listed below	55,185.2	52,099.8	55,848.7
Selling, general and administrative expenses	2,715.0	2,636.7	2,475.5
Depreciation of real estate, plants and equipment	1,837.3	1,458.1	1,236.9
Amortization of special tools	2,568.9	2,719.6	1,950.4
Provision for the Bonus Plan (Note 3)	—	—	133.8
Total Costs and Expenses	62,306.4	58,914.2	61,645.3
Operating Income (Loss)	392.1	(1,185.7)	4,665.9
Other income less income deductions—net (Note 4)	367.7	348.7	560.3
Interest expense (Note 1)	(897.9)	(531.9)	(368.4)
Income (Loss) before Income Taxes	(138.1)	(1,368.9)	4,857.8
United States, foreign and other income taxes (credit) (Note 6)	(123.1)	(385.3)	2,183.4
Income (Loss) after Income Taxes	(15.0)	(983.6)	2,674.4
Equity in earnings of nonconsolidated subsidiaries and associates (dividends received amounted to $189.7 in 1981, $116.8 in 1980 and $112.8 in 1979)	348.4	221.1	218.3
Net Income (Loss)	333.4	(762.5)	2,892.7
Dividends on preferred stocks	12.9	12.9	12.9
Earnings (Loss) on Common Stock	$ 320.5	($ 775.4)	$ 2,879.8
Average number of shares of common stock outstanding (in millions)	299.1	292.4	286.8
Earnings (Loss) Per Share of Common Stock (Note 7)	$1.07	($2.65)	$10.04

Consolidated Balance Sheet

December 31, 1981 and 1980
(Dollars in Millions Except Per Share Amounts)

ASSETS	1981	1980
Current Assets		
Cash	$ 204.1	$ 157.2
United States Government and other marketable securities and time deposits—at cost, which approximates market of $1,086.3 and $3,541.4	1,116.6	3,558.0
Accounts and notes receivable (including GMAC and its subsidiaries—$636.2 and $704.9)—less allowances	3,645.5	3,768.4
Inventories (less allowances) (Note 1)	7,222.7	7,295.0
Prepaid expenses	1,527.2	706.5
Total Current Assets	13,716.1	15,485.1
Equity in Net Assets of Nonconsolidated Subsidiaries and Associates (principally GMAC and its subsidiaries—Note 8)	3,379.4	2,899.8
Other Investments and Miscellaneous Assets—at cost (less allowances)	1,783.5	1,147.3
Common Stock Held for the Incentive Program (Note 3)	71.5	125.8
Property		
Real estate, plants and equipment—at cost (Note 9)	34,811.5	29,202.7
Less accumulated depreciation (Note 9)	16,317.4	15,217.1
Net real estate, plants and equipment	18,494.1	13,985.6
Special tools—at cost (less amortization)	1,546.6	937.4
Total Property	20,040.7	14,923.0
Total Assets	$38,991.2	$34,581.0

LIABILITIES AND STOCKHOLDERS' EQUITY		
Current Liabilities		
Accounts payable (principally trade)	$ 3,699.7	$ 3,967.7
Loans payable (principally overseas) (Note 11)	1,727.8	1,676.5
Accrued liabilities (Note 10)	7,127.6	6,628.8
Total Current Liabilities	12,555.1	12,273.0
Long-Term Debt (Note 11)	3,801.1	1,886.0
Capitalized Leases	242.8	172.3
Other Liabilities (including GMAC of $424.0 in 1981)	3.215.1	1.482.5
Deferred Credits (principally investment tax credits)	1,456.0	952.6
Stockholders' Equity (Notes 3 and 12)		
Preferred stocks ($5.00 series, $183.6; $3.75 series, $100.0)	283.6	283.6
Common stock (issued, 304,804,228 and 298,053,782 shares)	508.0	496.7
Capital surplus (principally additional paid-in capital)	1,589.5	1,297.2
Net income retained for use in the business	15,340.0	15,737.1
Total Stockholders' Equity	17,721.1	17,814.6
Total Liabilities and Stockholders' Equity	$38,991.2	$34,581.0

VII.   LEASES AND PENSIONS

NOTE 5: Pension Program

(Dollars in Millions)	1981	1980	1979
Other income:			
Interest	$427.9	$392.1	$507.0
Other	123.6	81.7	72.2
Income deductions	(183.8)	(125.1)	(18.9)
Net	$367.7	$348.7	$560.3

Total pension expense of the Corporation and its consolidated subsidiaries amounted to $1,493.8 million in 1981, $1,922.1 million in 1980 and $1,571.5 million in 1979. For purposes of determining pension expense, the Corporation uses a variety of assumed rates of return on pension funds in accordance with local practice and regulations, which rates approximated 6% in 1980 and 1979. In 1981, the assumed rate of return used in determining retirement plan costs in the United States and Canada was increased to 7%. The Corporation's independent actuary recommended this change, and other changes in actuarial assumptions, after taking into account the experience of the plans and reasonable expectations. The total effect of these changes was to reduce retirement plan costs for 1981 by $411.1 million and accordingly increase net income by $205.6 million ($0.69 per share). The following table compares accumulated plan benefits and plan net assets for the Corporation's defined benefit plans in the United States and Canada as of October 1 (generally, the plans' anniversary date) of both 1981 and 1980:

(Dollars in Millions)	1981	1980
Actuarial present value of accumulated plan benefits:		
Vested	$16,228.5	$17,438.5
Nonvested	1,890.3	2,234.1
Total	$18,118.8	$19,672.6
Market value of assets available for benefits:		
Held by trustees	$10,795.1	$10,584.6
Held by insurance companies	3,049.4	2,769.2
Total	$13,844.5	$13,353.8

The assumed rates of return used in determining the actuarial present value of accumulated plan benefits (shown in the table above) were based upon those published by the Pension Benefit Guaranty Corporation, a public corporation established under the Employee Retirement Income Security Act (ERISA). Such rates averaged approximately 10% for 1981 and 8¼% for 1980.

The Corporation's foreign pension plans are not required to report to governmental agencies pursuant to ERISA, and do not otherwise determine the actuarial value of accumulated benefits or net assets available for benefits as calculated and shown above. For those plans, the total of the plans' pension funds and balance sheet accruals, less pension prepayments and deferred charges, exceeded the actuarially computed value of vested benefits by approximately $200 million at December 31, 1981 and $215 million at December 31, 1980.

ACCOUNTANTS' REPORT

**Deloitte
Haskins Sells**
CERTIFIED PUBLIC ACCOUNTANTS

1114 Avenue of the Americas
New York 10036

General Motors Corporation, its Directors and Stockholders: February 8, 1982

We have examined the Consolidated Balance Sheet of General Motors Corporation and consolidated subsidiaries as of December 31, 1981 and 1980 and the related Statements of Consolidated Income and Changes in Consolidated Financial Position for each of the three years in the period ended December 31, 1981. Our examinations were made in accordance with generally accepted auditing standards and, accordingly, included such tests of the accounting records and such other auditing procedures as we considered necessary in the circumstances.

In our opinion, these financial statements present fairly the financial position of the companies at December 31, 1981 and 1980 and the results of their operations and the changes in their financial position for each of the three years in the period ended December 31, 1981, in conformity with generally accepted accounting principles applied on a consistent basis.

Deloitte Haskins & Sells

8.1. SEARS, ROEBUCK AND COMPANY*

Introduction to deferred income taxes.
(Straightforward: 45 minutes)

Sears, Roebuck and Company's principal business groups are Merchandise, Allstate, and Seraco. Merchandise consists of Merchandising, Credit, and International units for which separate financial statements are presented; Allstate engages in property-liability insurance, life insurance, and financial services; Seraco invests in, develops, and operates real estate and performs mortgage banking and savings and loan activities.

Study Sears's Consolidated Statements of Income and Statements of Financial Position, along with Note 7, "Income Taxes," to those statements. Also included are the Credit group's Statements of Income, Statements of Financial Position, Statements of Changes in Financial Position, and Note 3, "Income Taxes."

As explained in the annual report, credit sales accounted for 53.3, 54.2, and 52.1 percent of gross sales of merchandising in the years ended January 31, 1979, 1980, and 1981. However, due to a company decision to convert installment accounts to regular "revolving charge" (Sears Charge) accounts, installment sales contract revenues decreased 40.8 percent in the year ended January 31, 1980 and 39.8 percent in the year ended January 31, 1981.

Sears apparently uses the installment sales method of reporting its income for tax purposes. Under this method, the profit on a sale is recognized in proportion to the amount of the installment account receivable that is collected each period. However, for purposes of calculating income for the annual report, the company recognizes the full amount of income on the credit transaction in the period of sale.

---

*Based on earlier case by Robert K. Jaedicke.

1. Assume that on February 1, 1978, Sears recorded an installment sale of $1,500. Apart from interest, the customer was required to pay $500 per year for three years. The item—a large-screen projection TV set—cost Sears $600. On February 2, 1978, Sears decided to abandon its installment sales plan and, consequently, made no further sales on the installment basis.

   Prepare journal entries for fiscal years ended 1/31/79, 1/31/80, and 1/31/81 to record all changes in the deferred income taxes liability account. Use a 40 percent tax rate in your calculations.

2. With reference to Credit's 1981 Statement of Income, explain why income expense is a credit amount of $32.9 million, whereas Credit's current provision for federal income tax on 1981 income amounts to $136.5 million.

3. Does your answer to part 2 above also explain why Credit's deferred income tax account decreased from $1,165.8 million in 1980 to $980.6 million in 1981?

4. Compute Credit's Net Income (Loss) for the years 1979, 1980, and 1981, assuming that the flow-through method of accounting for income taxes had been used. Compute Sears's Consolidated Net Income (Loss) for the years 1979, 1980, and 1981, assuming that the flow-through method of accounting for income taxes had been used.

5. Comment on the nature of the $1,424.2 million liability for Deferred Income Taxes shown in Sears's Consolidated Statement of Financial Position for 1981. Is this liability ever likely to be paid?

Consolidated Statements of Income

millions, except per share data	Year Ended January 31		
	1981	1980	1979
Operating revenues			
Merchandise Group			
Merchandising	$16,865.0	$16,839.6	$17,284.4
Credit	968.3	934.1	914.2
International	873.8	775.4	888.9
Total Merchandise Group	18,707.1	18,549.1	19,087.5
Allstate Group	6,197.2	5,783.8	5,238.5
Seraco Group	419.4	361.3	303.7
Corporate	71.2	14.4	—
Intergroup transactions	(200.0)	(159.2)	(139.9)
Total operating revenues	$25,194.9	$24,549.4	$24,489.8
Operating expenses			
Costs and expenses	23,393.5	22,615.4	22,436.7
Nonrecurring expenses			
Retirement incentive (note 2)	66.7	—	—
Customs settlement provision (note 10)	19.8	—	—
Interest	1,133.9	912.0	737.5
Total operating expenses	24,613.9	23,527.4	23,174.2
Operating income	581.0	1,022.0	1,315.6
Realized capital gains and other	92.8	63.2	80.0
Income before income taxes, equity in net income of unconsolidated companies and minority interest	673.8	1,085.2	1,395.6
Income taxes	85.2	307.1	504.9
Equity in net income of unconsolidated companies and minority interest	17.4	32.0	30.8
Net income	$606.0	$810.1	$921.5
Net income consists of:			
Group income (loss)			
Merchandise Group			
Merchandising	208.6	366.8	422.4
Credit	(33.5)	14.5	36.2
International	29.7	49.9	39.1
Total Merchandise Group	204.8	431.2	497.7
Allstate Group	450.4	421.8	428.4
Seraco Group	48.8	41.2	64.1
Net corporate expense	(98.0)	(84.1)	(68.7)
Net income	$606.0	$810.1	$921.5
Per share	$1.92	$2.54	$2.86
Average shares outstanding	315.5	319.0	322.4

Sears, Roebuck and Co.
Consolidated Statements of Financial Position

millions		January 31
	1981	1980
Assets		
Receivables		
Retail customer	$ 7,110.5	$ 7,132.4
Finance installment notes	591.2	672.1
Insurance premium installment	589.2	528.9
Other	396.2	335.4
	8,687.1	8,668.8
Investments		
Bonds and redeemable preferred stocks (estimated market $4,542.8 and $4,899.2)	6,169.6	5,589.6
Common and preferred stocks (cost $1,166.4 and $944.2)	1,438.7	1,020.1
Mortgage loans	3,139.1	2,869.4
Real estate	578.1	468.7
Other	93.8	62.8
	11,419.3	10,010.6
Property and equipment, net	3,155.7	3,053.1
Merchandise inventories	2,721.6	2,719.2
Cash and invested cash	786.7	866.6
Investments in unconsolidated companies	533.6	517.0
Prepaid expenses and deferred charges	449.3	430.6
Other assets	300.5	321.0
Total assets	28,053.8	26,586.9
Liabilities		
Reserve for insurance claims and policy benefits	4,508.5	4,161.2
Short-term borrowings (note 3)	4,304.1	4,184.9
Long-term debt (note 4)	2,961.9	2,972.2
Savings accounts and advances from Federal Home Loan Bank	2,696.1	2,411.4
Unearned revenue	2,298.6	2,126.3
Accounts payable and other liabilities	2,171.6	1,772.4
Deferred income taxes	1,424.2	1,491.3
Total liabilities	20,365.0	19,119.7
Commitments and contingent liabilities (notes 2, 9 and 10)		
Shareholders' equity (note 5)		
Common shares ($.75 par value)	244.1	243.7
Capital in excess of par value	640.4	634.3
Retained income	6,840.5	6,663.9
Treasury stock (at cost)	(188.6)	(150.7)
Unrealized net capital gains on marketable equity securities	152.4	76.0
Total shareholders' equity	$ 7,688.8	$ 7,467.2
Total shares outstanding	315.357	317.328

VIII.   INCOME TAXES AND INVESTMENT TAX CREDIT

7. Income taxes

Income before income taxes, equity in net income of unconsolidated companies and minority interest is as follows:

	Year Ended January 31		
	1981	1980	1979
Domestic	$630.2	$1,010.3	$1,336.8
Foreign	43.6	74.9	58.8
Total	$673.8	$1.085.2	$1,395.6

Federal, state and foreign income taxes include:

	Year Ended January 31		
	1981	1980	1979
Provision			
Current			
Domestic	$285.8	$216.9	$425.7
Investment tax credit (flow-through method)	(18.5)	(20.1)	(18.8)
Foreign	16.9	36.4	35.6
Total current	284.2	233.2	442.5
Deferred			
Current			
Installment sales	(205.7)	47.2	(30.7)
Receivables reserves	3.5	29.4	26.8
Pension expense	23.9	(28.9)	5.8
Maintenance agreement income	(13.3)	(16.6)	(6.5)
Retirement incentive	(33.0)	—	—
Other	18.1	18.6	38.8
Long-term			
Depreciation	8.7	17.3	17.2
Other	(1.2)	6.9	11.0
Total deferred	(199.0)	73.9	62.4
Financial statement income tax provision	$ 85.2	$307.1	$504.9
Classification			
Federal income tax			
Current	$ 244.7	$185.0	$356.6
Deferred	(173.1)	52.5	51.7
State income tax			
Current	22.6	11.8	50.3
Deferred	(27.4)	21.7	9.1
Foreign income tax			
Current	16.9	36.4	35.6
Deferred	1.5	(.3)	1.6
Financial statement income tax provision	$ 85.2	$307.1	$504.9

A reconciliation of the statutory federal income tax rate to the effective income tax rate is as follows:

	Year Ended January 31		
	1981	1980	1979
Statutory federal income tax rate	46.0%	46.0%	47.8%
State income taxes, net of federal income taxes	(.7)	1.0	1.7
Tax exempt income	(20.3)	(11.2)	(8.2)
Dividends received exclusion	(6.9)	(4.1)	(2.2)
Investment tax credit	(2.7)	(1.9)	(1.4)
Capital gains deduction	(1.3)	(.1)	(.9)
Other	(1.5)	(1.4)	(.6)
Effective income tax rate	12.6%	28.3%	36.2%

Credit
Statements of Income

millions		Year Ended January 31	
	1981	1980	1979
Finance charge revenues			
Revolving charge accounts	$ 883.7	$793.5	$676.6
Installment sales contracts	84.6	140.6	237.6
Total finance charge revenues	968.3	934.1	914.2
Operating expenses			
Costs and expenses (note 1)	382.0	385.4	413.4
Retirement incentive	3.1	—	—
Provision for uncollectible accounts (note 2)	110.7	78.2	62.7
Interest expense	528.2	431.3	361.2
Total operating expenses	1,024.0	894.9	837.3
Operating income (loss)	(55.7)	39.2	76.9
Other income (loss)	(10.7)	(10.7)	(3.2)
Income (loss) before income taxes	(66.4)	28.5	73.7
Income taxes (benefit) (note 3)	(32.9)	14.0	37.5
Credit income (loss)	$ (33.5)	$ 14.5	$ 36.2

Credit
Statements of Financial Position

millions		January 31
	1981	1980
Assets		
Retail customer receivables		
Revolving charge accounts (note 1)	$6,226.9	$5,956.0
Installment sales contracts	724.0	1,068.9
	6,950.9	7,024.9
Less: Unearned finance charges	54.7	72.3
Allowance for uncollectible accounts (note 2)	102.2	94.9
	6,794.0	6,857.7
Cash	72.0	72.5
Other assets	11.3	79.0
Total assets	6,877.3	7,009.2
Liabilities		
Debt	4,757.0	4,747.0
Deferred income taxes	980.6	1,165.8
Accrued interest payable	73.1	67.9
Accounts payable and accrued expenses	86.0	14.4
Total liabilities	5,896.7	5,995.1
Capital	$ 980.6	$1,014.1

Statements of Changes in Financial Position

millions		Year Ended January 31	
	1981	1980	1979
Source of funds			
Credit income (loss)	$ (33.5)	$ 14.5	$ 36.2
Increase (decrease) in deferred income taxes	(185.2)	89.0	2.5
Depreciation	2.0	1.8	1.6
Increase (decrease) in other assets and liabilities	142.5	(80.3)	66.8
From operations	(74.2)	25.0	107.1
Additional borrowings	10.0	487.5	—
Sale of customer receivables	187.8	167.5	643.2
Total source	$ 123.6	$680.0	$750.3
Use of funds			
Increase in retail customer receivables, before sale of accounts	$ 124.1	$678.6	$700.4
Reduction in borrowings	—	—	45.3
Increase (decrease) in cash	(.5)	1.4	4.6
Total use	$ 123.6	$680.0	$750.3

3. Income taxes

Federal and state income taxes include:

	Year Ended January 31		
	1981	1980	1979
Provision			
Current	$157.0	$(57.9)	$41.5
Deferred			
Installment sales	(210.4)	37.9	(35.2)
Receivable reserves	7.4	35.5	31.2
Pension expense	—	(1.5)	—
Retirement incentive	(1.5)	—	—
Other	14.6	—	—
Financial statement income tax provision (benefit)	$(32.9)	$ 14.0	$37.5
Classification			
Federal income tax			
Current	$136.5	$(52.3)	$35.8
Deferred	(165.0)	64.6	(2.6)
State income tax			
Current	20.5	(5.6)	5.7
Deferred	(24.9)	7.3	(1.4)
Financial statement income tax provision (benefit)	$(32.9)	$ 14.0	$37.5

A reconciliation of the effective income tax rate on income before taxes with the statutory federal income tax rate is:

	Year Ended January 31		
	1981	1980	1979
Statutory federal income tax rate	46.0%	46.0%	47.8%
State income taxes, net of federal income taxes	3.6	3.1	3.1
Effective income tax rate	49.6%	49.1%	50.9%

8.2. ROCKWELL INTERNATIONAL

*Interpretation of tax expense per income statement,
explanation of deferred tax liability account.
(Straightforward: 30 minutes)*

Rockwell International is a diversified company with operations in four principal areas: (1) aerospace, including manned and unmanned space systems; (2) defense electronic systems and products, telecommunications, and avionics; (3) energy products and control systems, and components for oil, gas, and nuclear industries; and (4) graphics and industrial machinery.

1. Using the accompanying Statement of Consolidated Income for 1980–82 and Note 20 to the financial statements, "Income Taxes," identify the following for 1982:

   a. Tax expense

   b. Deferred income tax expense

   c. Current provision for federal U.S. income taxes

   d. Investment tax credits that reduce current provisions for income taxes

2. Assume that the company is using the completed contract method for tax purposes to measure profit on long-term contracts (and hence deducting certain costs as incurred) but is recording profit for reporting purposes on a percentage-of-completion basis. What is the likely impact of the 1982 Tax Equity and Fiscal Responsibility Act on the market value of the company's net assets? To what extent are such potential changes in the value of the company's net assets likely to be reflected in present and future historical-cost accounting statements? Comment.

Rockwell International Corporation and Consolidated Subsidiaries

STATEMENT OF CONSOLIDATED INCOME

	Years ended September 30	1982	1981*	1980
		(In millions)		
Sales and other income	Sales	$7,395.4	$7,039.7	$6,906.5
	Other income	214.1	219.5	146.2
	Total sales and other income	7,609.5	7,259.2	7,052.7
Costs and expenses	Cost of sales	5,992.9	5,778.1	5,605.3
	Selling, general and administrative	950.0	854.5	874.9
	Interest	35.7	40.5	46.8
	Total costs and expenses	6,978.6	6,673.1	6,527.0
	Income before income taxes	630.9	586.1	525.7
	Provision for income taxes	299.3	267.3	245.5
Net income		$ 331.6	$ 318.8	$ 280.2
		(In dollars)		
Earnings per common share	Primary	$ 4.33	$ 4.19	$ 3.77
	Fully diluted	$ 4.22	$ 4.07	$ 3.59

*The 1981 results have been restated to conform with the 1982 change in method of accounting for foreign currency translation (see Note 2).

See notes to financial statements.

20. Income taxes

Taxes are provided, at appropriate rates, on the basis of items included in the determination of income for financial reporting purposes regardless of the period when such items are reported for tax purposes. Investment tax credits are recognized as a reduction of the provision for income taxes in the year the assets which give rise to the credits are placed in service.

The components of the provision for income taxes were as follows (in millions):

	1982	1981	1980
Current:			
United States	$ (1.7)	$ 46.2	$ 33.5
Foreign	31.7	14.7	42.5
State and local	25.0	22.6	26.4
Total current	55.0	83.5	102.4
Deferred:			
United States	230.2	161.6	136.6
Foreign	(1.5)	12.1	0.6
State and local	15.6	10.1	5.9
Total deferred	244.3	183.8	143.1
Provision for income taxes	$299.3	$267.3	$245.5

Investment tax credits reduced the provision for income taxes by $23.8 million in 1982, $15.1 million in 1981 and $13.7 million in 1980.

The consolidated effective tax rate was different from the United States statutory rate for the reasons set forth in the table below:

	1982	1981	1980
Statutory tax rate	46.0%	46.0%	46.0%
State and local income taxes	3.5	3.0	3.3
Investment tax credits	(3.8)	(2.6)	(2.6)
Taxes on foreign operations	.6	(2.1)	(1.1)
Other – net	1.1	1.3	1.1
Effective tax rate	47.4%	45.6%	46.7%

The income tax provisions were calculated based upon the following components of income before income taxes (in millions):

	1982	1981	1980
United States income	$547.7	$480.2	$422.5
Foreign income	83.2	105.9	103.2
Total	$630.9	$586.1	$525.7

Deferred taxes result from timing differences in the recognition of revenue and expense for financial and tax reporting purposes. The principal timing difference results from the recognition, for financial reporting purposes, of income from long-term contracts that is being deferred for tax purposes until contract completion. Under the completed contract method as currently applied for tax purposes, certain costs, including general and administrative, research and development and employee benefits are deducted as incurred. However, under the Tax Equity and Fiscal Responsibility Act of 1982, a significant portion of such costs related to long-term contracts entered into after December 31, 1982 will not be deductible until completion of the contract to which they relate. This change will be phased in over a three-year period beginning in 1983 and will accelerate the timing of payments of income taxes beginning in 1984. Although use of the completed contract method for tax purposes results in deferral of the payment of income taxes, it is not expected to result in any significant increase or decrease in income taxes ultimately payable or have any significant effect on the Company's consolidated effective tax rate for financial reporting purposes.

The provision for deferred taxes consisted of the following (in millions):

	1982	1981	1980
Tax effects of timing differences arising from:			
Recognition of income from long-term contracts	$260.6	$164.6	$132.0
Excess of tax over book depreciation	23.1	15.6	11.5
Other – net	13.5	3.6	(7.3)
Total	297.2	183.8	136.2
Increase (decrease) to account for tax effects of carryforwards for:			
Tax net operating loss	(30.8)		
Investment and foreign tax credits	(22.1)		6.9
Provision for deferred taxes	$244.3	$183.8	$143.1

Principally because of the use of the completed contract method for tax purposes, the Company expects to report a United States tax net operating loss for 1982. Investment tax credits and foreign tax credits arising in 1982 will be carried back to prior tax years to the extent allowable with unused investment tax credits being carried forward (expiring in 1997). The Company intends to carryforward its tax net operating loss for 1982 of $67 million (expiring in 1997).

VIII. INCOME TAXES AND INVESTMENT TAX CREDIT

8.3. THE DOW CHEMICAL COMPANY

Deferred taxes, investment tax credit, effects of accounting changes on taxes. (Straightforward: 45 minutes)

The Dow Chemical Company operates its worldwide activities through four principal groups: industrial chemicals, plastics and metals, specialty products, and bioproducts and consumer items.

Study Dow Chemical's 1981 Consolidated Statement of Income and Notes B, E, F, and L to the 1981 financial statements.

1. Calculate Dow Chemical's 1981 income before provision for taxes on income assuming that the company

   a. Did not capitalize interest cost (Note B)

   b. Did not decide that the tax-deferred earnings of its domestic international sales corporation (DISC) would be permanently invested (Note E)

   c. Did not change its method of accounting for inventories

   d. Did not increase the investment return and pay increase assumptions (Note L)

   If necessary, assume that all earnings are subject to taxes (deferred or current) at the rate of 46 cents on the dollar.

2. Provide a journal entry (or entries) to record the 1981 tax expense of $176 million and investment credits of $115 million.

3. Assume that 1979 was the first year in which Dow Chemical purchased assets qualifying for the investment tax credit and that all such assets were being depreciated over eight years. Calculate the balance in the unamortized investment tax credit (liability) account on December 1981 if Dow Chemical had used the deferral

method of accounting for the investment tax credit, amortizing such credits over eight years.

4. How much tax is owing to the IRS as a result of Dow Chemical's change in accounting for inventories on the LIFO basis?

Consolidated Statement of Income

	1981	Year Ended December 31 1980	1979
		(In millions)	
Net Sales	$11,873	$10,626	$9,255
Operating Costs and Expenses			
Cost of sales	10,019	8,649	7,231
Selling and administrative	938	765	690
	10,957	9,414	7,921
Operating income	916	1,212	1,334
Other Income (Expense)			
Equity in earnings:			
Nonconsolidated subsidiaries (excluding translation)	13	24	18
Gains (losses) on translation			
for non-consolidated subsidiaries	(2)	(14)	2
20%-50% owned companies	132	127	103
Interest income	102	87	86
Interest and amortization of debt			
discount and expense	(532)	(385)	(358)
Gains (losses) on exchange and translation			
for consolidated subsidiaries	7	31	(8)
Sundry income — net	108	156	136
Income Before Provision for Taxes on Income	744	1,238	1,313
Provision for Taxes on Income	176	424	515
Income Before Minority Interest	568	814	798
Minority Interests' Share in Income	4	9	14
Net Income	$ 564	$ 805	$ 784
Earnings per Common Share	$ 3.00	$ 4.42	$ 4.33

The Dow Chemical Company

Notes to Financial Statements

B. INTEREST COST Effective January 1, 1980, the policy of capitalizing interest cost as a part of the cost of constructing capital assets was adopted in accordance with Statement of Financial Accounting Standards No. 34. Gross interest incurred in 1981 and 1980 was $605 million and $456 million, respectively, of which $73 million was capitalized in 1981 and $71 million was capitalized in 1980. The effect of the change was to increase earnings per common share in 1981 and 1980 by approximately $.20 each year.

E. TAXES ON INCOME Domestic and foreign components of pre-tax income, classified primarily by the domicile of the individual subsidiaries, were:

| | Year Ended December 31 | | |
	1981	1980	1979
	(In millions)		
Domestic	$ 526	$ 849	$ 851
Foreign	218	389	462
Income before tax	$ 744	$1,238	$1,313

This classification of profit before tax will differ from note R, page 28, which presents revenue and profits allocated by geographic area in accordance with area management organization.

The provision for taxes on income consisted of:

(In millions)	Federal	State and Local	Foreign	Total
1981				
Current ...	$(103)	$(1)	$ 62	$ (42)
Deferred ..	200	—	18	218
Total ...	$ 97	$(1)	$ 80	$176
1980				
Current ...	$ 125	$13	$117	$255
Deferred ..	153	—	16	169
Total ...	$ 278	$13	$133	$424
1979				
Current ...	$ 250	$15	$144	$409
Deferred ..	34	—	72	106
Total ...	$ 284	$15	$216	$515

The current tax provision was reduced by investment tax credits of $115 million in 1981, $94 million in 1980 and $98 million in 1979.

Deferred tax provisions related to the following:

	1981	1980	1979
	(In millions)		
Tax effects of foreign exchange transactions	$(44)	$ (9)	$ 49
Excess of depreciation and depletion claimed for tax purposes over book amounts	137	125	113
Undistributed earnings of foreign subsidiaries deemed not to be permanently invested	4	13	11
Income of export and shipping companies operating outside the United States	8	29	2
Difference between LIFO method claimed for tax purposes and book amounts	108	(2)	(39)
Other — net	5	13	(30)
Total	$218	$169	$106

Prior to 1981, the Company provided taxes on the full earnings of its domestic international sales corporation (DISC), including deferred taxes of $198 million which remain accrued at December 31, 1981. The Company has determined that commencing with the year ended December 31, 1981, the tax deferred earnings of the DISC will be permanently invested and that under present statutes no tax on those earnings will be payable. The effect of this change in estimate was to increase net income for the year ended December 31, 1981 by $17 million and increase earnings per common share by $.09.

Major differences between the effective rate and the United States statutory rate were:

| | Percent | | |
	1981	1980	1979
Statutory rate	46.0	46.0	46.0
U.S. investment credits	(11.8)	(6.1)	(6.3)
Taxes on income of foreign operations at tax rates different from U.S. statutory rate (including DISC)	(7.6)	(2.4)	0.7
Untaxed equity in income of companies whose accounts are not consolidated	(5.9)	(2.9)	(3.5)
State and local income taxes (net of federal tax)	0.3	0.5	0.6
Other	2.7	(0.8)	1.7
Effective rate	23.7	34.3	39.2

Unremitted earnings of subsidiary and 50% - owned companies which are deemed to be permanently invested amounted to approximately $1.5 billion, $1.3 billion and $1.2 billion at December 31, 1981, 1980 and 1979, respectively.

Income tax returns filed in the United States through 1975 have been settled.

VIII. INCOME TAXES AND INVESTMENT TAX CREDIT

F. INVENTORIES Beginning in 1974, inventories have been valued, for both tax and financial reporting purposes, under the last-in, first-out method (LIFO) using inventory pools corresponding to business segments. In 1981, the Internal Revenue Service changed its requirement that inventories be the same for both tax and financial reporting. As a result of that modification, the Company realigned its LIFO inventory pools for financial reporting purposes to correspond to product groups rather than business segments, thereby achieving, in the opinion of management, a better matching of cost and revenue. The change was made effective January 1, 1981. The effect of the change was to increase net income for the year ended December 31, 1981 by $101 million and increase earnings per common share by $.54. Pro forma amounts for retroactive application or the cumulative effect of this change are not determinable.

The amount of reserve required to reduce inventories from the first-in, first-out basis to the last-in, first-out basis at December 31, 1981 and 1980 was $713 million and $799 million.

L. RETIREMENT PLANS The Company and its subsidiaries have several retirement plans covering substantially all of their employees, including certain employees in foreign countries. The cost of all retirement plans was $121 million in 1981, $127 million in 1980 and $115 million in 1979. The Company makes annual contributions to the plans equal to the amounts accrued for pension expense, as determined by the aggregate cost method of valuation. A comparison of accumulated plan benefits and plan assets for the Company's domestic defined benefit plan, representing approximately 90 percent of accumulated pension plan benefits for the Company and its consolidated subsidiaries, follows:

| | January 1 | |
	1982	1981
	(In millions)	
Actuarial present value of accumulated plan benefits:		
Vested	$ 887	$ 894
Nonvested	188	184
. . . .	$1,075	$1,078
Net assets available for benefits	$1,026	$1,044

Effective January 1981, the Company changed its investment return assumption for the domestic defined benefit plan from 6.5 percent to 8.0 percent and changed its pay increase assumption from 3 percent to 6 percent. These changes were adopted to reflect assumptions which will more clearly match anticipated future experience and are reflected in the actuarial present value of accumulated plan benefits at January 1, 1982. The net effect of the changes was to reduce pension expense by $16 million and increase net income by $9 million, or $.05 per common share. Actuarial assumptions include an average retirement age of 62 and turnover based on experience.

The Company's foreign pension plans are not required to report to certain governmental agencies pursuant to ERISA, and have not determined for 1981 the actuarial value of accumulated benefits or net assets available for benefits as calculated and disclosed above. However, as of January 1, 1981 and 1980, available assets in other plans exceeded vested benefits by approximately $65 million and $50 million, respectively.

8.4. NORTHWEST AND UNITED AIRLINES*

Comparison between airlines of accounting for income taxes and the investment tax credit of FASB Interpretation No. 25, "Accounting for an Unused Investment Tax Credit." (Difficult: 45 minutes)

This case analyzes and evaluates how Northwest Airlines and United Airlines account for income taxes and the investment tax credit. Excerpts are from the annual reports for 1980 (with 1978 and 1979 comparative data where applicable).

NORTHWEST

1. Explain how Northwest was able to report net earnings after taxes of $7,084,000 when, in fact, it reported a loss before taxes of $36,103.

2. Northwest has reflected $27,396,000 and $24,554,000 of investment tax credits in earnings for 1979 and 1980, respectively. To what extent have these amounts been received in cash—i.e., as actual tax credits?

3. Restate Northwest's net earnings for 1979 and 1980 so that they exclude the effects of any unused investment tax credits. Given Northwest's present accounting policies, what will happen if the unused investment tax credits expire unused?

UNITED

1. Provide a journal entry to record the effect of the change in accounting for investment tax credits on prior years. Assume that the change took effect as of 1/1/79. If the change had not taken place on 1/1/79, what would United's 1979 net income (loss) be?

---

*Based on earlier case by James M. Patell.

2. Explain the two largest components of United's 1980 $31,480,000 debit to the Deferred Income Taxes liability account (rounding error accounts for the difference between $31,480,000 in the notes and $284,487,000 less $253,009,000 in the liabilities section of the Statement of Financial Position).

3. In language that would be understandable to readers of your local daily newspaper, explain how in 1979 United is able to report pretax losses of $185 million but after-tax losses of only $72 million; and how in 1980 United is able to report after-tax profits that are *greater* than its pretax profits.

Statements of Earnings

NORTHWEST AIRLINES, INC.

		Year Ended December 31	
(In Thousands)	**1980**	1979	1978*
Operating Revenues			
Passenger	**$1,347,830**	$1,067,214	$557,401
Cargo	**190,837**	160,716	87,077
Mail	**57,305**	38,685	18,944
Charter and other transportation	**16,303**	15,093	10,997
Mutual Aid	**-0-**	-0-	104,864
Nontransport	**27,055**	28,850	10,879
	1,639,330	1,310,558	790,162
Other Income (Expenses)			
Interest, net of capitalized interest of (1980—$3,393; 1979—$6,240; 1978—$4,679)—Note A	**(15,831)**	(1,635)	(3,376)
Gain on sale of flight equipment	**143**	15,544	34,290
Other	**3,719**	15,099	10,836
	(11,969)	29,008	41,750
EARNINGS (LOSS) BEFORE INCOME TAXES	**(36,103)**	84,360	109,035
Income taxes (credit)—Note D	**(43,187)**	11,885	47,194
NET EARNINGS	**$ 7,084**	$ 72,475	$ 61,841
Average shares of Common Stock outstanding during the year	**21,646**	21,632	21,618
Earnings per share of Common Stock	**$.33**	$3.35	$2.86

VIII.   INCOME TAXES AND INVESTMENT TAX CREDIT

Statements of Financial Position

NORTHWEST AIRLINES, INC.

	December 31	
(Dollars In Thousands)	**1980**	1979

ASSETS

Current Assets

	1980	1979
Cash and short-term investments	$ **20,514**	$ 74,583
Accounts receivable, less allowance of $1,600 (1979—$1,500)	**124,957**	111,432
Recoverable income taxes	**-0-**	21,726
Flight equipment spare parts, less allowance for depreciation of $19,883 (1979—$17,600)	**42,654**	32,461
Maintenance and operating supplies	**16,920**	9,238
Prepaid expenses	**7,332**	3,724
TOTAL CURRENT ASSETS	**212,377**	253,164

	December 31	
	1980	1979

LIABILITIES AND STOCKHOLDERS' EQUITY

Deferred Credits and Other Liabilities

	1980	1979
Income taxes—Note D	**260,100**	313,329
Other	**18,932**	14,179
	279,032	327,508

Stockholders' Equity—Note C

	1980	1979
Common Stock $1.25 par value, authorized 40,000,000 shares; issued and outstanding 21,647,280 shares (1979—21,639,589 shares)	**27,059**	27,049
Capital surplus	**124,940**	124,797
Retained earnings	**687,043**	697,276
	839,042	849,122

Commitments and Contingencies—Notes E and F

	$1,532,539	$1,528,921

Statements of Changes in Financial Position

NORTHWEST AIRLINES, INC.

			Year Ended December 31
(In Thousands)	**1980**	1979	1978
Funds Provided			
Net earnings	$ **7,084**	$ 72,475	$ 61,841
Items not affecting working capital:			
Depreciation and amortization	**124,078**	106,401	104,970
Increase (decrease) in deferred income taxes	**(53,228)**	22,669	29,311
TOTAL FROM OPERATIONS	**77,934**	201,545	196,122
Proceeds from sale of flight equipment less gain included in earnings	**433**	2,818	6,795
Other	**-0-**	-0-	5,509
TOTAL PROVIDED	**78,367**	204,363	208,426

VIII.   INCOME TAXES AND INVESTMENT TAX CREDIT

Notes to Financial Statements

NORTHWEST AIRLINES, INC.

NOTE D—TAXES ON EARNINGS
(In thousands)

Reconciliation of the Company's effective income tax rate and the statutory federal income tax rate (46% in 1980 and 1979; 48% in 1978) follows:

	Year Ended December 31		
	1980	1979	1978
Statutory rate applied to pre-tax income	$(16,607)	$38,806	$52,337
Add (deduct):			
Investment tax credit earned	(24,554)	(27,396)	(6,320)
Other	(2,026)	475	1,177
Total income tax expense (credit)	$(43,187)	$11,885	$47,194

Federal, foreign and state income taxes (credit) consisted of the following:

	1980		1979		1978	
	Current	Deferred	Current	Deferred	Current	Deferred
Federal provision	$9,274	$(52,222)	$(14,516)	$23,175	$14,730	$28,503
Foreign	620		695		690	
State	(825)	(34)	825	1,706	2,075	1,196
	$9,069	$(52,256)	$(12,996)	$24,881	$17,495	$29,699

The deferred income tax expense (credit), which results from timing differences in recognizing items for financial reporting and income tax purposes, consists of the following:

	1980	1979	1978
Accelerated depreciation	$ 3,273	$19,176	$11,768
Investment tax credit	(60,218)	(2,431)	16,104
Prepaid expenses	1,958		
Interest	6,217	6,101	3,407
Deferred employee benefits	(1,893)	2,752	(2,422)
Other	(1,593)	(717)	842
	$(52,256)	$24,881	$29,699

Investment tax credits not applied on tax returns but offset against deferred income taxes at December 31, 1980 will expire $4,379 in 1984; $6,320 in 1985; $27,396 in 1986; and $24,554 in 1987.

Application of Investment Tax Credit

NORTHWEST AIRLINES, INC.

(Period)	Available* and Reflected in Earnings	Applied† on Tax Returns
1979	$27,396,000	$24,964,000
1980	24,554,000	(35,663,000)
TOTAL	$51,950,000	(10,699,000)
Applied on Returns	(10,699,000)	
To be Applied	$62,649,000	

*The Company uses the flow-through method of accounting for investment credits and records the credits as a reduction of income tax expense in the year earned.

†Investment credits are applied on tax returns as allowed by income tax regulations. Credits not applied currently are offset against deferred taxes.

Statements of Consolidated Earnings

(In Thousands, Except Per Share)	1980	1979	1978
Operating revenues:			
Airline—			
Passenger	**$3,880,689**	$2,847,704	$3,102,161
Cargo	**331,204**	250,393	292,045
Contract services and other	**246,939**	197,181	191,975
Mutual Aid	**—**	—	(37,100)
	4,458,832	3,295,278	3,549,081
Hotels	**425,921**	383,740	330,231
Business services	**156,582**	152,505	136,100
	5,041,335	3,831,523	4,015,412
Operating expenses:			
Operations, exclusive of expenses listed separately	**2,635,448**	2,295,094	2,197,433
Aircraft fuel	**1,342,529**	804,380	646,864
Depreciation and amortization	**305,102**	283,061	260,793
Sales and advertising	**527,328**	417,523	373,876
General and administrative	**213,019**	192,246	181,974
	5,023,426	3,992,304	3,660,940
Earnings (loss) from operations	**17,909**	(160,781)	354,472
Other deductions (income):			
Interest expense	**123,238**	91,786	94,505
Interest capitalized	**(17,492)**	(12,061)	(3,728)
Temporary investments income	**(29,079)**	(38,404)	(42,816)
Gain on disposition of property	**(47,717)**	(10,030)	(24,778)
Foreign exchange losses (gains)	**(1,427)**	667	218
Other, net	**(13,822)**	(7,025)	(6,749)
	13,701	24,933	16,652
Earnings (loss) before income taxes	**4,208**	(185,714)	337,820
Provision (credit) for income taxes:			
Income taxes before investment tax credits	**6,400**	(83,000)	175,165
Investment tax credits	**(23,200)**	(29,900)	(139,600)
	(16,800)	(112,900)	35,565
Net earnings (loss)	**$ 21,008**	$ (72,814)	$ 302,255
Net earnings (loss) per share:			
Primary	**$ .70**	$ (2.50)	$ 11.93
Fully diluted	**.70**	(2.50)	10.20

Statements of Consolidated Financial Position

December 31

(In Thousands)	1980	1979
Assets		
Current assets:		
Cash	$ **24,910**	$ 35,027
Temporary investments	**294,013**	320,094
Receivables, less allowance for doubtful accounts		
(1980—$7,852,000; 1979—$7,770,000)	**605,219**	565,272
Flight equipment spare parts, less obsolescence and valuation		
allowances (1980—$76,231,000; 1979—$72,806,000)	**143,274**	119,055
Aircraft fuel and maintenance and operating supplies	**83,021**	59,006
Prepaid expenses	**59,537**	54,545
Refundable federal income tax	**2,556**	11,051
	1,212,530	1,164,050

UAL Inc.
December 31

(In Thousands)	1980	1979
Liabilities		
Current liabilities:		
Commercial paper	$ **152,192**	$ —
Long-term debt maturing within one year	**59,034**	52,074
Current obligations under capital leases	**46,213**	50,040
Advance ticket sales and customer deposits	**396,680**	360,812
Accounts payable	**356,500**	354,750
Accrued salaries and wages	**199,315**	176,287
Accrued and deferred income taxes	**23,409**	13,840
Accrued interest	**15,173**	12,369
Other accrued liabilities	**181,844**	156,284
	1,430,360	1,176,456
Long-term debt	**546,317**	768,002
Long-term obligations under capital leases	**623,969**	462,022
Deferred credits and other liabilities:		
Deferred income taxes	**253,009**	284,487
Other	**11,728**	9,732
	264,737	294,219

Statements of Changes
in Consolidated Financial Position

UAL Inc.
Year Ended December 31

(In Thousands)	1980	1979	1978
Cash and temporary investments at beginning of year	**$355,121**	$ 616,245	$679,128
Funds provided:			
Net earnings (loss)	**21,008**	(72,814)	302,255
Add (deduct) items not requiring (providing) funds—			
Depreciation and amortization	**305,102**	283,061	260,793
Deferred income taxes	**(31,480)**	(97,325)	11,985
Other	**6,098**	3,436	4,446
Funds provided from operations	**300,728**	116,358	579,479

VIII. INCOME TAXES AND INVESTMENT TAX CREDIT

Income Taxes

The provisions (credits) for income taxes, net of investment tax credits, are summarized as follows:

(In Thousands)	1980	1979	1978
Current:			
Federal	$ 8,500	$(18,100)	$ 9,255
State	1,663	(283)	12,220
Foreign	4,517	2,808	2,105
	14,680	(15,575)	23,580
Deferred:			
Federal	(35,700)	(100,600)	45
State	1,217	1,321	10,936
Foreign	3,003	1,954	1,004
	(31,480)	(97,325)	11,985
	$(16,800)	$(112,900)	$35,565

Deferred taxes are provided for timing differences between reported income and income for tax purposes. The most significant recurring timing difference is for depreciation. Depreciation differences are caused by the use of shorter lives and different depreciation methods for tax purposes than the lives and straight-line depreciation method used for accounting purposes, resulting in tax depreciation exceeding book depreciation in some years and the reverse in other years. Other recurring differences relate to interest capitalized, gain on disposal of depreciable assets, and capitalized leases.

The components of the provision (credit) for deferred income taxes were as follows:

(In Thousands)	1980	1979	1978
Deferred tax provision (credit) for timing differences:			
Depreciation and capitalized interest	$ 3,492	$(10,086)	$14,609
Gain on disposal of depreciable assets	(4,165)	(3,390)	(7,573)
Capitalized leases	(11,884)	44	(585)
Other, net	(4,923)	(8,193)	5,534
	(17,480)	(21,625)	11,985
Investment tax credits:			
Current year's generations allocated to deferred taxes	(22,100)	(31,600)	—
Applied to accrued federal income tax liability	8,100	—	—
Restored by carryback of 1979 net operating loss	—	(44,100)	—
	(14,000)	(75,700)	—
	$(31,480)	$(97,325)	$11,985

Income tax provisions differed from "expected" amounts computed at the statutory federal income tax rate, as follows:

(In Thousands)	1980	1979	1978
Income tax provision (credit) at statutory rate:			
Pretax earnings (loss)—			
Domestic	$(16,650)	$(200,004)	$327,490
Foreign	20,858	14,290	10,330
Total	4,208	(185,714)	337,820
Statutory rate	x 46%	x 46%	x 48%
	1,936	(85,428)	162,154
Investment tax credits	(23,200)	(29,900)	(139,600)
State income taxes, net of federal income tax benefit	1,555	561	12,041
Other, net	2,909	1,867	970
Income tax provision (credit) as reported	$(16,800)	$(112,900)	$ 35,565

As of December 31, 1980, the tax benefit of all prior losses has been fully reflected in the provision (credit) for income taxes, and no loss remains to be carried over to future years.

On a per-share basis, the investment tax credits included in earnings amounted to $.78 in 1980, $1.02 in 1979 and $5.52 in 1978. Approximately $94,000,000 of the investment tax credits recognized in earnings in 1978 represented a carryforward because of inadequate earnings in earlier years.

Effective January 1, 1979, UAL complied with Financial Accounting Standards Board Interpretation No. 25, "Accounting for an Unused Investment Tax Credit," issued in September 1978. Interpretation No. 25 requires current recognition of investment tax credits (even though there is a pretax loss) that relate to post-1978 additions of qualified properties, to the extent that they would offset existing deferred tax credits that are expected to reverse during the investment tax credit carryforward period. The effect of this 1979 change in accounting was to increase the credit for income taxes, and thus decrease the net loss, by $31,600,000 ($1.08 per share) for the year ended December 31, 1979. As of December 31, 1980, there were no investment tax credits remaining to be included in future earnings.

To the extent that any investment tax credits recognized for financial reporting purposes cannot be deducted on the federal income tax return before they expire, future earnings could be adversely affected under certain circumstances.

For federal income tax return purposes there were unused investment tax credits of approximately $89,700,000 available at December 31, 1980 to reduce federal income taxes payable in future years, including the contested liability noted below. Of these unused credits, approximately $35,900,000 will be available to be utilized in tax returns through 1985, $34,300,000 through 1986 and $19,500,000 through 1987. The Tax Reform Act of 1976 and The Revenue Act of 1978 provide that, in the case of air

carriers, investment tax credits may be applied, to
the extent available, against 80% of federal income
tax liability for 1980 and 1981 and 90% for
subsequent years.

During 1979, the Internal Revenue Service concluded
an examination of UAL's federal income tax returns
through 1975. At the end of the examination, UAL
indicated its agreement with certain IRS adjustments
which represent a net tax liability of $8,300,000 (after
application of approximately $8,300,000 of invest-
ment tax credits) and indicated its disagreement
with, and is currently protesting, other IRS adjustments which represent a potential net tax liability
of approximately $14,000,000 (after application of
approximately $14,000,000 of investment tax
credits). Substantially all of the agreed and unagreed
adjustments involve the timing of tax deductions
(principally depreciation), and, in the opinion of
management, their impact on the consolidated
earnings and financial position of UAL will not be
material.

The Internal Revenue Service is currently conducting
a routine examination of UAL's federal income tax
returns for 1976 and 1977. While several adjustments
have been proposed, mainly dealing with the timing of
tax deductions, the impact of such adjustments on
the consolidated earnings and financial position
of UAL will not, in the opinion of management,
be material.

8.5. BOISE CASCADE CORPORATION

Measurement and disclosure of proceeds from sale of depreciation tax benefits. (Moderate: 30 minutes)

Boise Cascade is an integrated forests products company engaged principally in the manufacture, distribution, and sale of paper, packaging and office products, wood products, and building materials. In addition, the company has one of the industry's more extensive timber bases on which it grows and harvests timber to support these operations. Its timberlands and manufacturing facilities are located primarily in the United States and Canada.

Study Boise Cascade's 1981 Statement of Income, 1981 Statement of Changes in Financial Position, and excerpts from Notes 1 and 2 to the 1981 financial statements. A clipping from the *Wall Street Journal*, February 10, 1982, is also included.

1. Provide a journal entry to record Boise's sale of depreciation tax benefits for approximately $60 million. Distinguish between the before-tax and after-tax effects of this transaction. Approximately how much tax is owing as a result of this $60 million transaction?

2. a. How much 1981 federal U.S. income tax is Boise likely to pay in 1982? State this amount as a percentage of Boise's domestic (U.S.) 1981 earnings before tax of $92,160,000. Foreign pretax earnings for 1981 were $92,580,000.

   b. Would this percentage alter significantly in future years if Boise could no longer sell its depreciation tax benefits to other companies? Explain.

3. a. What would you expect to be the stock market's reaction to the disclosure of sale of depreciation tax benefits by Boise?

b. As a financial vice-president of Boise, what strategy for reporting the effects of tax benefit sales would be in the best interests of Boise's stockholders?

STATEMENTS OF INCOME

Boise Cascade Corporation and Subsidiaries

	Year Ended December 31		
	1981	1980	1979
	(expressed in thousands)		
Revenues			
Sales	$3,107,360	$3,018,940	$2,916,610
Other income, net (Note 1)	67,360	14,250	31,830
	3,174,720	3,033,190	2,948,440
Costs and expenses			
Cost of sales	2,451,800	2,378,470	2,280,310
Depreciation and cost of company timber harvested	134,390	121,610	108,990
Selling and administrative expenses	322,080	323,550	297,410
Interest expense (Note 1)	81,710	48,960	40,560
	2,989,980	2,872,590	2,727,270
Income before income taxes and extraordinary gain	184,740	160,600	221,170
Income taxes (Note 2)	64,660	25,160	47,100
Income before extraordinary gain	120,080	135,440	174,070
Extraordinary gain (Note 4)	—	12,500	—
Net income (Notes 1 and 8)	$ 120,080	$ 147,940	$ 174,070
Per common share (Note 1)			
Income before extraordinary gain	$4.50	$5.08	$6.48
Extraordinary gain (Note 4)	—	.47	—
Net income (Notes 1 and 8)	$4.50	$5.55	$6.48

STATEMENTS OF CHANGES IN FINANCIAL POSITION

Boise Cascade Corporation and Subsidiaries

	Year Ended December 31		
	1981	1980	1979
	(expressed in thousands)		
Sources of Working Capital			
Income before extraordinary gain	$120,080	$135,440	$174,070
Items in income not affecting working capital			
Depreciation and cost of company timber harvested	134,390	121,610	108,990
Deferred income tax provision (benefit) (Note 2)	21,297	(14,860)	14,807
Equity in earnings of joint ventures (Note 3)	(1,967)	(6,561)	(19,658)
Total from operations	273,800	235,629	278,209
Extraordinary gain (Note 4)	—	12,500	—
Additions to long-term debt (Note 6)	57,967	259,250	222,420
Sales of property and equipment	25,442	15,580	27,674
Net increase in other long-term liabilities	10,931	14,553	7,319
Distributions received from joint ventures	2,945	2,430	8,808
All other, net	1,838	(2,509)	4,164
Total sources of working capital	372,923	537,433	548,594
Uses of Working Capital			
Additions to property and equipment	140,606	311,475	402,760
Expenditures for timber and timberlands	9,262	86,752	37,743
Payments and current portion of long-term debt	91,805	26,248	63,352
Cash dividends declared	50,900	46,849	40,461
Net increase (decrease) in other assets	40,368	22,298	(73)
Capital contributions to joint ventures (Note 3)	22,326	7,232	—
Decrease (increase) in deferred income taxes	18,522	7,733	(35,233)
Purchase of common stock (Note 9)	122	29	14,882
Total uses of working capital	373,911	508,616	523,892
Increase (decrease) in working capital	$ (988)	$ 28,817	$ 24,702
Changes in Working Capital			
Increase (decrease) in current assets			
Cash and short-term investments	$ 5,237	$ (3,844)	$ (21,377)
Receivables	(22,523)	28,034	26,209
Inventories	32,266	13,632	36,810
Other	(22,009)	3,687	(5,847)
	(7,029)	41,509	35,795
(Increase) decrease in current liabilities			
Notes payable	770	24,166	17,794
Current portion of long-term debt	2,316	3,969	(312)
Income taxes payable	5,983	(23,352)	(2,328)
Accounts payable	7,705	(13,903)	(16,933)
Accrued liabilities	(10,733)	(3,572)	(9,314)
	6,041	(12,692)	(11,093)
Increase (decrease) in working capital	$ (988)	$ 28,817	$ 24,702

NOTES TO FINANCIAL STATEMENTS

Boise Cascade Corporation and Subsidiaries

1. Summary of Significant Accounting Policies

Other Income. "Other income, net" in the Statements of Income includes the sale of depreciation tax benefits, foreign exchange gains and losses, interest income, equity in earnings of joint ventures, gains and losses on the sale of property and other miscellaneous income and expense items.

Sale of Tax Benefits. Following the passage of the Economic Recovery Tax Act of 1981, the Company sold certain depreciation tax benefits for approximately $60,000,000. In accordance with the tentative decision of the Financial Accounting Standards Board, referenced in its recent announcement, the net proceeds of $31,100,000 after taxes, or $1.17 per common share, were included in income.

2. Income Taxes

The Company provides income taxes for all items included in the Statements of Income, regardless of when such items are reported for tax purposes and when the taxes are actually paid. Investment tax credits are recognized currently as a reduction of income tax expense. Approximately $67,115,000 of investment tax credits recognized in current and prior years is available to reduce income taxes expected to be paid in future years. The Company expects to utilize these credits prior to their statutory expiration. The Company uses the progress expenditure method for taking investment tax credits on projects which will be under construction for more than two years.

Income tax expense includes the following:

	Year Ended December 31		
	1981	1980	1979
	(expressed in thousands)		
Current income taxes			
Federal	$ 3,552	$ 5,740	$22,764
State	4,101	7,480	8,116
Foreign	35,710	26,800	1,413
	43,363	40,020	32,293
Deferred income taxes			
Federal	11,542	(27,599)	10,182
State	3,072	1,107	2,582
Foreign	6,683	11,632	2,043
	21,297	(14,860)	14,807
Total income tax expense	$64,660	$25,160	$47,100

A reconciliation of the theoretical tax expense, assuming all income had been taxed at the statutory U.S. Federal income tax rate, and the Company's actual tax expense is as follows:

	Year Ended December 31					
	1981		1980		1979	
	Amount	Percentage of Pretax Income	Amount	Percentage of Pretax Income	Amount	Percentage of Pretax Income
	(expressed in thousands, except percentages)					
Theoretical tax expense	$84,980	46.0%	$73,876	46.0%	$101,738	46.0%
Increases (decreases) in taxes resulting from						
Income taxed at the capital gains rate	(24,273)	(13.1)	(23,725)	(14.8)	(22,568)	(10.2)
U.S. investment tax credits	(19,420)	(10.5)	(44,339)	(27.6)	(38,519)	(17.4)
Tax on foreign dividends, net of foreign tax credits	10,761	5.8	10,460	6.5	1,242	.6
Foreign income taxed at less than theoretical tax rate	(1,571)	(.9)	(2,470)	(1.5)	(3,077)	(1.4)
State tax	3,874	2.1	4,640	2.9	5,777	2.6
Minimum tax on preference items	4,403	2.4	4,755	3.0	1,889	.8
Other	5,906	3.2	1,963	1.2	618	.3
Actual tax expense	$64,660	35.0%	$25,160	15.7%	$ 47,100	21.3%

The deferred income tax provision (benefit) results from timing differences in recognition of revenue and expense for tax and financial reporting purposes. The nature of these differences and the tax effect of each are as follows:

	Year Ended December 31		
	1981	1980	1979
	(expressed in thousands)		
Sale of depreciation tax benefits (Note 1)	$28,906	$ —	$ —
Investment tax credits carried forward	(15,626)	(28,334)	(14,797)
Deferred expense, net of amortization	15,128	8,573	8,310
Book depreciation less than tax depreciation	8,066	19,024	24,672
Provision for pensions not funded	(4,619)	(16,866)	—
Foreign exchange loss (Note 1)	(4,249)	—	—
Decrease (increase) in tax basis of inventories resulting from timber capital gains	(1,093)	202	53
Other	(5,216)	2,541	(3,431)
Deferred income tax provision (benefit)	$21,297	$(14,860)	$14,807

Tax-Credit Sales Enabled Some Firms To Post Higher Rather Than Lower Net

A WALL STREET JOURNAL *News Roundup*

For much of what good news is found in some companies' fourth quarter reports, the credit goes to the sale of tax credits.

Potlatch Corp., for example, reported a 115% surge in quarterly net to $30.6 million from $14.2 million a year earlier. Included in the latest figure was a $19.2 million gain on tax-credit sales; without that gain, profit of the forest-products company would have dropped 20%. With the tax-credit sales, net for the year rose 19%; without them, it would have declined 21%.

Similarly, Boise Cascade Corp., another forest-products concern, posted a 14% slide in fourth quarter net to $37.2 million, including a $31.1 million after-tax gain from tax-benefit sales. Without that gain, net would have slumped 86% from the year-earlier $43.4 million (which included a $5.7 million extraordinary credit from settlement of litigation with China).

Both companies were taking advantage of provisions of the federal tax law passed last August. Under the new law, a company owing little or no federal tax may sell unusable depreciation deductions and investment tax credits to profitable concerns wanting to reduce their taxes. The company with the unusable benefits sells its capital equipment and then leases it back. The company buying the equipment gets the related tax benefits, while the seller gets cash and continued use of the equipment. The only money that really changes hands is the buyer's down payment for the tax benefits.

Such transactions have had particularly dramatic effects on the earnings reports of companies in troubled industries. Like forest-products companies, cement makers also have been hard hit by the construction slump, and at least two of them took full advantage of the new law in the fourth quarter. Ideal Basic Industries Inc. sold for $77 million the tax breaks on $372 million in capital spending for two cement plants. It thus turned what one securities analyst estimates would have been an 80% drop in quarterly profit into a 70% increase. And Lone Star Industries Inc. indicated that a $60 million sale of benefits might have held its fourth quarter net even with a year earlier even though its operating profit slumped an estimated 50%.

Tax-benefit transactions have been a godsend to the recession-battered metals companies, too. Asarco Inc., a producer of silver, lead, zinc and copper, sold $34 million in tax benefits relating to $108 million of equipment; as a result, it posted a $26.7 million pretax gain and turned what would have been a fourth quarter net loss into a $15.3 million profit. Phelps Dodge Corp., the second-largest U.S. copper producer, says similar transactions accounted for about $4 million of its $12.4 million quarterly net income.

Among other big gainers from tax-benefit sales were Chrysler Corp. and Ford Motor Co. Sources at Chrysler say such transactions gave the auto maker gains of about $15 million in the fourth quarter and of more than $40 million for the year. Ford also is expected to report a sizable gain. Last fall, it announced the sale of tax credits on more than $1 billion of equipment to International Business Machines Corp. and said it expected to realize $100 million to $200 million from the transaction. Despite these gains, however, the two auto companies are expected to report huge losses for the quarter.

Boise Cascade Corporation

8.6. POTLATCH CORPORATION AND CONSOLIDATED SUBSIDIARIES

Impact of interest and income tax accounting on net earnings. (Moderate: 30 minutes)

Potlatch is an integrated forest products company with 1.4 million acres of timberland in Arkansas, Idaho, and Minnesota. Facilities convert wood fiber into two main lines of products: solid wood items (lumber, plywood, oriented strand board, particleboard, and wood specialties) and bleached fiber products (bleached kraft pulp and paperboard, printing and business papers, packaging, and household tissue products).

Study Potlatch's 1979–81 Statements of Earnings and Retained Earnings, Statements of Changes in Financial Position, Note 6 on taxes, and Note 14 on capitalization of interest. Refer also to the *Wall Street Journal* article of February 10, 1982, following Case 8.5 (Boise Cascade Corporation).

Analyze Potlatch's earnings trend from 1979 to 1981, paying particular attention to the effects of accounting rules for reporting (1) income tax payments and related benefits and (2) interest expense. Are the income statements comparative? Did Potlatch really enjoy an increase in earnings in 1981?

Statements of Earnings and Retained Earnings

For the years ended December 31	1981	1980	1979
Net sales	$880,493	$818,301	$808,213
Costs and expenses:			
Depreciation, amortization and cost of fee timber harvested	54,640	44,984	40,454
Materials, labor and other operating expenses	700,389	652,784	611,415
Selling, administrative and general expenses	52,315	54,276	52,501
	807,344	752,044	704,370
Earnings from operations	73,149	66,257	103,843
Interest expense (Note 14)	(19,100)	(17,756)	(22,348)
Interest income	4,688	7,743	12,631
Other income (expense), net (Note 15)	32,713	4,875	(268)
Earnings before taxes on income	91,450	61,119	93,858
Provision for taxes on income (Note 6)	33,646	12,368	22,847
Net earnings (Note 9)	$ 57,804	$ 48,751	$ 71,011
Net earnings per common share	$3.25	$3.21	$4.69

For the years ended December 31	1981	1980	1979
Balance at beginning of year (Note 9)	$411,479	$383,074	$330,248
Net earnings	57,804	48,751	71,011
Dividends:			
Common ($1.42 per share in 1981; $1.34 per share in 1980; $1.20 per share in 1979)	(21,690)	(20,346)	(18,185)
Preferred ($12.375 per share) (Note 10)	(8,223)	–	–
Balance at end of year	$439,370	$411,479	$383,074

Potlatch Corporation and Consolidated Subsidiaries   **221**

For the years ended December 31	1981	1980	1979
Net earnings	$ 57,804	$ 48,751	$ 71,011
Current charges (credits) to income not involving funds:			
Depreciation, amortization and cost of fee timber harvested	54,640	44,984	40,454
Deferred taxes on income, net noncurrent	32,832	17,748	9,458
Equity in (earnings) losses of unconsolidated subsidiaries	1,444	(1,258)	(637)
Other, net	23	(3,720)	(246)
Funds provided by operations	146,743	106,505	120,040
Decrease (increase) in investments of unexpended revenue bond funds	20,752	46,752	(65,328)
Disposition of plant and properties	5,535	7,159	13,715
Proceeds from new long-term debt	33,196	41,000	120,269
Decrease (increase) in noncurrent receivables	5,123	6,089	(8,864)
Proceeds from sale of preferred stock	75,000	–	–
	286,349	207,505	179,832
Dividends	29,913	20,346	18,185
Additions to land, other than timberlands, and buildings and equipment	64,596	138,838	168,354
Additions to timber, timberlands and related logging facilities	153,315	10,595	13,934
Reduction of long-term debt	14,246	14,039	10,868
Increase (reduction) of investment in unconsolidated subsidiaries	1,054	(13,690)	323
Other, net	3,434	2,151	3,475
	266,558	172,279	215,139
Increase (decrease) in working capital	$ 19,791	$ 35,226	$(35,307)
Detail of increase (decrease) in working capital:			
Cash and short-term investments	$ 11,780	$(12,420)	$ (9,489)
Receivables	1,079	20,656	(2,524)
Inventories	13,479	1,535	12,229
Prepaid expenses	(1,834)	(4,911)	3,424
Current notes payable	(1,697)	17,857	(29,857)
Current installments on long-term debt	(51)	(3,159)	(3,076)
Accounts payable and accrued liabilities	(2,965)	15,668	(6,014)
Increase (decrease) in working capital	$ 19,791	$ 35,226	$(35,307)

SUMMARY OF PRINCIPAL ACCOUNTING POLICIES

NOTE 6: Taxes on Income

The company's federal income tax returns have been examined for all years through 1976. Certain assessments including interest have been paid for 1971 and 1972. During 1980, these assessments were successfully litigated; however, the court's decision has been appealed by the government. The amounts paid are included in "Receivables." Settlements have been reached for the years 1973 through 1976. At December 31, 1981, the company had investment tax and other credit carryforwards of approximately $8,800 (expiring in 1996) available as credits against future federal income taxes. There are no available credit carryforwards for financial statement purposes at December 31, 1981.

The provision for taxes on income is divided between current and deferred portions as follows:

	1981	1980	1979
Current federal income tax	$ —	$(6,762)	$11,028
Current state income tax	499	1,997	5,256
Total current	499	(4,765)	16,284
Deferred income tax on:			
Difference in timber market values over cost, included in inventories	(797)	799	(546)
Difference between tax and financial depreciation	13,882	13,112	10,045
Difference between tax and financial accounting for insurance	(913)	331	(1,617)
Difference between tax and financial accounting for capitalized interest	7,762	4,973	—
Difference between tax and financial accounting for sale of depreciation tax benefits	14,491	—	—
All other timing differences	(1,278)	(2,082)	(1,319)
Total deferred	33,147	17,133	6,563
Provision for taxes on income	$33,646	$12,368	$22,847

The 1981 provision for taxes on income represents an effective rate of 36.8 percent (20.2 percent in 1980 and 24.3 percent in 1979) of financial income before taxes, and is less than the amount which would normally be expected by applying the statutory federal income tax rate of 46 percent to such income. The reasons for the difference are as follows:

	1981	1980	1979
Computed "expected" tax expense	$42,067	$28,673	$ 43,165
Benefits from income taxed as capital gains	—	—	(10,580)
Investment tax credit	(7,910)	(8,267)	(13,814)
Energy tax credit	(2,117)	(3,142)	(2,061)
State and local taxes, net of federal income tax benefit	269	1,134	2,862
Reversal of prior years overaccruals of federal income taxes	—	(6,000)	—
All other items	1,337	(30)	3,275
Provision for taxes on income	$33,646	$12,368	$ 22,847

Deferred income taxes of $102,686 and $69,854 at December 31, 1981 and 1980, respectively, resulted principally from deducting depreciation allowances for federal tax purposes in amounts greater than the allowances determined using the straight-line method for financial reporting purposes. Depreciation for tax purposes reflects use of Internal Revenue Service guidelines and permissible accelerated depreciation of certain assets.

Included in the balance sheet caption "Prepaid expenses" are the tax effects of other timing differences in the amount of $10,587 and $10,827 at December 31, 1981 and 1980, respectively.

NOTE 14: Capitalization of Interest

Effective January 1, 1980, the company changed its method of accounting for interest costs to comply with Financial Accounting Standards Board Statement No. 34, "Capitalization of Interest Cost," which requires the capitalization of interest on certain assets during construction. The company previously followed the policy of expensing such interest costs as incurred.

Interest expense for the years ended December 31, 1981 and 1980, does not include $17,307 and $10,850, respectively, of interest charges which have been capitalized. Interest expense for 1979 has not been restated as the Statement does not require retroactive application.

223

8.7. HEWLETT-PACKARD COMPANY

Reporting the impact of the tax credit for incremental research and development expenditures.
(Straightforward: 15 minutes)

The Hewlett-Packard Company is a major designer and manufacturer of precision electronic equipment for measurement, analysis, and computation. The company's principal products include computers and computer systems, calculators and related products, test and measuring instrumentation, and solid-state components.

On August 4, 1981, Congress passed the Economic Recovery Tax Act of 1981, which provided for, among other things, a nonrefundable income tax credit of 25 percent of certain qualifying expenses incurred by a taxpayer after June 30, 1981 (and before January 1, 1986). The credit is limited to 25 percent of the "incremental" research expenditures (over the average expenditures during a base period of the three preceding years).

Using the accompanying Consolidated Statement of Earnings for 1980–82 and the note, "Taxes on Earnings," calculate the effect of the research and development tax credits on cash flows, reported earnings, and the company's current (1981 and 1982) provisions for federal income taxes.

Consolidated Statement of Earnings

For the years ended October 31

(Millions except per share amounts)	1982	1981	1980
Net sales	$4,254	$3,578	$3,099
Costs and expenses:			
Cost of goods sold	2,032	1,709	1,480
Research and development	424	349	273
Marketing	631	529	461
Administrative and general	491	424	372
	3,578	3,011	2,586
Earnings before taxes	676	567	513
Provision for taxes	293	262	250
Net earnings	$ 383	$ 305	$ 263
Net earnings per share	$ 3.05	$ 2.49	$ 2.19

Taxes on Earnings

The provision for taxes is composed of the following elements:

(Millions)	1982	1981	1980
Federal taxes:			
Current	$ 90	$113	$143
Deferred	84	25	(8)
State taxes	30	28	26
Foreign taxes	89	96	89
	$293	$262	$250

Deferred federal taxes result from timing differences in the recognition of revenues and expenses for tax and financial reporting purposes. The major sources of these timing differences are as follows:

(Millions)	1982	1981	1980
DISC earnings..........	$ 33	$ 22	$ 16
Undistributed earnings of certain foreign subsidiaries	15	16	14
Other timing differences..	12	(13)	(22)
Adjustments to prior years' estimates:*			
DISC earnings........	6	—	(12)
Other	18	—	(4)
	$ 84	$ 25	$ (8)

*Reflects reclassification between the current and deferred provisions for taxes

The difference between taxes computed by applying the federal income tax rate to earnings before taxes and the actual provision for taxes is reconciled as follows:

(Millions)	1982	1981	1980
Taxes on earnings at the United States statutory rate	$311	$261	$236
State income taxes, net of federal tax benefit	16	15	14
Investment tax credits ...	(15)	(9)	(5)
Research and development tax credits	(15)	(7)	—
Other	(4)	2	5
	$293	$262	$250

The company has reached tentative agreement with the Internal Revenue Service regarding certain additional assessments on the company's foreign earnings for fiscal years 1976 and 1977. The Internal Revenue Service has not completed its examination of returns for years subsequent to 1977. The company believes that adequate accruals have been provided for all years.

The company has not provided for United States taxes on the undistributed earnings of foreign subsidiaries that amounted to $299 million at October 31, 1982. If these earnings were distributed to the parent company in the United States, foreign tax credits should become available to reduce or eliminate the resulting United States income tax liability. Normally such earnings are reinvested in subsidiary operations. However, where excess cash has accumulated and it is advantageous for tax or foreign exchange reasons, subsidiary earnings are remitted.

9.1. KOPPERS COMPANY, INC.

Equity vs. cost accounting for affiliated companies.
(Straightforward: 45 minutes)

Koppers Company, Inc., is a diversified manufacturing corporation offering specialized engineering and construction capabilities. The company comprises four main operating groups: (1) organic materials (e.g., chemicals, coke, resins), (2) road materials, (3) forest products, and (4) engineered metal products.

The accompanying Balance Sheet (assets only), Income Statement, and Statement of Changes in Financial Position have been extracted from Koppers Company's 1980 Consolidated Annual Report.

Koppers accounts for companies owned 50 percent or less but 20 percent or more (termed Affiliated Companies) on the equity method.

1. What was the dollar amount of dividends that Koppers received from those Affiliated Companies during 1979 and 1980?

2. Did Koppers purchase more shares in Affiliated Companies during 1980 or sell off part of its holdings (in aggregate)? Give the dollar amount of the transaction and label it as a purchase or a sale. (Ignore the account "Affiliated and Other" in your analysis.)

3. During 1980, Koppers sold or otherwise disposed of (scrapped) certain capital assets. What were the total proceeds of the sales?

4. During 1978, Koppers purchased *and* sold its investment in Cutler-Hammer, Inc. What was the sales price and purchase price of Koppers's (21 percent) interest in the stock of Cutler-Hammer?

Consolidated Balance Sheet

ASSETS

December 31, 1980	1979	Koppers Company, Inc. and Subsidiaries
($ Thousands)		
		Current assets:
$ 84,377	$ 10,712	Cash, including short-term investments of $64,755 in 1980 and $5,143 in 1979
298,370	295,207	Accounts receivable, principally trade, less allowance for doubtful accounts of $4,875 in 1980 and $4,295 in 1979 (Note 1)
		Inventories (Note 2):
		At cost—FIFO (first-in, first-out) basis:
177,512	156,308	Product
50,112	49,795	Work in process
122,020	98,905	Raw materials and supplies
349,644	305,008	
109,305	93,128	Less excess of FIFO cost over LIFO (last-in, first-out)
240,339	211,880	
18,171	14,864	Prepaid expenses
641,257	532,663	Total current assets
		Investments (Note 3):
50,780	21,159	Affiliated companies, at equity
2,697	3,287	Affiliated and other, at cost
53,477	24,446	
		Fixed assets, at cost:
115,849	87,581	Buildings
857,413	745,924	Machinery and equipment
973,262	833,505	
438,900	373,461	Less accumulated depreciation
534,362	460,044	
16,438	18,241	Assets under capital leases, net of accumulated amortization of $9,609 in 1980 and $12,336 in 1979 (Note 5)
81,795	51,888	Depletable properties, less accumulated depletion of $19,667 in 1980 and $15,865 in 1979
34,420	25,598	Land
667,015	555,771	
24,139	25,239	Other assets
$1,385,888	$1,138,119	

　　IX.　INTERCORPORATE INVESTMENTS AND CONSOLIDATIONS

Consolidated Statement of Income

	Years ended December 31,		Koppers Company, Inc. and Subsidiaries
1980	1979	1978	
($ Thousands, except per share figures)			
$1,929,190	$1,828,268	$1,581,876	Net sales
			Operating expenses:
1,537,880	1,435,698	1,247,162	Cost of sales
78,860	63,599	52,651	Depreciation, depletion and amortization
44,320	40,084	33,005	Taxes, other than income taxes
174,152	154,229	132,061	Selling, research, general and administrative expenses
1,835,212	1,693,610	1,464,879	
93,978	134,658	116,997	Operating profit
			Other income:
—	—	15,118	Profit from investment in Cutler-Hammer, Inc. (Note 3)
2,483	8,877	2,221	Profit on sales of capital assets
5,138	2,527	3,806	Equity in earnings of affiliates (dividends received: 1980—$4,328; 1979—$1,994; 1978—$2,375)
5,177	4,883	3,752	Miscellaneous
12,798	16,287	24,897	
106,776	150,945	141,894	Income before interest expense and provision for income taxes
			Interest expense:
23,192	17,800	10,699	Term debt
9,998	2,796	2,491	Other
33,190	20,596	13,190	
73,586	130,349	128,704	Income before provision for income taxes
18,597	43,878	52,693	Provision for income taxes (Note 9)
$ 54,989	$ 86,471	$ 76,011	Net income for the year
26,989	26,228	25,031	Average number of shares of common stock outstanding during year (in thousands)
$2.02	$3.27	$3.01	Earnings per share of common stock

Consolidated Statement of Changes in Financial Position

1980	Years ended December 31, 1979	1978	Koppers Company, Inc. and Subsidiaries
	($ Thousands)		
			Source of funds:
			Operations:
$ 54,989	$ 86,471	$ 76,011	Net income
78,860	63,599	52,651	Depreciation, depletion and amortization
5,044	8,506	4,789	Deferred income taxes and other expenses
(810)	(533)	(1,431)	Equity in earnings of affiliated companies, less dividends received
138,083	158,043	132,020	Funds provided from operations
134,558	29,565	94,125	Term debt and obligations under capital leases issued
—	—	62,102	Book value of investment in Cutler-Hammer, Inc. sold
26,413	32,243	2,532	Common stock issued
72,590	—	—	Preference stock issued, net of associated expenses
10,899	15,247	23,513	Book value of fixed assets and other noncurrent assets disposed of or sold
382,543	235,098	314,292	
			Disposition of funds:
230,871	177,125	144,452	Capital investments
—	—	62,102	Investment in Cutler-Hammer, Inc.
50,065	39,018	12,484	Term debt and capital leases retired
38,387	33,174	28,758	Dividends paid
2,347	—	—	Treasury stock acquired
253	1,006	4,563	Other
321,923	250,323	252,359	
$ 60,620	$ (15,225)	$ 61,933	Increase (decrease) in working capital
			Changes in components of working capital:
			Increase (decrease) in current assets:
$ 73,665	$ (95)	$ (16,981)	Cash and short-term investments
3,163	(52,452)	114,511	Accounts receivable
28,459	48,927	(5,790)	Inventories
3,307	7,714	(2,120)	Prepaid expenses
$108,594	4,094	89,620	
			Increase (decrease) in current liabilities:
(2,713)	16,337	1,133	Accounts payable
18,223	116	42,291	Accrued liabilities
2,674	(4,767)	(10,473)	Advance payments received on contracts
4,521	7,608	(5,283)	Term debt and capital leases due within one year
25,269	25	19	Short-term debt
47,974	19,319	27,687	
$ 60,620	$ (15,225)	$ 61,933	Increase (decrease) in working capital

IX. INTERCORPORATE INVESTMENTS AND CONSOLIDATIONS

9.2. ALLEGHENY LUDLUM INDUSTRIES, INC.

Equity vs. cost accounting for affiliated companies.
(Moderate: 45 minutes)

Allegheny Ludlum Industries, Inc., manufactures and markets special-ized products worldwide for a diversity of industrial and consumer uses. The range of Allegheny's businesses includes consumer products, specialty metals, industrial specialties, safety and protection equip-ment, and railway products.

Study Allegheny's Consolidated Statements of Earnings for 1978–80, Consolidated Statements of Changes in Financial Position for 1978–80, and a section from Note 6 to the consolidated financial state-ments. The number of common shares issued as of January 1, 1978, 1979, and 1980, respectively, was 7,323,608, 7,579,532, and 7,669,772.

1. State Allegheny's Equity Earnings for the years 1978–80. Why are equity earnings considered distinct from earnings from continuing operations (before equity earnings)?

2. State dividends received by Allegheny from unconsolidated affili-ated companies in 1978–80.

3. Allegheny accounts for its investments in affiliated companies on the "equity basis." Restate Allegheny's Net Earnings *and* Earnings (loss) per Share of Common Stock as if they had been computed on the "cost basis" of accounting for unconsolidated affiliated companies.

4. Excluding Earnings (loss) from discontinued operations, to what extent did Allegheny's profit position improve from 1979 to 1980? Do you feel that the "Pro Forma Summaries of Sales and Earn-ings" as shown in the accompanying Financial Review provide a better picture of the earnings change from 1979 to 1980? Com-ment.

Consolidated Statements of Earnings

For the Years 1980, 1979 and 1978	1980	1979*	1978*
	(In thousands, except per share amounts)		
Net sales	$923,528	$850,290	$753,753
Other income, net	13,963	12,266	4,337
Provision for closedown of foreign operations	(3,900)	(2,100)	—
	933,591	860,456	758,090
Costs and expenses:			
Cost of goods sold	674,014	621,647	540,272
Depreciation and amortization	20,188	18,936	20,534
Selling, general and administrative	163,359	143,055	140,987
Interest	41,840	35,733	32,875
	899,401	819,371	734,668
Earnings from continuing operations			
before income taxes and equity earnings	34,190	41,085	23,422
Income taxes	13,153	23,108	9,492
Earnings from continuing operations			
before equity earnings	21,037	17,977	13,930
Equity earnings	45,839	28,126	12,255
Earnings from continuing operations	66,876	46,103	26,185
Earnings (loss) from discontinued operations,			
net of applicable income taxes	(20,981)	25,424	7,189
Net earnings	$ 45,895	$ 71,527	$ 33,374

Earnings (loss) per share of Common Stock:						
Primary:						
Continuing operations	$	7.02	$	3.86	$	1.11
Discontinued operations		(2.91)		3.44		.99
Net earnings	$	4.11	$	7.30	$	2.10
Fully diluted:						
Continuing operations	$	5.78	$	3.30	$	**
Discontinued operations		**		2.47		.70
Net earnings	$	3.56	$	5.77	$	2.04

Consolidated
Statements of Changes
in Financial Position
For the Years 1980, 1979 and 1978

	1980	1979*	1978*
		(In thousands)	
Source of funds:			
Earnings from continuing operations	$ 66,876	$ 46,103	$ 26,185
Items not requiring (providing) funds:			
Depreciation and amortization	20,188	18,936	20,534
Deferred income taxes	3,159	4,623	4,225
Equity earnings	(45,839)	(28,126)	(12,255)
Funds provided from consolidated continuing operations	44,384	41,536	38,689
Earnings (loss) from discontinued operations	(20,981)	25,424	7,189
Items not requiring (providing) funds:			
Depreciation and amortization	14,579	13,551	15,323
Deferred income taxes	3,964	1,406	4,806
Loss (gain) on sale or disposal of discontinued operations	32,409	(17,823)	(3,027)
Funds provided from consolidated discontinued operations	29,971	22,558	24,291
Total funds provided from consolidated operations	74,355	64,094	62,980
Proceeds from sale or exchange of businesses	154,188	106,716	94,449
Long-term borrowings	30,034	78,919	1,574
Long-term liabilities assumed in connection with acquisitions:			
Long-term debt	67,001	2,069	700
Minority interests and other	59,069	4,162	—
Dividends from unconsolidated affiliated companies	7,771	31,799	1,196
Capital stock issued for acquired companies	—	8,358	52
Other, net:			
Continuing operations	7,764	6,130	4,325
Discontinued operations	(3,107)	3,493	3,954
	397,075	305,740	169,230
Use of funds:			
Capital expenditures:			
Continuing operations	36,119	34,083	39,260
Discontinued operations	7,231	17,376	25,420
Dividends	25,318	26,357	27,385
Reduction of long-term debt	30,256	91,566	24,697
Non-current assets of businesses acquired, including property, plant and equipment of $167,345,000 in 1980 and goodwill of $7,215,000 in 1980 and $24,983,000 in 1979	201,119	30,569	4,136
Working capital of businesses sold or exchanged	70,657	25,501	49,739
Increase (decrease) in long-term receivables and other investments and other assets	111,031	(5,112)	3,273
Increase (decrease) in investments in and advances to unconsolidated affiliated companies	(107,794)	64,215	66,219
Purchase of capital stock for treasury or sinking fund	17,042	16,305	17,395
	390,979	300,860	257,524
Increase (decrease) in working capital	$ 6,096	$ 4,880	$ (88,294)

Allegheny Ludlum Industries, Inc.

233

NOTE 6

At December 28, 1980 the quoted market price of the 3,335,000 shares of Liquid Air's common stock owned by Allegheny aggregated $99,216,000 and Allegheny's carrying value thereof was $78,101,000. Allegheny's carrying value exceeded its proportionate share of Liquid Air's net assets by $10,116,000 at December 28, 1980 and $10,466,000 at December 30, 1979.

Wilkinson Match Limited
Condensed Consolidated Balance Sheets

	September 30, 1980	March 31, 1979		September 30, 1980	March 31, 1979
	(In thousands)			(In thousands)	
Assets			**Liabilities and Shareholders' Equity**		
Current assets	$277,248	$330,068	Current liabilities	$167,787	$190,192
Property, plant and equipment	147,183	115,851	Long-term debt	53,535	85,618
Other assets	24,910	14,683	Deferred income taxes and other long-term liabilities	29,420	6,625
			Minority interests	29,559	31,894
			Shareholders' equity	169,040	146,273
	$449,341	$460,602		$449,341	$460,602

Wilkinson's September 30, 1980 balance sheet is consolidated in Allegheny's December 28, 1980 balance sheet.

Condensed Consolidated Summaries of Earnings

	Year Ended September 30, 1980	Six Months Ended September 30, 1979	Year Ended March 31, 1979
		(In thousands)	
Net sales	$611,765	$280,174	$556,383
Earnings before minority interests	$ 20,100	$ 4,886	$ 15,922
Minority interests	3,945	1,066	2,050
Net earnings	$ 16,155	$ 3,820	$ 13,872
Equity earnings recognized by Allegheny after giving effect to dividend requirements on Wilkinson's preference stock	$ 7,079	$ 1,669	$ 6,105

The condensed financial statements of Wilkinson were translated by Allegheny into U.S. dollars and adjusted to reflect Allegheny's cost bases (at a 44.4% ownership level prior to September 30, 1980 and 100% ownership effective on such date) in Wilkinson's net assets pursuant to Accounting Principles Board Opinion No. 16 and United States generally accepted accounting principles.

Wilkinson's consolidated balance sheets as of September 30, 1980 and March 31, 1979 and summaries of earnings for the years ended September 30, 1980 and March 31, 1979 and the six months ended September 30, 1979, before translation and the adjustments described above, were examined by auditors other than Allegheny's independent public accountants.

The excess of Allegheny's proportionate share of Wilkinson's net assets over Allegheny's investment therein, aggregating $11,398,000 at December 28, 1980 and $12,740,000 at December 30, 1979, has been applied as an adjustment to appropriate noncurrent assets of Wilkinson.

Dividends received by Allegheny from all of its unconsolidated affiliated companies aggregated $7,771,000 in 1980, $31,799,000 in 1979 and $1,196,000 in 1978. Allegheny's consolidated retained earnings as of December 28, 1980 and December 30, 1979 includes undistributed earnings of unconsolidated affiliated companies of $67,754,000 and $45,142,000, respectively.

Because of the accounting treatment afforded major corporate transactions completed in 1980, the consolidated statement of earnings for 1980, shown elsewhere in this report, does not reflect the level of sales and earnings of the Corporation as we entered 1981.

Allegheny Ludlum Steel Corporation, which was owned for all of last year but sold at year-end, was treated as a discontinued operation. As a result, its sales and earnings for the year 1980 were *excluded* from the results of Allegheny's continuing operations.

Full ownership of Wilkinson Match Limited was achieved in October, 1980. However, because Wilkinson is reflected in the Corporation's results on a three month delayed basis, Allegheny's earnings statement includes *only the equity earnings from the 44.4% interest* for twelve months ended September 30, 1980.

In order to portray the Corporation as it exists today, pro forma summaries of sales and earnings for 1980 and 1979 are shown on this page. Wilkinson is reflected as though it were wholly-owned for both years, as is Schenuit Industries, Inc., a much smaller but dynamic enterprise acquired in mid-1980. Operations of Allegheny Ludlum Steel Corporation are excluded from the summaries for both 1979 and 1980; the steel company is treated as though it had been sold at the end of 1978.

Pro forma Summaries of Sales and Earnings

	1980	1979
	(In millions, except per share amounts)	
Net sales	$1,591.1	$1,516.6
Earnings from continuing operations before minority interests and equity earnings	$41.2	$35.0
Minority interests	(4.0)	(2.6)
Equity earnings	38.8	22.5
Earnings from continuing operations	76.0	54.9
Earnings (loss) from discontinued operations	(3.8)	6.4
Net earnings	$72.2	$61.3
Earnings per share of Common Stock:		
Primary:		
Continuing operations	$8.28	$5.04
Net earnings	7.76	5.91
Fully diluted:		
Continuing operations	$6.74	$4.15
Net earnings	6.34	4.77

9.3. HERSHEY FOODS CORPORATION

Introduction to accounting for acquisitions, goodwill amortization. (Straightforward: 45 minutes)

Hershey Foods Corporation is a major U.S. producer of chocolate and confectionery products. It also operates a chain of restaurants (Friendly's), is a major producer of pasta products, and operates an office coffee service plan.

Study Hershey's 1980 Consolidated Statement of Income and Retained Earnings, assets section of the Consolidated Balance Sheet, and Consolidated Statement of Changes in Financial Position (with comparative statements). Also included are the 1980 Six-Year Financial Summary and Notes 2 and 5 to Hershey's 1979 financial statements. Notes 2 and 5 provide information regarding Hershey's acquisition of Skinner Macaroni Company and Friendly Ice Cream Corporation.

1. Provide a journal entry dated April 9, 1979, that would record Hershey's purchase for cash of the Friendly Ice Cream Corporation.

2. Are Hershey's results of operations for 1978–80 comparable in the sense that they adequately recognize the impact of the Friendly acquisition in 1979? Explain.

3. The 1979 Consolidated Statement of Income and Retained Earnings included the item "Adjustment for Pooled Company (Note 3)." Explain in words what this number means and how it might have arisen in the pooling procedure. Approximately, what was the fair market value of the Skinner Macaroni Company on January 3, 1979?

4. Assuming that there were no purchases of companies involving goodwill in 1980 and that goodwill is being amortized on a

straight-line basis over forty years, estimate goodwill relating to acquisitions made prior to 1970, which is carried at cost until such time as there may be evidence of diminution.

CONSOLIDATED STATEMENTS OF
INCOME AND RETAINED EARNINGS

(in thousands of dollars except per share amounts)

	For the Years Ended December 31		
	1980	1979	1978
Net Sales	$1,335,289	$1,161,295	$ 767,880
Costs and Expenses:			
Cost of sales	971,714	855,252	560,137
Selling, administrative and general	224,615	184,186	128,520
Total costs and expenses	1,196,329	1,039,438	688,657
Income from Operations	138,960	121,857	79,223
Interest expense (income)—net (Note 1)	14,100	17,764	(2,683)
Income before Taxes	124,860	104,093	81,906
Provision for income taxes (Note 2)	62,805	50,589	40,450
Net Income	62,055	53,504	41,456
Retained Earnings at January 1	304,316	268,475	243,855
Adjustment for Pooled Company (Note 3)	—	1,444	—
Less—Cash Dividends	21,240	19,107	16,836
Retained Earnings at December 31	$ 345,131	$ 304,316	$ 268,475
Net Income per Common Share (Note 1)	$ 4.38	$ 3.78	$⋅ 3.02
Cash Dividends per Common Share	$ 1.50	$ 1.35	$ 1.225

CONSOLIDATED BALANCE SHEETS

(in thousands of dollars)

	December 31	
	1980	1979

ASSETS

Current Assets:

	1980	1979
Cash and short-term investments	**$ 48,906**	$ 17,185
Accounts receivable—trade (less allowances for doubtful accounts of $1,890 and $1,351)	**45,964**	37,423
Inventories (Note 1)ʼ	**113,701**	106,078
Other current assets	**12,796**	9,564
Total current assets	**221,367**	170,250

Property, Plant and Equipment, at cost:

	1980	1979
Land	**42,682**	40,610
Buildings	**139,611**	130,268
Machinery and equipment	**316,421**	275,630
Capitalized leases	**16,316**	16,237
	515,030	462,745
Less—accumulated depreciation and amortization	**135,589**	113,480
	379,441	349,265

	1980	1979
Excess of Cost Over Net Assets of Businesses Acquired (Notes 1 and 3)	**55,214**	56,516
Investments and Other Assets	**28,450**	31,168
	$684,472	$607,199

Hershey Foods Corporation

CONSOLIDATED STATEMENTS OF CHANGES
IN FINANCIAL POSITION

(in thousands of dollars)

	For the years ended December 31		
	1980	1979	1978
Financial Resources Provided			
Net income	**$ 62,055**	$ 53,504	$41,456
Depreciation and amortization	**26,378**	21,568	8,850
Deferred income taxes	**13,561**	11,283	3,764
Resources provided from operations	**101,994**	86,355	54,070
Increase in long-term debt	**15,000**	75,000	7,000
Disposals of property, plant and equipment	**4,393**	1,854	1,023
Other	**2,939**	(1,423)	(541)
Total resources provided	**124,326**	161,786	61,552
Financial Resources Applied			
Capital additions	**59,029**	56,437	37,425
Cash dividends	**21,240**	19,107	16,836
Increase in investments	**274**	8,710	2,200
Reduction in long-term debt	**500**	7,600	900
Acquisition of Friendly Ice Cream Corporation (net of working capital acquired of $18,248) represented by—			
Property, plant and equipment	**—**	141,494	—
Other assets	**—**	2,500	—
Long-term debt assumed	**—**	(38,031)	—
Excess of cost over net assets acquired	**—**	39,789	—
	—	145,752	—
Total resources applied	**81,043**	237,606	57,361
Increase (Decrease) In Working Capital	**$ 43,283**	$(75,820)	$ 4,191
Increase (Decrease) in Working Capital			
Cash and short-term investments	**$ 31,721**	$(94,571)	$(5,482)
Receivables	**8,541**	5,636	(3,969)
Inventories	**7,623**	40,467	3,661
Other current assets	**3,232**	2,059	1,247
Accounts payable	**(862)**	(7,940)	11,954
Accrued liabilities	**(4,207)**	(15,353)	(6,701)
Accrued income taxes	**(9,561)**	2,318	3,481
Current portion of long-term debt	**6,796**	(8,436)	—
Increase (Decrease) in Working Capital	**$ 43,283**	$(75,820)	$ 4,191

SIX-YEAR FINANCIAL SUMMARY

Hershey Foods Corporation and Subsidiaries

(all dollar and share amounts in thousands except market price and per share statistics)

	1980	1979	1978	1977	1976	1975
Summary of Earnings						
Continuing Operations						
Net Sales	$1,335,289	1,161,295	767,880	671,227	601,960	576,165
Cost of Sales	$ 971,714	855,252	560,137	489,802	417,673	413,134
Operating Expenses	$ 224,615	184,186	128,520	110,554	94,683	77,573
Interest Expense	$ 16,197	19,424	2,620	2,422	2,240	3,126
Interest Income	$ 2,097	1,660	5,303	2,931	1,883	1,862
Income Taxes	$ 62,805	50,589	40,450	35,349	45,562	43,292
Income from Continuing Operations	$ 62,055	53,504	41,456	36,031	43,685	40,902
Income (Loss) from Discontinued Operations	$ —	—	—	—	1,112	(1,457)
Gain (Loss) Related to Disposal of						
Discontinued Operations	$ —	—	—	5,300	—	(4,898)
Net Income	$ 62,055	53,504	41,456	41,331	44,797	34,547
Income Per Share of Common Stock						
Continuing Operations	$ 4.38	3.78	3.02	2.62	3.18	2.99
Discontinued Operations	$ —	—	—	—	.08	(.11)
Gain (Loss) Related to Disposal	$ —	—	—	.39	—	(.36)
Net Income	$ 4.38	3.78	3.02	3.01	3.26	2.52
Dividends Per—Common Share	$ 1.50	1.35	1.225	1.14	1.03	.85
Preferred Share	$ —	—	—	—	—	.60
Average Number of Common Shares and						
Equivalents Outstanding During						
the Year	14,160	14,153	13,742	13,722	13,720	13,698
Per Cent of Income from Continuing						
Operations to Sales	4.6%	4.6%	5.4%	5.4%	7.3%	7.1%
Financial Statistics						
Capital Additions	$ 59,029	56,437	37,425	27,535	20,722	10,542
Depreciation	$ 24,896	20,515	8,850	7,995	7,539	7,541
Advertising	$ 42,684	32,063	21,847	17,637	13,330	9,499
Current Assets	$ 221,367	170,250	216,659	221,202	169,872	157,579
Current Liabilities	$ 111,660	103,826	74,415	83,149	47,309	53,808
Working Capital	$ 109,707	66,424	142,244	138,053	122,563	103,771
Current Ratio	2.0:1	1.6:1	2.9:1	2.7:1	3.6:1	2.9:1
Long-Term Debt and Lease Obligations	$ 158,758	143,700	35,540	29,440	29,440	29,856
Debt-to-Equity Per Cent	44%	45%	13%	11%	13%	15%
Stockholders' Equity	$ 361,550	320,730	284,389	259,668	233,529	202,466
Stockholders' Data						
Outstanding Common Shares at Year-End	14,160	14,159	13,745	13,730	13,720	13,720
Market Price of Common Stock						
At Year-End	$ 23$^{1/2}$	24$^{5/8}$	20$^{5/8}$	19$^{7/8}$	22$^{3/8}$	18$^{5/8}$
Range During Year	$ 26–20	26$^{1/2}$–17$^{3/8}$	23$^{1/2}$–18$^{1/2}$	22$^{3/8}$–16$^{5/8}$	27$^{1/2}$–18$^{1/2}$	20$^{7/8}$–10$^{1/8}$
Number of Common Stockholders	17,774	18,417	18,735	19,694	20,421	19,686
Employees' Data						
Payrolls	$ 253,297	227,987	112,135	99,322	88,848	78,973
Number of Full-Time Employees—Year-End	12,430	11,700	8,100	7,660	7,670	7,580

Hershey Foods Corporation

2. Acquisitions

On January 3, 1979, the Company, in a pooling of interests transaction, acquired all of the outstanding shares of common stock of Skinner Macaroni Company in exchange for 398,680 shares of the Company's common stock. Prior year consolidated financial statements have not been restated as the effect would not be material. The adjustment to Retained Earnings of $1,444,000 represents the retained earnings of Skinner at January 1, 1979.

On January 18, 1979, the Company entered into a joint venture agreement in Brazil with S. A. Industrias Reunidas F. Matarazzo to manufacture, market and distribute pasta, biscuits and margarine and also distribute certain products manufactured by the food division of Matarazzo. The Company's initial investment amounted to approximately $7,500,000 representing a 40% equity interest.

During January, 1979, the Company acquired for cash substantially all of the outstanding common stock of Friendly Ice Cream Corporation and Friendly became a wholly-owned subsidiary through a merger effective April 9, 1979. The total acquisition cost amounted to approximately $164,000,000. The acquisition has been accounted for as a purchase and the excess of the acquisition cost over the fair value of the assets acquired and liabilities assumed approximated $39,800,000. Accordingly, the results of Friendly are included in the Consolidated Statements of Income and Retained Earnings for eleven months of 1979. Had the January, 1979 results of Friendly been included in the consolidated results of operations, the effect would not have been material.

Had Friendly been acquired on January 1, 1978, the unaudited combined results of operations for 1978 including amortization and depreciation adjustments based on the final asset appraisal and interest expense on funds expended for the acquisition would have reflected net sales of approximately $986,000,000; net income of $43,000,000 and net income per common share of $3.13. These unaudited pro forma amounts are based on the Company's audited results of operations for the year ended December 31, 1978, and Friendly's unaudited results of operations for the twelve months ended December 31, 1978.

5. Long-Term Debt

Long-term debt at December 31, 1979 and 1978 consisted of the following:

	1979	1978
	(In thousands of dollars)	
9½% Sinking Fund Debentures due 2009	$ 75,000	$ —
7¼% Sinking Fund Debentures due 1997	27,000	28,500
Less-Debentures repurchased	(3,060)	(3,960)
8.7% Senior Notes due 1992	20,000	—
8⅞% Promissory Notes due 1980	—	7,000
6⅞% Industrial Revenue Bonds due 2000–2005	4,000	4,000
Other obligations	4,946	—
	$127,886	$35,540

In December, 1978, in connection with the acquisition of Friendly Ice Cream Corporation (see Note 2), the Company obtained a revolving credit and term loan agreement with four banks which provided for borrowings of up to $200,000,000 (reduced to $100,000,000 on January 22, 1979). This agreement was cancelled on March 15, 1979, with the issuance of $75,000,000 of 9½% Sinking Fund Debentures due 2009 used to finance long-term, a portion of the acquisition price. Sinking Fund payments on the Debentures begin in 1985 with an annual payment of $3,000,000. The total amount borrowed under the revolving credit and term loan agreement averaged $96,576,000 with a weighted average interest rate of 11.6%.

During 1979, the Company purchased $600,000 of its 7¼% Sinking Fund Debentures. A total of $1,500,000 of previously purchased Debentures were utilized to meet the 1979 Sinking Fund requirement. The Company intends to use the $3,060,000 of repurchased Debentures at December 31, 1979, to meet future Sinking Fund requirements.

On November 20, 1979, the Company issued $20,000,000 of 8.7% Senior Notes due January 15, 1992, in exchange for similar notes issued by Friendly in 1977. Annual payments of $2,000,000 begin in 1983.

The aggregate annual payments of long-term debt, net of repurchased debentures of $1,500,000 in 1980 and 1981 and $60,000 in 1982 and exclusive of capitalized lease obligations for the succeeding five years are: 1980, $7,406,000; 1981, $311,000; 1982, $1,732,000; 1983, $3,817,000; 1984, $3,844,000.

9.4. DANA CORPORATION AND CONSOLIDATED SUBSIDIARIES

*Overview of acquisition and equity accounting
for affiliates. (Moderate: 60 minutes)*

Dana Corporation is a diverse, worldwide enterprise that designs, manufactures, and markets hundreds of different products for the transmission and control of power. Dana's principal lines of business are truck parts, service parts, and distribution systems, and industrial power products.

Study Dana's 1978–79 Balance Sheet, Statement of Changes in Financial Position, Comment to the Financial Statements on Business Combinations, and details of 1978–79 Shareholders' Equity. Also included are Dana's 1979–80 Balance Sheet, Statement of Changes in Financial Position, and Statement of Earnings.

1. Provide a detailed journal entry that would record Dana's acquisition of Wix Corporation in June 1979. Assume that no other material acquisitions took place during 1979.

2. How much did Dana receive as dividends from international affiliates?

3. Explain numerically how the combined accounts, Investments at Cost and Investments at Equity, changed from 1979 to 1980. Assume that $3,820,000 was used to purchase "other assets" in 1980.

BALANCE SHEET

	August 31	
	1979	**1978**
	(in thousands)	

ASSETS

Current Assets

Cash, including certificates of deposit of $31,000,000 in 1978 ....$	11,143	$ 52,796
Marketable securities, at cost plus accrued interest which approximates market	16,577	17,331
Accounts receivable, less allowance for doubtful accounts of $8,486,000		
(1978 — $7,010,000)...	360,857	280,929
Inventories		
Raw materials	137,306	116,880
Work in process and finished goods	466,121	354,182
Total inventories	603,427	471,062
Other current assets	21,604	23,171
Total current assets	1,013,608	845,289

Investments and Other Assets

Investments at cost	24,053	60,392
Investments at equity...	92,062	68,889
Goodwill	93,938	21,084
Other	9,144	10,889
Total investments and other assets..................................	219,197	161,254

Property, Plant and Equipment, at cost

Land and improvements to land..	23,634	18,924
Buildings and building fixtures	184,874	152,877
Machinery and equipment	652,847	508,211
	861,355	680,012
Less — Accumulated depreciation	338,284	284,684
Total property, plant and equipment.................................	523,071	395,328
Total Assets	$1,755,876	$1,401,871

LIABILITIES AND SHAREHOLDERS' EQUITY

Current Liabilities

Notes payable ....$	80,054	$ 77,328
Accounts payable	171,303	155,526
Accrued payroll and employee benefits	79,572	77,460
Other accrued liabilities...	46,059	28,916
Dividends payable	13,346	10,678
Taxes other than taxes on income	15,388	13,492
Taxes on income	23,457	38,127
Total current liabilities	429,179	401,527
Deferred Income Taxes	59,275	40,391
Deferred Compensation	14,979	12,877
Long-Term Debt..	292,158	192,575
Minority Interest in Consolidated Subsidiaries	24,426	21,261
Shareholders' Equity	935,859	733,240
Total Liabilities and Shareholders' Equity	$1,755,876	$1,401,871

STATEMENT OF CHANGES IN FINANCIAL POSITION

	Year ended August 31	
	1979	**1978**
	(in thousands)	
Financial Resources were Provided by		
Net income	**$164,177**	$134,225
Provision for depreciation	**52,827**	45,984
Deferred income taxes	**12,083**	10,120
Increase in minority interest in consolidated subsidiaries	**3,165**	1,628
Working capital provided by operations	**232,252**	191,957
Disposals of property, plant and equipment	**3,620**	1,661
Issuance of common stock		
Relating to acquisitions	**81,260**	32,941
Exercise of stock options	**2,047**	3,603
Under deferred compensation plans	**307**	55
Contribution to Dana Corporation Foundation	**1,000**	498
Contribution to employees' pension plans	**5,537**	
Increase in deferred compensation	**2,102**	2,564
Increase in long-term debt	**106,177**	12,105
Long-term debt assumed in acquisitions	**4,023**	18,678
Deferred income taxes of subsidiaries consolidated	**6,801**	
Decrease in investments and other assets, including $21,166,000 due to consolidation of subsidiaries in 1979	**32,354**	
	477,480	264,062
Financial Resources were Used for		
Additions to property, plant and equipment, including $27,630,000 in 1979 and $30,103,000 in 1978 relating to acquisitions	**184,190**	120,055
Cash dividends	**46,843**	40,226
Additions to investments and other assets, including $63,229,000 of goodwill relating to the Wix acquisition in 1979	**90,297**	41,025
Decrease in long-term debt	**10,617**	39,882
Purchase of treasury stock	**4,866**	1,033
	336,813	242,221
Increase in working capital, including $19,226,000 in 1979 and $28,716,000 in 1978 due to acquisitions	**$140,667**	$ 21,841
Analysis of Changes in Working Capital		
Cash	**$(41,653)**	$ 35,252
Marketable securities	**(754)**	(39,373)
Accounts receivable	**79,928**	84,533
Inventories	**132,365**	90,679
Other current assets	**(1,567)**	15,401
Notes payable	**(2,726)**	(73,288)
Accounts payable	**(15,777)**	(45,524)
Accrued payroll and employee benefits	**(2,112)**	(20,175)
Dividends and other accruals	**(21,707)**	(17,988)
Taxes on income	**14,670**	(7,676)
Increase in working capital	**$140,667**	$ 21,841

　IX.　INTERCORPORATE INVESTMENTS AND CONSOLIDATIONS

DETAILS OF SHAREHOLDERS' EQUITY

SHAREHOLDERS' EQUITY

	August 31	
	1979	1978
	(in thousands)	
Common stock of $1 par value — Authorized — 80,000,000 shares Issued — 36,675,854 shares in 1979; 33,327,425 shares in 1978	$ 36,676	$ 33,327
Additional paid-in capital	222,631	136,984
Retained earnings	700,697	583,363
	960,004	753,674
Less — Cost of common shares held in treasury — 1,414,773 shares in 1979; 1,322,816 shares in 1978	24,145	20,434
	$935,859	$733,240

COMMON STOCK $1 PAR VALUE

	Issued	Treasury
	(in thousands)	
Balance at August 31, 1977	$ 31,679	$ 19,740
Issuance of common stock — Employees' stock option plans	238	
Deferred compensation plans		(42)
Contribution to Dana Corporation Foundation		(297)
Acquisition of The Weatherhead Company	1,410	
Cost of 42,804 shares reacquired		1,033
Balance at August 31, 1978	33,327	20,434
Issuance of common stock — Employees' stock option plans	130	
Deferred compensation plans		(162)
Contribution to Dana Corporation Foundation		(406)
Employees' pension plans	200	
Acquisition of Wix Corporation	3,019	(587)
Cost of 173,900 shares reacquired		4,866
Balance at August 31, 1979	$ 36,676	$ 24,145

ADDITIONAL PAID-IN CAPITAL

	Year ended August 31	
	1979	1978
	(in thousands)	
Balance at beginning of year	$136,984	$101,874
Issuance of common stock — Employees' stock option plans	1,216	2,551
Deferred compensation plans	145	13
Contribution to Dana Corporation Foundation	594	201
Employees' pension plans	5,337	
Acquisition of Wix Corporation in 1979 and The Weatherhead Company in 1978	77,654	31,531
Tax benefits arising from exercise of non-qualified stock options and disqualifying dispositions	701	814
Balance at end of year	$222,631	$136,984

COMMENTS

ON FINANCIAL STATEMENTS

BUSINESS COMBINATIONS

Wix Corporation, a producer of oil, air and fuel filters for use in automobiles, trucks and industrial equipment, was acquired by Dana in June 1979. The cost to acquire Wix was $114,272,000 which included $33,012,000 paid in cash and $81,260,000 representing the fair market value of 3,052,000 shares of Dana common stock exchanged for Wix. This acquisition has been accounted for as a purchase and accordingly, the results of operations have been included in the consolidated accounts since the date of acquisition. Goodwill resulting from this acquisition amounting to $63,229,000 is being amortized over 40 years. The pro forma combined results of operations of Dana and Wix for the years ended August 31, 1979 and 1978 after giving effect to adjustments recording the combination, none of which was material, were:

	1979	1978
Net Sales and Other Income	$ 2,902,747,000	$ 2,384,600,000
Net Income	170,157,000	139,922,000
Net Income Per Common Share	$4.84	$4.02

BALANCE SHEET

	August 31	
	1980	**1979**
	(in thousands)	
ASSETS		
Current Assets		
Cash .... $	16,225	$ 11,143
Marketable securities, at cost plus accrued interest which approximates market	28,168	16,577
Accounts receivable, less allowance for doubtful accounts of $9,591,000		
(1979 — $8,486,000)...	376,771	360,857
Inventories		
Raw materials	132,229	137,306
Work in process and finished goods	486,824	466,121
Total inventories	619,053	603,427
Other current assets	33,524	21,604
Total current assets	1,073,741	1,013,608
Investments and Other Assets		
Investments at cost	31,518	24,053
Investments at equity...	74,294	92,062
Goodwill	109,982	93,938
Other	10,221	9,144
Total investments and other assets.................................	226,015	219,197
Property, Plant and Equipment, at cost		
Land and improvements to land	31,803	23,634
Buildings and building fixtures	233,638	184,874
Machinery and equipment	793,080	652,847
	1,058,521	861,355
Less — Accumulated depreciation	422,817	338,284
Total property, plant and equipment...............................	635,704	523,071
Total Assets	**$1,935,460**	$1,755,876

LIABILITIES AND SHAREHOLDERS' EQUITY

Current Liabilities		
Notes payable .... $	171,708	$ 80,054
Accounts payable	148,611	171,303
Accrued payroll and employee benefits	74,293	79,572
Other accrued liabilities...	67,715	46,059
Dividends payable	14,106	13,346
Taxes other than taxes on income	20,174	15,388
Taxes on income	11,816	23,457
Total current liabilities	508,423	429,179
Deferred Income Taxes	65,314	59,275
Deferred Compensation	11,378	14,979
Long-Term Debt	337,090	292,158
Minority Interest in Consolidated Subsidiaries	53,448	24,426
Shareholders' Equity	959,807	935,859
Total Liabilities and Shareholders' Equity	**$1,935,460**	$1,755,876

IX. INTERCORPORATE INVESTMENTS AND CONSOLIDATIONS

STATEMENT OF CHANGES IN FINANCIAL POSITION

	Year ended August 31	
	1980	**1979**
	(in thousands)	
Financial Resources were Provided by		
Net income	$ 95,727	$164,177
Provision for depreciation	69,560	52,827
Unremitted equity in earnings of international affiliates	(21,228)	(16,004)
Deferred income taxes	5,630	12,083
Increase in minority interest in consolidated subsidiaries	5,937	3,165
Working capital provided by operations	155,626	216,248
Disposals of property, plant and equipment	3,990	3,620
Issuance of common stock		
Relating to acquisitions	38,323	81,260
Exercise of stock options	546	2,047
Under deferred compensation and stock award plans	374	307
Contribution to Dana Corporation Foundation		1,000
Contribution to employees' pension plans		5,537
Increase in deferred compensation		2,102
Increase in long-term debt	53,902	106,177
Long-term debt assumed in acquisitions	7,790	4,023
Deferred income taxes of subsidiaries consolidated	409	6,801
Minority interest of subsidiaries consolidated	23,085	
Decrease in investments and other assets, including $45,568,000 in 1980 and $21,166,000 in 1979 due to consolidation of subsidiaries	54,172	32,354
	338,217	461,476
Financial Resources were Used for		
Additions to property, plant and equipment, including $56,756,000 in 1980 and $27,630,000 in 1979 relating to acquisitions and subsidiaries consolidated	186,183	184,190
Cash dividends	53,981	46,843
Additions to investments and other assets, including goodwill of $21,905,000 in 1980 and $63,229,000 in 1979 relating to acquisitions	39,762	74,293
Decrease in deferred compensation	3,601	
Decrease in long-term debt	16,760	10,617
Repurchase of common stock	57,041	4,866
	357,328	320,809
Increase (decrease) in working capital, including $34,991,000 in 1980 and $19,226,000 in 1979 due to acquisitions and subsidiaries consolidated	$ (19,111)	$140,667
Analysis of Changes in Working Capital		
Cash	$ 5,082	$(41,653)
Marketable securities	11,591	(754)
Accounts receivable	15,914	79,928
Inventories	15,626	132,365
Other current assets	11,920	(1,567)
Notes payable	(91,654)	(2,726)
Accounts payable	22,692	(15,777)
Accrued payroll and employee benefits	5,279	(2,112)
Dividends and other accruals	(27,202)	(21,707)
Taxes on income	11,641	14,670
Increase (decrease) in working capital	$ (19,111)	$140,667

STATEMENTS OF INCOME AND RETAINED EARNINGS

STATEMENT OF INCOME

	Year ended August 31	
	1980	**1979**
	(in thousands)	
Net sales	**$2,524,008**	$2,761,135
Equity in earnings of international affiliates and other income	**37,512**	28,302
Foreign currency translation adjustments	**(11,518)**	(902)
	2,550,002	2,788,535
Costs and expenses		
Cost of sales	**2,106,234**	2,262,801
Selling, general and administrative expenses	**247,123**	189,272
Interest expense	**49,613**	29,650
Minority interest in net income of consolidated subsidiaries	**8,475**	4,035
	2,411,445	2,485,758
Income before income taxes	**138,557**	302,777
Estimated taxes on income		
Current, net of investment tax credits of $6,200,000 in 1980 and $7,500,000 in 1979	**46,145**	124,056
Deferred	**(3,315)**	14,544
	42,830	138,600
Net income	**$ 95,727**	$ 164,177
Net income per common share	**$2.78**	$5.03

STATEMENT OF RETAINED EARNINGS

	Year ended August 31	
	1980	**1979**
	(in thousands)	
Balance at beginning of year	**$ 700,697**	$ 583,363
Net income for the year	**95,727**	164,177
Cash dividends declared ($1.57 per share in 1980; $1.42 in 1979)	**(53,981)**	(46,843)
Balance at end of year	**$ 742,443**	$ 700,697

9.5. GOULD, INC.

Preacquisition and postacquisition performance evaluation, merger analysis, and goodwill. (Difficult: 60 minutes)

Gould Inc. is a diversified electrical/electronic company engaged in the manufacture of electronics components, medical products, government defense systems, electrical products (e.g., motors), batteries, and other industrial products. Gould is a leader in the manufacture of copper foil used in electronic printed circuits.

On December 17, 1980, Gould shareholders approved a plan of reorganization whereby System Engineering Laboratories, Inc. (SYSTEMS), of Fort Lauderdale became a part of Gould. SYSTEMS is a major manufacturer of 32-bit minicomputers.

Study Gould's 1980 Statement of Financial Position, Statement of Earnings, Statement of Stockholders' Equity, and Note B, "Mergers, Acquisitions, and Dispositions." Also included is Gould's 1979 Consolidated Statement of Financial Position (as originally presented in the 1979 annual report).

1. During 1978–80, Gould merged with or acquired ownership of several companies, including SYSTEMS. How did Gould incorporate the performance of those companies in the years 1978–80? Distinguish between preacquisition and postacquisition profits and sales.

2. Provide a journal entry to show the effect of the SYSTEMS merger on the 1979 Consolidated Statement of Financial Position. Use major classifications only (i.e., current assets; investments and other assets; property, plant, and equipment; cost of acquired businesses in excess of net assets, etc.).

3. Estimate the amount of goodwill (or asset revaluation or both) that would have been recorded in December 1980 if the merger had

been consummated as a purchase instead of a pooling. Assuming the estimate is 100 percent goodwill (not asset revaluation), estimate the 1980 pretax earnings that would have been reported if the purchase method had been used. Gould amortizes goodwill over forty years on a straight-line basis.

Consolidated Statements of Financial Position

Gould Inc. and Consolidated Subsidiaries

Assets (All amounts in thousands)	December 31	1980	1979
Current Assets:			
Cash and marketable securities—at cost, which approximates market		$ 7,768	$ 20,174
Accounts receivable, less allowances (1980—$9,571; 1979—$7,905)		342,010	347,156
Inventories, less LIFO reserve (1980—$64,059; 1979—$68,553)		408,318	439,823
Other current assets		56,035	75,280
Total Current Assets		814,131	882,433
Investments and Other Assets:			
Unconsolidated financial subsidiary		32,746	24,722
Unconsolidated real estate subsidiary		20,316	18,296
Unconsolidated joint venture		—	37,498
Affiliated companies and other investments		59,199	48,914
Other assets		47,278	53,667
Total Investments and Other Assets		159,539	183,097
Property, Plant and Equipment:			
Land		28,571	27,086
Buildings		241,224	228,868
Machinery and equipment		499,328	460,523
Construction in progress		76,724	68,932
		845,847	785,409
Less allowances for depreciation and amortization		286,915	260,219
Total Property, Plant and Equipment		558,932	525,190
Cost of Acquired Businesses in Excess of Net Assets at Acquisition Dates— Net of amortization		75,906	76,693
Total Assets		$1,608,508	$1,667,413

Liabilities and Stockholders' Equity			
Current Liabilities:			
Notes payable		$ 16,346	$ 35,967
Trade accounts payable		189,252	182,198
Salaries, wages and other compensation		.40,243	36,634
Accrued pension		21,874	17,614
Other liabilities and accrued expenses		78,417	70,506
Current maturities of long-term debt		31,502	12,975
Total Current Liabilities		377,634	355,894
Long-Term Debt		376,021	474,120
Deferred Income Taxes		38,955	45,697
Other Deferred Credits		12,837	20,899
Stockholders' Equity:			
Preferred Stock		280	539
Common Stock		138,512	134,832
Additional paid-in capital		192,526	188,010
Earnings retained for use in the business		471,904	447,583
Less cost of Common Stock in treasury		161	161
Total Stockholders' Equity		803,061	770,803
Total Liabilities and Stockholders' Equity		$1,608,508	$1,667,413

Consolidated Statements of Earnings

Gould Inc. and Consolidated Subsidiaries

For the Year Ended December 31 (All amounts in thousands except per share amounts)	1980	1979	1978
Revenues:			
Net sales	$2,199,862	$2,094,893	$1,931,554
Equity earnings	16,901	5,333	8,605
Royalty income	5,589	5,123	2,958
Interest income	5,201	11,059	2,460
Gain on involuntary conversion	—	9,038	—
Gain on disposition of certain operations and joint venture	19,575	—	—
Total Revenues	2,247,128	2,125,446	1,945,577
Costs and Expenses:			
Cost of products sold	1,574,694	1,483,058	1,337,943
Selling, administrative and general expenses (includes internally funded research and development expenditures; 1980—$86,205; 1979—$75,569; 1978—$78,536)	478,461	421,422	388,413
Interest expense	60,726	52,908	35,874
Other (income)	4,026	(3,313)	2,414
Total Costs and Expenses	2,117,907	1,954,075	1,764,644
Pretax earnings	129,221	171,371	180,933
Federal, state and foreign income taxes	56,747	61,008	74,491
Net Earnings	$ 72,474	$ 110,363	$ 106,442
Per Share of Common Stock:			
Net earnings	$ 2.10	$ 3.27	$ 3.27
Net earnings assuming full dilution	$ 2.06	$ 3.18	$ 3.10

Consolidated Statements of Stockholders' Equity

Gould Inc. and Consolidated Subsidiaries

For the Three Years Ended December 31, 1980 (All dollar amounts in thousands)

	$7.50 Cumulative Preferred Stock Outstanding		$1.35 Cumulative Preferred Stock Outstanding		Common Stock Issued		Additional Paid-In Capital	Earnings Retained for Use in the Business	Common Stock in Treasury	
	Shares	Amount	Shares	Amount	Shares	Amount			Shares	Amount
Balance January 1, 1978— as previously reported	200,000	$20,000	1,808,605	$1,809	24,392,648	$ 97,571	$167,365	$322,293	32,346	$ 548
Adjustments arising from pooling of interests with Systems Engineering Laboratories, Inc.					5,508,258	22,033	(4,349)	(6,511)		
As restated	200,000	20,000	1,808,605	1,809	29,900,906	119,604	163,016	315,782	32,346	548
Net earnings								106,442		
Cash dividends: Preferred								(2,220)		
Common								(39,215)		
Common Stock issued in connection with acquisitions					1,082,630	4,330	9,759	3,395	(23,531)	(387)
Conversions and redemptions	(200,000)	(20,000)	(1,086,839)	(1,087)	1,709,233	6,837	9,929			
Exercise of stock options and other			1,750	2	396,899	1,588	2,502	82	999	
Balance December 31, 1978	—	—	723,516	724	33,089,668	132,359	185,206	384,266	9,814	161
Net earnings								110,363		
Cash dividends: Preferred								(812)		
Common								(46,234)		
Conversions			(184,732)	(185)	180,001	720	(535)			
Exercise of stock options and other					438,234	1,753	3,339			
Balance December 31, 1979	—	—	538,784	539	33,707,903	134,832	188,010	447,583	9,814	161
Net earnings								72,474		
Cash dividends: Preferred								(534)		
Common								(48,846)		
Conversions			(258,940)	(259)	252,429	1,010	(751)			
Common Stock issued in connection with acquisitions					450,305	1,801	3,832	1,228		
Exercise of stock options and other					217,243	869	1,435	(1)		
Balance December 31, 1980	—	$ —	279,844	$ 280	34,627,880	$138,512	$192,526	$471,904	9,814	$ 161

Notes to Consolidated Financial Statements

Note B: Mergers, Acquisitions and Dispositions

In December 1980, the Company issued 5,880,822 shares of Common Stock in exchange for all of the outstanding shares of Systems Engineering Laboratories, Incorporated (SYSTEMS), which designs, manufactures, markets and services medium-scale, high-speed digital computer systems and related products. The merger was accounted for as a pooling of interests and the accompanying consolidated financial statements have been restated to include the accounts of SYSTEMS for 1980 and prior years. The separate results of operations of SYSTEMS which have been included in the consolidated statements of earnings are as follows (in thousands):

Year Ended December 31	1980	1979	1978
Net Sales	$89,099	$71,008	$61,610
Net earnings	$ 6,501	$ 4,476	$ 5,409

In addition, the Company and SYSTEMS incurred ancillary costs of the merger of approximately $2,700,000 ($.08 per share) which were charged to earnings during the year ended December 31, 1980.

In 1980, the Company issued 205,305 shares of Common Stock in exchange for all of the outstanding shares of Deltec Corporation and 50,000 shares of Common Stock in exchange for all of the outstanding shares of Marjol Battery and Equipment Co. These mergers were accounted for as poolings of interests. Sales and earnings of the Company were not materially affected by these transactions and prior years amounts have not been restated.

In 1979, the Company acquired the remaining 54% of Imperial Trans Europe N.V., a European manufacturer of fluid power products, for approximately $12,000,000 and in 1978, the Company issued 489,117 shares of Common Stock valued at $13,573,000 in exchange for all the outstanding shares of Hoffman Electronics Corporation. These acquisitions were treated as purchases.

Proforma amounts of net sales, net earnings and earnings per share, assuming the aforementioned purchases had taken place on January 1, 1978, would not differ significantly from the reported amounts.

In 1978, the Company issued 617,044 shares of Common Stock for certain companies primarily in the electronics segment. These acquisitions were accounted for as poolings of interests.

In January 1981, the Company exchanged 414,927 shares of Common Stock for all the outstanding shares of SRL Medical, Inc. In February 1981, the Company exchanged 799,986 shares of Common Stock for all the outstanding shares of Gettys Manufacturing Company, Inc. Had these mergers been consummated during 1980 and included in the consolidated financial statements, the results would not have been materially affected.

The sale of certain Industrial Group operations was consummated during 1980. Proceeds from the sale of such operations aggregated approximately $58,773,000, resulting in a net gain of approximately $6,300,000 ($.18 per share). Net sales and earnings before interest and taxes of these operations for the year ended December 31, 1980 were approximately $95,000,000 and $2,500,000, respectively. At December 31, 1980, the Company had guaranteed $11,777,000 of bank term loans and lines of credits of one of the disposed operations. It is anticipated that the Company will be relieved of these guarantees in early 1981, when the purchaser establishes lines of credit.

The Company intends to dispose of all, or a significant portion, of the remaining businesses carried on by the Industrial Group and is presently negotiating the terms of the potential sale. The Company does not anticipate that it will incur a net loss as a result of the intended disposition of the remaining operations of its Industrial Group. However, because of significant presently unresolved contingencies affecting the proposed disposition, the financial position and results of operations of the Industrial Group have not been disaggregated and presented as discontinued in the accompanying consolidated financial statements.

On December 18, 1980, the Company sold its 50% share in the joint venture partnership (Gould-Brown Boveri) to its coventurer BBC, Brown Boveri and Company, Limited ("BBC") for $24,000,000 in cash and retained certain inventory and fixed assets associated with the Navy business. The Company is presently contractually obligated under $8,313,000 of capitalized lease agreements that have been transferred to BBC. The Company and BBC are currently negotiating with the lessors to transfer these obligations to BBC. The sale resulted in a net loss of approximately $4,600,000 ($.13 per share). In addition the Company granted BBC an option to purchase the assets of the Electrical Systems Group ("ESG") Canadian Operations and the stock of the related Australian subsidiary for substantially the book value thereof.

Consolidated Statements of Financial Position
Gould Inc. and Consolidated Subsidiaries

Assets (All amounts in thousands) December 31	1979	1978
Current Assets:		
Cash	$ 18,105	$ 32,440
Marketable securities—at cost, which approximates market	906	1,908
Accounts receivable, less allowances (1979–$7,732; 1978–$6,148)	324,593	284,355
Inventories, less LIFO reserve (1979–$68,553; 1978–$21,178)	429,203	388,810
Other current assets	73,558	50,870
Total Current Assets	846,365	758,383
Investments and Other Assets:		
Unconsolidated financial subsidiary	24,722	19,559
Unconsolidated real estate subsidiary	18,296	5,659
Unconsolidated joint venture	37,498	—
Affiliated companies and other investments	48,914	45,327
Other assets	45,992	58,595
Total Investments and Other Assets	175,422	129,140
Property, Plant and Equipment:		
Land	26,669	23,215
Buildings	226,546	209,013
Machinery and equipment	448,137	389,503
Construction in progress	68,932	66,225
	770,284	687,956
Less allowances for depreciation and amortization	255,701	231,684
Total Property, Plant and Equipment	514,583	456,272
Cost of Acquired Businesses in Excess of Net Assets at Acquisition Dates—Net of amortization	76,693	77,168
Total Assets	$1,613,063	$1,420,963

Liabilities and Stockholders' Equity (All amounts in thousands) December 31	1979	1978
Current Liabilities:		
Notes payable	$ 33,856	$ 55,504
Accounts payable and accrued expenses	286,515	272,706
Income taxes	9,152	25,131
Current maturities of long-term debt	12,608	13,600
Total Current Liabilities	342,131	366,941
Long-Term Debt	455,717	300,828
Deferred Income Taxes	45,697	47,623
Other Deferred Credits	20,899	20,101
Stockholders' Equity:		
Preferred Stock	539	724
Common Stock	111,850	109,780
Additional paid-in capital	192,182	189,759
Earnings retained for use in the business	444,209	385,368
Less cost of Common Stock in treasury	161	161
Total Stockholders' Equity	748,619	685,470
Total Liabilities and Stockholders' Equity	$1,613,063	$1,420,963

IX.   INTERCORPORATE INVESTMENTS AND CONSOLIDATIONS

9.6. DENNY'S, INC.

Introduction to divestiture and disposal of acquisitions.
(Straightforward: 30 minutes)

Denny's, Inc., is one of the largest food-service companies in the world. Its domestic operations include approximately 840 Denny's Restaurants in forty-four states and Canada, 870 Winchell's Donut Houses in eighteen states, and supporting services in manufacturing, processing, warehousing, and distribution.

In 1980, Denny's decided to dispose of over one hundred of its Donut stores and provided $9,930,000 in the 1980 Statement of Income as expenses to be incurred. Study Denny's Consolidated Balance Sheets for 1980–81, Statements of Income for 1979–81, and a financial comment entitled "Other Liabilities."

1. Provide a journal entry to describe the 1980 decision to dispose of the more than one hundred Winchell's Donut Houses. Specify whether the accounts are long-term, short-term, assets, liabilities, expenses, etc.

2. Provide a journal entry to record actual charges or costs incurred in the current (1981) year.

3. Comment on the accounting policy adopted by Denny's. How appropriate is it that expenses be charged against revenues for losses not actually incurred? What might be the reaction of investors and bankers to news of this kind?

Consolidated Balance Sheets

Denny's, Inc. ASSETS	June 26 1981	June 27 1980
Current assets:		
Cash	$ 1,249,000	$ 6,752,000
Short-term investments	87,829,000	26,087,000
Notes and accounts receivable	9,597,000	11,216,000
Inventories	31,244,000	30,620,000
Prepaid expenses	6,828,000	7,527,000
Deferred income tax benefit	6,400,000	5,600,000
Total current assets	143,147,000	87,802,000
Investments in foreign affiliated companies	4,430,000	4,213,000
Property, equipment and improvements, at cost:		
Land	53,971,000	50,940,000
Buildings	119,458,000	106,956,000
Equipment	176,636,000	163,478,000
Leasehold improvements	43,928,000	41,155,000
	393,993,000	362,529,000
Less accumulated depreciation and amortization	120,187,000	97,538,000
Net property, equipment and improvements	273,806,000	264,991,000
Leased property under capital leases	163,635,000	160,405,000
Less accumulated amortization	44,424,000	37,074,000
Net leased property under capital leases	119,211,000	123,331,000
Other assets:		
Notes and accounts receivable	5,133,000	3,250,000
Miscellaneous	5,585,000	5,448,000
Total other assets	10,718,000	8,698,000
	$551,312,000	$489,035,000

Denny's, Inc. LIABILITIES AND SHAREHOLDERS' EQUITY	June 26 1981	June 27 1980
Current liabilities:		
Accounts payable	$ 19,389,000	$ 21,339,000
Income taxes	6,384,000	2,118,000
Accrued payroll and related expenses	20,520,000	17,207,000
Other accrued liabilities	34,952,000	30,694,000
Current maturities of notes and obligations under capital leases	11,299,000	9,545,000
Total current liabilities	92,544,000	80,903,000
Long-term notes	92,674,000	94,093,000
5½% subordinated convertible debentures	8,881,000	9,489,000
Obligations under capital leases	135,780,000	136,971,000
Other liabilities	18,485,000	16,312,000
Deferred income taxes	7,518,000	4,778,000
Shareholders' equity:		
Common stock, $1 par value; 9,899,306 shares issued and outstanding (8,714,787 shares in 1980)	9,899,000	8,715,000
Additional paid-in capital	50,850,000	22,065,000
Retained earnings	134,681,000	115,709,000
Total shareholders' equity	195,430,000	146,489,000
	$551,312,000	$489,035,000

Consolidated Statements of Income

Denny's, Inc.	Years ended		
	June 26 1981	June 27 1980	June 29 1979
REVENUES:			
Company restaurant and donut house sales	$840,701,000	$708,796,000	$615,921,000
Rent, management fees and other income	8,329,000	7,713,000	7,956,000
Total revenues	849,030,000	716,509,000	623,877,000
COSTS AND EXPENSES:			
Restaurants and donut houses:			
Cost of sales	635,718,000	539,246,000	465,839,000
Operating expenses	46,200,000	40,398,000	33,090,000
Rent, insurance and property taxes	31,047,000	27,382,000	23,125,000
Depreciation and amortization	32,242,000	28,672,000	23,351,000
Provision for donut house closing expenses	—	9,930,000	—
	745,207,000	645,628,000	545,405,000
Rent, insurance, property taxes and depreciation applicable to rent income	1,716,000	1,990,000	1,968,000
Selling, general and administrative expenses	32,095,000	22,709,000	14,966,000
Employee profit sharing	3,028,000	1,912,000	2,736,000
Interest expense	24,808,000	21,751,000	17,678,000
Interest capitalized	(534,000)	(1,051,000)	(512,000)
Interest income	(5,808,000)	(2,194,000)	(1,582,000)
Total costs and expenses	800,512,000	690,745,000	580,659,000
INCOME BEFORE INCOME TAXES	48,518,000	25,764,000	43,218,000
PROVISION FOR INCOME TAXES	21,600,000	8,800,000	18,150,000
NET INCOME	$ 26,918,000	$ 16,964,000	$ 25,068,000
NET INCOME PER SHARE:			
Primary	$3.04	$1.95	$2.89
Fully diluted	2.96	1.93	2.82

Denny's, Inc.

OTHER LIABILITIES

Other liabilities includes estimated liabilities related to the sale or other disposition of units and estimated accruals for partial self-insurance for workers compensation claims, employee medical benefits and property damage and liability claims. The provision for estimated losses on the sale or other disposition of units is charged to income in the period the decision is made to dispose of such units.

Included in other accrued liabilities are accruals for partial self-insurance of $6,318,000 and $5,891,000 at June 26, 1981 and June 27, 1980 respectively, and accruals for real estate taxes of $6,554,000 and $5,868,000 at June 26, 1981 and June 27, 1980 respectively.

In the year ended June 27, 1980, a $9,930,000 charge to income was made to provide for the disposal of over 100 Donut Houses. The charge consisted of a write-down of assets, estimated lease termination costs and estimated direct disposal costs of $4,590,000, $4,240,000 and $1,100,000 respectively. Of the 108 Donut Houses closed during the current year approximately one-half have been disposed of, resulting in charges of $4,330,000 to the reserve. The remaining reserve of $5,600,000 relates to estimated asset valuation, lease termination and direct disposal costs of $2,200,000, $2,800,000 and $600,000 respectively.

9.7. PHELPS DODGE CORPORATION

Divestiture of acquisition by sale with present value accounting. (Moderate: 60 minutes)

Phelps Dodge mines each year about 20 percent of the copper produced in the United States and fabricates a portion of that copper into a wide variety of products. The company also produces silver, gold, and molybdenum as byproducts of its copper operations.

Study Phelps Dodge's 1980 Statement of Consolidated Income, 1980 Consolidated Balance Sheet, and Notes 3 and 5 to the consolidated financial statements.

1. Prepare a table showing (a) the amount of cash flows and (b) the timing of cash flows associated with the company's sale of its 40 percent interest in Consolidated Aluminum Corporation (Conalco) to Swiss Aluminium Ltd. in installments through 1985.

2. Calculate the present value of the cash flows identified above using a 15 percent discounting factor.

3. Prepare a journal entry to record the sale on December 30, 1980.

4. Approximately how much of Phelps Dodge's 1980 Net Income (after taxes) is attributable to profit and gains from the Consolidated Aluminum Corporation? Is this number a fair reflection of Phelps Dodge's performance in 1980? Explain in quantitative terms, to the extent possible. Use a 46 percent tax rate (if necessary).

Statement of Consolidated Income

(In thousands of dollars)

	1980	1979	1978
Sales and other operating revenues	**$1,440,137**	1,280,830	1,007,490
Operating costs and expenses			
Cost of products sold	**1,191,922**	987,997	818,556
Depreciation, depletion and amortization	**70,441**	67,303	58,889
Selling and general administrative expense	**54,228**	46,326	42,247
Exploration and research expense	**22,994**	20,768	18,821
	1,339,585	1,122,394	938,513
Operating income	**100,552**	158,436	68,977
Interest expense	**(43,737)***	(40,117)*	(53,174)
Interest and miscellaneous income, net	**39,239**	8,341	10,185
Income before taxes and equity earnings	**96,054**	126,660	25,988
Provision for taxes on income	**(25,454)**	(36,880)	(4,390)
Equity earnings, net of income tax effect	**20,714**	20,991	8,514
Net income	**$ 91,314**	110,771	30,112
Per common share after preferred dividend requirement	**$4.20**	5.06	1.16
Average number of shares outstanding	**20,831,647**	20,698,414	20,672,795

*Excludes interest capitalized.

Statement of Consolidated Retained Earnings

(In thousands of dollars)

	1980	1979	1978
Retained earnings at beginning of year	**$ 821,112**	741,248	729,602
Net income	**91,314**	110,771	30,112
Dividends declared and paid:			
Preferred shares	**(4,038)**	(6,062)	(6,062)
Common shares	**(32,305)**	(24,845)	(12,404)
Retained earnings at end of year	**$ 876,083**	821,112	741,248

Consolidated Balance Sheet

(In thousands of dollars)

	December 31,		
	1980	1979	1978
Assets			
Current assets:			
Cash and short-term investments, at cost	**$ 19,576**	12,034	22,758
Receivables, less allowance for doubtful accounts (1980—$5,674; 1979—$3,874; 1978—$4,211)	**202,728**	166,855	139,896
Inventories	**176,257**	152,046	144,496
Supplies, at cost or less	**116,598**	120,141	90,578
Prepaid expenses	**4,682**	6,774	3,686
Income tax prepayments	**5,274**	4,330	6,969
Current assets	**525,115**	462,180	408,383
Investments and long-term receivables	**171,904**	176,635	173,308
Property, plant and equipment	**1,408,244**	1,354,772	1,326,678
Deferred charges	**6,841**	6,631	7,292
	$2,112,104	2,000,218	1,915,661
Liabilities			
Current liabilities:			
Short-term borrowings	**$ 40,263**	—	—
Current portion of long-term debt	**11,195**	45,958	12,057
Accounts payable and accrued expenses	**199,639**	165,338	135,057
Uranium delivery obligations	**—**	—	29,547
Income taxes	**34,421**	35,197	23,008
Current liabilities	**285,518**	246,493	199,669
Long-term debt	**626,749**	605,554	664,713
Deferred income taxes	**112,553**	95,296	81,343
Other liabilities and deferred credits	**9,561**	9,092	6,765
	1,034,381	956,435	952,490
Redeemable Preferred Shares			
Redemption value $100, par value $1; 2,000,000 shares authorized; 470,000 shares outstanding (1979 and 1978—750,000)	**48,290**	74,590	74,590
Common Shareholders' Equity			
Common shares, par value $6.25; 30,000,000 shares authorized; 20,880,971 shares outstanding (1979—20,717,838; 1978—20,691,305)	**130,506**	129,486	129,320
Capital in excess of par value	**22,844**	18,595	18,013
Retained earnings	**876,083**	821,112	741,248
	1,029,433	969,193	888,581
	$2,112,104	2,000,218	1,915,661

Phelps Dodge Corporation

3. Sale of Consolidated Aluminum Corporation Stock

The Corporation agreed in 1980 to sell its 40% equity interest in Consolidated Aluminum Corporation ("Conalco") to Swiss Aluminium Ltd. ("Alusuisse") in installments through 1985. Pursuant to this agreement, Alusuisse paid the Corporation $11 million on December 30, 1980 and $29 million on January 2, 1981 for slightly more than half of such equity interest. Alusuisse is obligated to make successive annual payments for the balance of such interest from December 31, 1981 through December 31, 1985 of $14 million, $17.5 million, $26.5 million, $24.5 million and $27.5 million.

The Corporation has waived all rights to dividends and other distributions by Conalco and granted to Alusuisse an irrevocable proxy for the shares the Corporation retains. The Corporation has also been released from all obligations as minority stockholder and will no longer participate in the management of Conalco.

The Corporation accounted for the transaction as a sale in 1980 of its entire interest for $110.5 million, representing the 1980 present value of the various cash payments. The resultant capital gain of $26.2 million before taxes is included in miscellaneous income. At December 31, 1980, the Corporation had recorded a receivable from Alusuisse for $99.5 million, $32.4 as current.

5. Investments and Long-term Receivables

Investments and long-term receivables are as follows:

	1980	1979	1978
Equity basis:			
Black Mountain (49%)	$ 22,133	19,199	19,120
Manufacturing interests abroad	46,660	41,949	36,513
Consolidated Aluminum (40%)	—	76,462	73,501
Other	3,146	2,959	2,880
Cost basis:			
Southern Peru (16.2%)	13,157	13,157	13,157
Receivable from Alusuisse ..	67,088	—	—
Alumina supply loans	17,655	19,960	22,134
Other	2,065	2,949	6,003
	$171,904	176,635	173,308

Equity earnings (losses) were as follows:			
Black Mountain	$ 2,975	(1,486)	(784)
Manufacturing interests abroad	9,859	10,351	7,025
Consolidated Aluminum	7,832	2,961	137
Gains on restructure of foreign investments	2,378	4,288	3,406
Other	236	197	140
Income taxes (Note 6)	(2,566)	4,680	(1,410)
	$ 20,714	20,991	8,514

Retained earnings of the Corporation include undistributed earnings of equity investments of (in millions): 1980—$36.3; 1979—$19.6; 1978—$10.5.

Condensed financial information pertaining to major equity investments is as follows:

Manufacturing Interests Abroad

Equity basis investments in manufacturing interests abroad represent companies which are engaged primarily in the manufacture of wire and cable and related products. The following table presents summary financial statement information for those companies:

	1980	1979	1978
Net current assets	$ 61,467	54,378	38,226
Fixed assets—net	57,162	46,462	42,561
Long-term debt	(46,655)	(38,766)	(25,928)
Other assets, net	12,248	10,268	7,182
Net assets	$ 84,222	72,342	62,041
Phelps Dodge's share of net assets	$ 46,534	41,949	34,561
Sales	$226,232	184,701	150,431
Net income	18,129	15,526	9,492
Phelps Dodge's share of net income	9,859	10,351	7,025
Dividends received	1,889	1,878	964

Consolidated Aluminum Corporation

	1980	1979	1978
Net sales	$928,397	824,821	743,228
Extraordinary item-utilization of a tax loss carryforward	—	646	1,344
Net income	19,870	4,056	3,398

See Note 3 for a description of the sale by the Corporation of its equity interest in Consolidated Aluminum.

Consolidated Aluminum's 1980, 1979 and 1978 net income was increased (in millions) by approximately $10.5, $3.0 and $1.8, respectively, as a result of reductions of LIFO inventory quantities valued at lower costs prevailing in prior years.

Consolidated Aluminum had (in millions) purchases of $53.6, $62.7 and $55.3 from, and sales of $93.8, $44.1 and $51.4 to, its shareholders and their affiliates in 1980, 1979 and 1978, respectively.

9.8. CATERPILLAR TRACTOR COMPANY

*Purchase accounting, amortization of intangibles,
accounting for affiliated companies.
(Moderate: 45 minutes)*

Caterpillar Tractor Company designs, manufactures, and markets products in two principal categories: (1) earthmoving, construction, and materials handling machinery and equipment and (2) engines and electric power generating systems.

Study Caterpillar's Consolidated Statements of Results of Operations, Financial Position, and Changes in Financial Position. Note 10, "Acquisitions," and Note 11, "Investments in Unconsolidated Companies," are also included.

1. Provide a journal entry that would show the effects on consolidated financial position of the July 1981 purchase of Solar Turbines International.

2. Provide a journal entry, dated December 31, 1981, that would record the amortization of intangibles purchased in July 1981.

3. Assuming that the market value of tangible assets purchased approximated their book value and that taxes approximated 46 percent of pretax net income, estimate Caterpillar's 1981 net income had it been able to use the *pooling* method of accounting for the acquisition of Solar Turbines International.

4. If Caterpillar had used the cost method for reporting its share of profit in affiliated companies, what would have been reported as Consolidated Profit for the years 1979, 1980, and 1981? Ignore any tax effects.

5. How would the answers given in part 4 change if all affiliated companies had paid exactly 50 percent of profits after tax as dividends to stockholders? Ignore any tax effects.

STATEMENT 1

Consolidated Results of Operations for the Years Ended December 31
(Millions of dollars except amounts stated on a per share basis)

	1981	1980	1979
Sales	**$9,154.5**	**$8,597.8**	**$7,613.2**
Operating costs:			
Cost of goods sold	6,933.3	6,627.1	5,888.5
Selling, general, and administrative expenses	869.7	769.5	662.0
Depreciation and amortization	448.4	370.2	311.8
	8,251.4	7,766.8	6,862.3
Operating profit	903.1	831.0	750.9
Deduct: Interest expense	224.8	173.2	139.1
	678.3	657.8	611.8
Add: Other income	107.3	112.6	80.0
	785.6	770.4	691.8
Deduct: Taxes based on income (note 6)	223.9	231.9	233.9
Profit of consolidated companies	561.7	538.5	457.9
Equity in profit of affiliated companies (note 11)	16.3	23.5	30.2
Profit of subsidiary credit companies	.9	2.8	3.5
Profit for year — consolidated	**$ 578.9**	**$ 564.8**	**$ 491.6**
Profit per share of common stock (note 7):			
Assuming no dilution	$ 6.64	$ 6.53	$ 5.69
Assuming full dilution	$ 6.44	$ 6.32	$ 5.50
Dividends per share of common stock	$2.400	$2.325	$2.100

STATEMENT 2

Consolidated Ownership
(Dollars in millions)

	1981	1980	1979
Common stock:			
Balance at beginning of year	$ 180.0	$ 177.1	$ 174.0
Shares issued under stock options:			
1981 — 55,621; 1980 — 34,584; 1979 — 68,746	3.0	1.7	3.1
Shares issued upon conversion of convertible debentures:			
1981 — 1,042,891; 1980 — 24,351; 1979 — 198	52.2	1.2	—
Balance at end of year	235.2	180.0	177.1
Profit employed in the business:			
Balance at beginning of year	3,252.0	2,888.2	2,578.1
Add: Profit for year — consolidated	578.9	564.8	491.6
Deduct: Dividends paid	209.3	201.0	181.5
Balance at end of year	3,621.6	3,252.0	2,888.2
Ownership	$3,856.8	$3,432.0	$3,065.3

STATEMENT 3

Consolidated Financial Position at December 31

(Dollars in millions)

	1981	1980	1979
Current assets:			
Stated on basis of realizable values:			
Cash	$ 59.8	$ 74.9	$ 58.4
Short-term investments	21.2	29.1	88.8
Receivable from customers and others	994.3	912.4	692.7
Prepaid expenses and income taxes allocable to the following year	255.3	166.9	96.8
	1,330.6	1,183.3	936.7
Stated on basis of cost using principally "last-in, first-out" method:			
Inventories (notes 1C and 8)	2,213.8	1,749.6	1,670.2
	3,544.4	2,932.9	2,606.9
Deduct: Current liabilities:			
Notes payable (note 12)	747.0	430.3	404.2
Payable to material suppliers and others	1,120.9	890.0	645.0
Wages, salaries, and contributions for employee benefits	211.6	176.8	144.5
Taxes based on income	189.4	198.1	133.4
Long-term debt due within one year	100.6	16.3	59.0
	2,369.5	1,711.5	1,386.1
Net current assets (statement 4)	1,174.9	1,221.4	1,220.8
Buildings, machinery, and equipment — net (notes 1D and 9)	3,299.7	2,927.9	2,571.7
Land — at original cost	96.5	80.6	66.1
Patents, trademarks, and other intangibles (note 1E)	146.4	—	—
Investments in affiliated companies (notes 1A and 11)	104.8	87.7	71.3
Investments in subsidiary credit companies (notes 1A and 11)	15.2	15.8	14.0
Other assets	77.9	53.3	49.8
Total assets less current liabilities	4,915.4	4,386.7	3,993.7
Deduct:			
Long-term debt due after one year (note 13)	960.9	931.6	951.9
Deferred taxes based on income	97.7	23.1	(23.5)
Net assets	$3,856.8	$3,432.0	$3,065.3
Ownership (statement 2):			
Preferred stock of no par value:			
Authorized shares: 5,000,000			
Outstanding shares: none			
Common stock of no par value (note 14):			
Authorized shares: 105,000,000			
Outstanding shares: 1981 — 87,591,148; 1980 — 86,492,636; 1979 — 86,433,701	$ 235.2	$ 180.0	$ 177.1
Profit employed in the business	3,621.6	3,252.0	2,888.2
	$3,856.8	$3,432.0	$3,065.3

Caterpillar Tractor Company

STATEMENT 4

Changes in Consolidated Financial Position
(Millions of dollars)

	1981	1980	1979
Additions to net current assets from:			
Operations:			
Profit for year	$ 578.9	$ 564.8	$ 491.6
Items affecting profit for year, but not affecting net current assets:			
Depreciation and amortization	448.4	370.2	311.8
Deferred taxes based on income	74.6	46.6	(47.4)
Equity in profit of unconsolidated companies	(17.2)	(26.3)	(33.7)
Net current assets provided from operations	1,084.7	955.3	722.3
Long-term debt	222.4	9.1	2.8
Common stock issued under stock options and			
upon conversion of convertible debentures	55.2	2.9	3.1
Dividends from unconsolidated companies	8.3	8.1	7.0
Reclassification of other assets	—	—	10.8
Other	.1	4.8	9.9
	1,370.7	980.2	755.9
Reductions of net current assets for:			
Cash dividends	209.3	201.0	181.5
Land, buildings, machinery, and equipment	713.2	749.2	675.9
Long-term debt	193.1	29.4	68.9
Purchase of tax benefits through tax lease	10.1	—	—
Investment in affiliated company	6.5	—	—
Acquisition of Solar Turbines International Division (exclusive of net current assets) (note 10):			
Land, buildings, machinery, and equipment	123.1	—	—
Patents, trademarks, and other intangibles	161.9	—	—
	1,417.2	979.6	926.3
Increase (decrease) in net current assets during year	(46.5)	.6	(170.4)
Net current assets at beginning of year	1,221.4	1,220.8	1,391.2
Net current assets at end of year	$1,174.9	$1,221.4	$1,220.8
Increase (decrease) in components of net current assets:			
Cash and short-term investments	$ (23.0)	$ (43.2)	$ (97.3)
Receivable from customers and others	81.9	219.7	(75.1)
Prepaid expenses and income taxes allocable			
to the following year	88.4	70.1	3.1
Inventories	464.2	79.4	147.9
Net change in current assets	611.5	326.0	(21.4)
Notes payable	316.7	26.1	291.6
Payable to material suppliers and others	230.9	245.0	(79.0)
Wages, salaries, and contributions for employee benefits	34.8	32.3	15.0
Taxes based on income	(8.7)	64.7	(103.3)
Long-term debt due within one year	84.3	(42.7)	24.7
Net change in current liabilities	658.0	325.4	149.0
Increase (decrease) in net current assets during year	$ (46.5)	$ .6	$ (170.4)

10. Acquisition

In July 1981, the company acquired the assets constituting the Solar Turbines International Division of International Harvester Company for approximately $505 in cash. The company assumed substantially all of the liabilities of Solar, but no indebtedness for borrowed money except minor short-term borrowings.

The acquisition has been accounted for as a purchase. The company's consolidated results of operations include Solar's results beginning with those for August 1981. Unaudited pro forma consolidated results of operations, as though the company had acquired Solar on January 1, 1980, are as follows:

	1981	1980
Sales	$9,401.4	$8,928.6
Profit	$ 588.1	$ 513.5
Profit per share of common stock	$ 6.75	$ 5.94

These pro forma data reflect adjustments for amortization of intangibles, additional depreciation on purchased assets, imputed interest costs on borrowed funds, and associated income taxes. The intangibles acquired include assets such as patents, designs, drawings, and trademarks.

In accordance with U.S. law, the acquisition was subject to review by the Antitrust Division of the U.S. Department of Justice. In December 1981, the department announced it had completed its study and would not challenge the purchase.

11. Investments in unconsolidated companies

Affiliated companies

The company's investments in affiliated companies consist of 50% interests in two companies and 49% interests in two others. The principal such investment is a 50% interest in Caterpillar Mitsubishi Ltd., Japan ($96.4). The other 50% owner of this company is Mitsubishi Heavy Industries, Ltd., Tokyo, Japan.

Combined financial information of the affiliated companies, as translated to U.S. dollars, is as follows:

	September 30,		
	1981	1980	1979
Financial Position			
Assets:			
Current assets	$752.9	$688.2	$661.9
Land, buildings, machinery, and equipment — net	165.9	122.4	108.4
Other assets	32.5	33.9	33.2
	951.3	844.5	803.5
Deduct: Liabilities:			
Current liabilities	464.2	481.1	472.8
Long-term debt	223.0	131.7	142.6
Other liabilities	52.4	53.6	43.1
	739.6	666.4	658.5
Ownership	$211.7	$178.1	$145.0
Company share of ownership	$105.7	$ 89.1	$ 72.5
Intercompany adjustments	(.9)	(1.4)	(1.2)
Investments in affiliated companies	$104.8	$ 87.7	$ 71.3

	Years ended September 30,		
	1981	1980	1979
Results of Operations			
Sales	$865.0	$884.8	$901.3
Profit after tax	$ 31.6	$ 47.3	$ 60.8
Company share of profit	$ 15.8	$ 23.7	$ 30.4
Intercompany adjustments	.5	(.2)	(.2)
Equity in profit of affiliated companies	$ 16.3	$ 23.5	$ 30.2

Profit after tax for the combined affiliated companies in 1981, 1980, and 1979 would have been approximately $20.2, $48.6, and $43.7, respectively, if exchange gains and losses were excluded. The intercompany adjustments result from the exclusion of unrealized profit from inventory.

At December 31, 1981, the company's consolidated "Profit employed in the business" included $70.4 representing its share of undistributed profit of the affiliated companies.

Certain products are sold to and purchased from the affiliated companies at intercompany prices. In addition, the company receives license fees under license agreements with the affiliated companies. These transactions were not material in relation to consolidated results of operations.

10.1. LEVI STRAUSS AND COMPANY*

Introduction to Statement of Changes in Financial Position.
(Straightforward: 45 minutes)

Study the Consolidated Statement of Changes in Financial Position for Levi Strauss and Company for the year ended November 30, 1980, and a note summarizing changes in the shares of common stock.

1. Determine fiscal 1980 Net Income (Loss).

2. Determine Cash Provided by Operations—i.e., determine the funds generated from operations assuming funds are defined as *cash* (not working capital).

3. The November 25, 1979, balance of Long-Term Debt less Current Maturities was $99,126,000. Determine the balance in this account as of November 30, 1980.

4. Refer to the accompanying note, "Common Stock." Approximately how much did the company pay *per share* to repurchase its common stock during the year ended November 30, 1980?

---

*Based on earlier case by Mark A. Wolfson.

Levi Strauss & Co. and Subsidiaries

(In Thousands)	Year Ended		
	November 30, 1980 (53 weeks)	November 25, 1979 (52 weeks)	November 26, 1978 (52 weeks)
Working Capital Provided By:			
Operations:			
Net income	$	$191,454	$144,969
Add items not currently involving working capital:			
Depreciation and amortization	30,004	20,430	17,606
Other, net	13,066	5,380	(2,140)
Working capital provided by operations	266,759	217,264	160,435
Common stock issued in acquisition of Koracorp Industries Inc.	—	37,261	—
Proceeds from long-term debt	54,586	8,400	14,411
Common stock issued to employees	6,322	4,999	5,077
Working capital provided	327,667	267,924	179,923
Working Capital Used For:			
Additions to property, plant and equipment	119,824	51,254	42,863
Cash dividends declared	53,442	40,391	34,972
Acquisition of Koracorp Industries Inc. (less working capital of $34,961):			
Property, plant and equipment	—	17,702	—
Other assets	—	4,885	—
Goodwill	—	39,341	—
Long-term liabilities assumed	—	(26,054)	—
Purchases of treasury stock	26,130	87,451	3,611
Reductions in long-term debt	14,958	15,505	11,766
Other, net	640	1,862	(4,379)
Working capital used	214,994	232,337	88,833
Increase in working capital	$ 112,673	$ 35,587	$ 91,090

Changes in shares of common stock are summarized below:

	Issued	Treasury Stock	Outstanding
Balance November 27, 1977	21,999,404	(238,938)	21,760,466
Purchases of treasury stock	—	(110,889)	(110,889)
Shares issued to employees	—	238,206	238,206
Balance November 26, 1978	21,999,404	(111,621)	21,887,783
Purchase of treasury stock	—	(2,000,000)	(2,000,000)
Shares issued to employees	—	201,259	201,259
Shares issued in the acquisition of Koracorp Industries Inc.	—	555,413	555,413
Balance November 25, 1979	21,999,404	(1,354,949)	20,644,455
Two-for-one stock split	21,999,404	(1,349,710)	20,649,694
Purchase of treasury stock	—	(700,000)	(700,000)
Shares issued to employees	—	299,177	299,177
Balance November 30, 1980	43,998,808	(3,105,482)	40,893,326

10.2. R. J. REYNOLDS INDUSTRIES, INC.—II

Reconstruction of Statement of Changes in Financial Position. (Moderate: 60 minutes)

R. J. Reynolds is a diversified, international corporation with major interests in domestic and international tobacco, processed foods, fresh fruit and beverages, containerized ocean shipping, energy, and packing. About one-third of the corporation's revenue is generated abroad.

Study the Consolidated Balance Sheets; Note 12, "Series A Cumulative Preferred Stock"; Note 16, "Acquisitions"; and the Consolidated Statements of Changes in Financial Position for 1980, along with the applicable comparative data.

1. Determine Net Earnings for 1980.

2. Does it appear that Reynolds defers or flows through the investment tax credit (assuming some asset purchases to which the investment credit would apply)? Does Reynolds defer any income tax? Explain.

3. Determine Current Assets and Current Liabilities as of December 31, 1980.

4. If Reynolds had prepared consolidated statements on February 2, 1979, various balance sheet accounts would have been affected by the Del Monte acquisition. Show the numerical effects of the Del Monte acquisition on all relevant balance sheet accounts (or groups of accounts). What method of accounting for business combinations was used by Reynolds in this transaction? Explain.

5. Explain the asset account "Cost in Excess of Net Assets of Businesses Acquired." Does it appear that this account increased as a result of acquisitions during 1980? (Note: This account is being amortized over forty years.)

Consolidated Balance Sheets

December 31

(Dollars in Millions)	1980	1979
ASSETS		
Current assets:		
Cash and short-term investments (Note 3).................................	$ 188.3	$ 164.8
Accounts and notes receivable		
(less allowances of $40.2 and $27.4, respectively).........................	1,019.6	815.1
Inventories (Note 4)...	2,371.8	2,178.9
Prepaid expenses..	61.8	42.4
Total current assets	**3,641.5**	3,201.2
Property, plant and equipment — at cost (Notes 5 and 14)	**4,901.2**	4,111.3
Less allowances for depreciation, depletion and amortization	1,636.5	1,327.3
Net property, plant and equipment	**3,264.7**	2,784.0
Cost in excess of net assets of businesses acquired	**160.3**	162.0
Other assets and deferred charges	**288.8**	274.7
	$7,355.3	$6,421.9
LIABILITIES AND STOCKHOLDERS' EQUITY		
Current liabilities:		
Notes payable (Note 6)..	$ 514.3	$ 395.3
Accounts payable and accrued accounts (Note 7)	1,068.3	883.0
Current maturities of long-term debt (Note 8)	123.2	87.0
Income taxes accrued...	104.0	119.3
Total current liabilities	**1,809.8**	1,484.6
Long-term debt (less current maturities) (Note 8)	**1,045.9**	988.9
Other noncurrent liabilities	**213.0**	183.5
Deferred income taxes	**495.3**	411.4
Commitments and contingencies (Note 11)		
Series A Cumulative Preferred Stock (Note 12)	**342.1**	342.1
$2.25 Convertible Preferred Stock (Note 13)	**3.8**	13.6
Common stockholders' equity:		
Common Stock — net (Note 13)	253.2	244.8
Paid-in capital (Note 13)...	213.5	190.2
Earnings retained (Note 8)..	2,978.7	2,562.8
Total common stockholders' equity	**3,445.4**	2,997.8
	$7,355.3	$6,421.9

Note 12
Series A Cumulative Preferred Stock

In connection with the Del Monte Corporation merger (see Note 16), the Company issued 7,053,478 shares (authorized 7,053,660 shares) of Series A Cumulative Preferred Stock (without par value), stated value of $48.50. The terms of the Preferred Stock provide for redemption by the Company, pursuant to a mandatory sinking fund, at a redemption price of $48.50 per share plus any accrued dividends, in an amount equal to approximately one-seventh of such shares issued in connection with the merger in each year commencing on March 1, 1985. The Company has the non-cumulative option to double the amount redeemed pursuant to such mandatory redemption in any year.

Each share of the Series A Cumulative Preferred Stock entitles the holder to receive cumulative dividends payable quarterly at the rate of $4.10 per share per annum. The Series A Cumulative Preferred Stock ranks senior to the Common Stock, and on a parity with the outstanding $2.25 Convertible Preferred Stock, as to dividends and upon liquidation and entitles the shareholder to receive $48.50 per share plus accrued dividends (whether or not earned or declared) before any distribution upon liquidation is made to holders of a junior stock.

Each share entitles the holder to three-quarters of one vote on all matters on which holders of the Common Stock have the right to vote, voting together with all other shares entitled to vote and not as a class.

Dividends paid on the Series A Cumulative Preferred Stock amounted to $28.9 million in 1980 and $26.4 million in 1979.

Note 16
Acquisitions

On February 1, 1979, the shareholders of Del Monte Corporation approved an Agreement and Plan of Merger under which Del Monte became a wholly owned subsidiary of the Company on February 2, 1979. Under the terms of the merger, approximately 45 percent of the Del Monte capital stock was acquired for cash of $48.50 per share, and the remainder of the Del Monte capital stock was converted on a share-for-share basis into the Company's Series A Cumulative Preferred Stock. (See Note 12.) The total cost of the merger, which was accounted for as a purchase, was approximately $618 million. The consolidated results of operations of the Company include the operations of Del Monte from the date of the merger.

The unaudited pro forma combined results of operations shown in the following table assume that the Del Monte merger had taken place on January 1, 1978 and that the cash portion of the purchase price had been borrowed at the short-term interest rates prevailing during the respective periods.

	1979	1978
Net sales and revenues	$9,057.3	$8,345.5
Net earnings	551.7	483.5
Net earnings per common share:		
Primary	5.21	4.64
Fully diluted	5.03	4.41

The effects of the Del Monte merger on the Consolidated Statement of Changes in Financial Position are shown in the following table:

	1979
Acquisition:	
Property, plant and equipment	$301.4
Other assets	953.3
Liabilities assumed	(637.1)
Total cost of acquisition	617.6
Less working capital at date of acquisition	449.9
Net increase in long-term assets	$167.7

On December 17, 1979, the Company acquired, for cash of $25 million, the remaining 49 percent minority interest in Signal Petroleum, a Louisiana oil and gas producing concern. Consolidated operating results since December 17, 1979 include the effects of this acquisition, which did not have a material effect on the Company's consolidated financial statements.

Consolidated Statements of Changes in Financial Position

For the Years Ended December 31

(Dollars in Millions)	1980	1979	1978
Working capital was provided by:			
Operations:			
Net earnings	$	$ 550.9	$441.9
Depreciation, depletion and amortization	**363.2**	312.2	226.0
Deferred income taxes	**83.5**	72.0	58.6
Other	**53.9**	41.7	32.6
Total from operations	**1,171.0**	976.8	759.1
Proceeds from long-term debt	**198.2**	165.6	43.5
Proceeds from issuance of Company's stocks (Notes 12 and 13)	**31.6**	388.8	9.5
Other (principally disposals of property, plant and equipment)	**34.4**	70.6	28.2
	1,435.2	1,601.8	840.3
Working capital was used for:			
Net increase in long-term assets from			
acquisition of Del Monte Corporation (Note 16)	—	167.7	—
Capital expenditures	**897.9**	684.3	383.4
Cash dividends	**254.5**	224.7	179.3
Long-term debt becoming currently payable	**138.5**	114.9	79.8
Retirement of $2.25 Convertible Preferred Stock			
upon conversion (Note 13)	**9.8**	14.8	3.1
Other	**19.4**	17.2	35.9
	1,320.1	1,223.6	681.5
Increase in working capital	**$ 115.1**	$ 378.2	$158.8
Analysis of change in working capital:			
Increase (decrease) in current assets:			
Cash and short-term investments	**$ 23.5**	$ 50.5	$ 20.1
Accounts and notes receivable	**204.5**	232.5	42.9
Inventories	**192.9**	757.8	67.3
Prepaid expenses	**19.4**	19.5	(9.9)
Decrease (increase) in current liabilities:			
Notes payable	**(119.0)**	(321.0)	100.4
Accounts payable and accrued accounts	**(185.3)**	(324.7)	(3.9)
Current maturities of long-term debt	**(36.2)**	(21.8)	9.3
Income taxes accrued	**15.3**	(14.6)	(67.4)
Increase in working capital	**$ 115.1**	$ 378.2	$158.8

X.   STATEMENT OF CHANGES IN FINANCIAL POSITION

10.3. HOLIDAY INNS, INC., AND CONSOLIDATED SUBSIDIARIES

Statement of Changes in Financial Position, acquisition, and accounting methods. (Moderate: 75 minutes)

Holiday Inns comprises four main business segments. The company operates more than 1,750 hotels, two gambling casinos (Harrah's), a fast-food restaurant chain (Cake & Steak), and a shipping and transportation company (Delta Steamship).

Study the Statements of Changes in Financial Position for the years ended 12/29/78, 12/28/79, and 1/2/81.

1. What is Holiday Inns' definition of *funds*?

2. Determine the company's earnings (Income from Continuing Operations) for fiscal year 1980.

3. On the Balance Sheet, the balances in Long-Term Debt Due after One Year and Long-Term Debt Due within One Year on 1/2/81 and 12/28/79 are $564,613,000 and $45,653,000, respectively. Estimate combined Long-Term Debt as of 12/28/79. (Assume that none of the Increase in Other Current Liabilities [of $39,278,000] relates to long-term debt transactions.)

4. Assume that Holiday Inn's dividends during fiscal years 1979 and 1980 were paid in four equal installments in the quarter following that to which they relate: For example, assume that a dividend on fourth-quarter earnings is paid in the first quarter of the following year. Estimate dividends paid in cash during 1980.

5. The Property and Equipment accounts in the balance sheets appeared as follows:

	January 2, 1981	December 28, 1979
Property and equipment, at cost *less*	$1,486,298,000	$1,023,983,000
Accumulated depreciation and amortization	338,648,000	286,911,000
	$1,147,650,000	$ 737,072,000

Estimate the cost of property and equipment purchased as part of Holiday Inns' purchases of other companies (labeled *Acquisitions* in the Statement of Changes in Financial Position). Assume that the phrase "Depreciated Value of Property Dispositions" means "Book Value of Property Dispositions."

6. Does it appear that Holiday Inns defers or flows through the investment tax credit (assuming some asset purchases to which the investment credit would apply)? Does Holiday Inns defer any income tax? Explain.

7. On August 22, 1979, the company completed its acquisition of "Perkins" Cake & Steak, Inc., a restaurant chain, for 2 million common shares of $1.50 par value per share. Make all required entries to record this issuance of common stock.

Statements of Changes in Financial Position

Holiday Inns, Inc., and Consolidated Subsidiaries
Fifty-three Weeks Ended January 2, 1981 and Fifty-two Weeks
Ended December 28, 1979 and December 29, 1978

	1980	1979	1978
		(In thousands)	
Cash and Temporary Cash Investments — Beginning of Year	$161,213	$156,471	$ 84,385
Sources of Funds			
Income from Continuing Operations		71,296	52,504
Add (Deduct) Items Not Affecting Funds			
Depreciation, Amortization and Allowance for Property Dispositions	84,186	60,493	54,639
Deferred Income Taxes	3,497	876	(8,221)
Other	(2,078)	1,152	2,242
Funds Provided from Continuing Operations	193,880	133,817	101,164
Funds Provided from Discontinued Operations	—	84,078	6,963
Common Stock Issued in Acquisition	—	37,810	—
Proceeds from Financing	298,367	25,038	64,699
Deferred Gain on Sale of Real Estate	—	—	21,550
Depreciated Value of Property Dispositions	23,279	31,322	38,440
Increase in Unterminated Voyage Gross Profit	4,091	3,334	9,025
Increase (Decrease) in Accrued Federal and State Income Taxes	(2,380)	(22,367)	12,542
Increase in Other Current Liabilities	39,278	21,132	61,496
Total Sources	556,515	314,164	315,879
Applications of Funds			
Acquisitions, Net of Funds Acquired of $15,061,000 and $190,000	287,344	37,620	—
Expenditures for Property and Equipment	207,062	133,434	147,752
Reduction of Long-Term Debt	68,325	57,786	58,176
Cash Dividends Declared	22,438	20,460	16,657
Increase (Decrease) in Investments and Long-Term Receivables	2,629	57,038	(6,469)
Increase (Decrease) in Restricted Funds	4,659	(2)	(21,692)
Increase (Decrease) in Receivables	8,105	(7,170)	48,570
Other	(4,059)	10,256	799
Total Applications	596,503	309,422	243,793
Cash and Temporary Cash Investments — End of Year	$121,225	$161,213	$156,471

10.4. NATIONAL DISTILLERS AND CHEMICAL CORPORATION*

Consolidated Statement of Changes in Working Capital,
equity investments, and purchase accounting.
(Moderate: 45 minutes)

National Distillers and Chemical Corporation (NDCC) and its subsidiaries are engaged in the production and marketing of petrochemicals, alcoholic beverages, wines and brandy (Almaden Vineyards, Inc.), metal products, and insurance. NDCC's Associated Companies produce and market natural gas liquids, polyethylene, titanium, chemical raw materials, and carbon monoxide. The company employs approximately fourteen thousand people.

Study the Consolidated Statement of Changes in Working Capital and Notes 1, 2, and 9 to the financial statements of National Distillers and Chemical Corporation.

1. Your attention is directed to Note 1, "Summary of Accounting Policies, Principles of Consolidation," and Note 9, "Investments in Associated Companies."

   a. What amounts are reported (as assets) for "Investments in Associated Companies" in NDCC's balance sheets for 1979 and 1980?

   b. By how much would NDCC's reported Net Income for 1980 of $103,348 change if NDCC's share of dividends received from "associated companies" suddenly doubled (from $34,910 to twice that amount)?

   c. Ignoring tax effects, if NDCC were to account for "Investments in Associated Companies" on the *cost* basis, how would the 1980 Balance Sheet change? (Hint: Only two account balances are affected.)

---

*Based on earlier case by Mark A. Wolfson.

d. Ignoring tax effects, if NDCC were to account for "Investments in Associated Companies" on the *cost* basis, by how much would 1979 Net Income for NDCC change?

2. Prepare a journal entry dated May 19, 1978, to record the purchase of Emery Industries, Inc. The total acquisition price, as indicated, was $196 million, paid for by issuing new preferred stock and providing the remaining balance in cash. Note that the $72.3 million cash paid for Emery Industries does not incorporate certain other "expenses" of the deal which were required to be paid by NDCC as part of the $196.0 million deal.

   Note also that in addition to the items purchased (as shown in the Statement of Changes in Working Capital), NDCC acquired certain of Emery's current assets and liabilities (i.e., working capital).

CONSOLIDATED STATEMENT OF CHANGES IN WORKING CAPITAL

(dollar amounts in thousands)

	Year Ended December 31		
	1980	1979	1978
Working capital was provided by:			
Net income	$103,348	$135,753	$106,814
Charges (credits) to income not requiring (providing) working capital			
Depreciation and amortization	46,772	45,908	37,943
Deferred taxes on income	(5,338)	14,635	9,463
Unremitted earnings — insurance subsidiaries	(14,450)	(15,538)	(15,828)
Unremitted earnings — associated companies	(4,471)	(843)	(10,625)
Portion of plant shutdown costs	30,924		
Portion of loss on discontinued operation	14,779		
Other	1,409	9,279	3,827
Tax (expense) benefit attributable to partnership operations included in share of earnings of associated companies	(15,272)	1,337	4,064
Total from operations	157,701	190,531	135,658
Sale of investment in associated company	20,144		
Issuance of common stock upon conversion of debentures	10,117	5,804	648
Sales or issuance of common stock under stock option, employee savings and dividend reinvestment plans	6,128	1,042	1,076
Additional long-term debt and capital lease obligations	692	922	108,039
Sale of European operations		15,498	
Preference stock issued for business acquisition			120,474
Plant assets disposed of or held for sale	14,806	3,672	2,633
Sale or collection of investments and other receivables — net	4,585	2,496	15,036
	214,173	219,965	383,564
Working capital was used for:			
Dividends to stockholders	72,787	63,669	50,484
Additions to property, plant and equipment	49,372	57,802	105,730
Reduction of long-term debt	31,715	25,208	31,830
Conversion of subordinated debentures	10,129	5,811	650
Additions to investments in associated companies	1,368	21,439	23,895
Addition to miscellaneous investments	15,752		
Acquisition of preferred and preference stocks	192	11,450	4,292
Net non-current assets of company acquired			87,790
Goodwill arising from acquisition of Emery Industries			47,126
Other	3,206	(1,940)	1,026
	184,521	183,439	352,823
Increase in working capital	$ 29,652	$ 36,526	$ 30,741
Working capital changes — increases (decreases):			
Cash and short-term investments	$ 19,145	$(20,203)	$(40,960)
Accounts and notes receivable — net	(15,834)	11,786	29,966
Inventories	(11,557)	10,148	72,743
Prepaid expenses and other assets	30,629	3,385	91
Accounts payable	(3,075)	26,201	(12,127)
Federal excise taxes payable	(6,246)	28,709	973
Taxes on income	10,888	(26,616)	4,525
Other accrued liabilities	(1,012)	1,765	(20,992)
Loans payable to banks and others	5,484	(1,969)	3,026
Long-term debt payable within one year	1,230	3,320	(6,504)
	$ 29,652	$ 36,526	$ 30,741

NOTES TO CONSOLIDATED FINANCIAL STATEMENTS

(dollar amounts in thousands except for per share data)

Note 1 — Summary of Accounting Policies

Principles of Consolidation

The financial statements include the accounts of all majority-owned companies except those subsidiaries engaged in insurance operations. Unconsolidated insurance subsidiaries and associated companies are accounted for under the equity method, i.e., at cost, increased or decreased by the Company's share of earnings or losses, less dividends. Associated companies include significant companies in which National has at least a 20%, but not more than a 50%, interest.

Inventories

Inventories are valued at the lower of cost or market. Cost is determined for the various categories of inventory using the first-in, first-out; last-in, first-out; or average cost method as deemed appropriate. Whiskey in storage for aging over a number of years is included in current assets in accordance with the general practice in the distilling industry.

Property, Plant and Equipment

Property, plant and equipment are stated at cost. Depreciation is determined for related groups of assets under the straight line method based upon their estimated useful lives; however, for income tax purposes, depreciation is based on accelerated methods and shorter useful lives where permitted. Minor renewals or replacements and maintenance and repairs are expensed. Major replacements and improvements are capitalized. Gains or losses on disposal of assets in the normal course of business are credited or charged to accumulated depreciation. Gains or losses from abnormal dispositions are credited or charged to income.

Goodwill

The excess of the cost of acquired businesses over values assigned to net assets is classified as goodwill, and with respect to acquisitions made after 1970 is being amortized to income for a period of not more than 40 years. In the opinion of management, goodwill which arose from acquisitions made prior to 1970 has not diminished in value and is not being amortized.

Taxes on Income

The provision for taxes on income includes the tax effects of revenue and expense transactions included in the determination of financial statement income. Where such transactions are included in the determination of taxable income in a different year, the tax effects are deferred. Investment tax credits are recognized in the year in which they are allowed for tax purposes, which is generally the year the qualified assets are placed in service.

Pensions

With respect to principal pension plans, the Company accrues and funds costs annually. Costs of all principal plans are actuarially determined under projected benefit cost methods and include amounts for current service, amortization of prior service cost over periods varying up to 40 years, and interest on unfunded prior service cost.

Earnings per Common Share

Earnings per common share were computed by dividing net income applicable to common stock by the weighted average number of shares of common stock outstanding during the year. For purposes of this computation certain unissued shares subject to stock options have been included in the weighted average.

Note 2 — Business Combinations

On April 23, 1979, the Company acquired by merger Indiana Group, Inc. ("Indiana"), an insurance holding company. In the merger the Company issued 4,974,870 shares of its common stock in exchange for all of the outstanding shares of Indiana. The consolidated financial statements for 1978 give effect to the merger of Indiana on the pooling of interests method of accounting. The earnings of Indiana for periods prior to the merger which have been included in the consolidated statement of income are $3,808 (unaudited) for the period January 1 – April 23, 1979 and $13,707 for the year ended December 31, 1978.

On May 19, 1978, the Company acquired by merger Emery Industries, Inc. ("Emery"), a manufacturer of chemicals principally derived from natural fats and oils. In connection with the merger, the Company issued 5,414,544 shares of $1.85 Preference Stock (redemption price $22.25 per share) and paid $72,300 in cash. The total cost of the acquisition, including expenses, was approximately $196,000. The transaction has been accounted for as a purchase and the excess of the purchase cost over the fair value of net assets acquired of $47,126 (Goodwill) is being amortized on the straight-line basis over 40 years. The results of operations of Emery have been included in the Company's consolidated financial statements from the date of merger. The following summarizes unaudited pro forma operating results for the year ended December 31, 1978, as if the operations of the Company (after giving effect to the pooling of interests with Indiana) and Emery had been consolidated for the entire year:

Net sales	$1,942,454
Net income	$ 107,304
Net income per common share	$3.12

Note 9 — Investments in Associated Companies

Summary financial information for associated companies as a group is as follows:

Balance sheet data	December 31	
	1980	1979
Current assets	$286,394	$287,453
Property, plant and equipment		
— net	258,204	248,221
Other assets	89,835	60,515
	$634,433	$596,189
Current liabilities	$132,570	$106,963
Long-term debt	80,311	67,530
Other liabilities	60,770	61,430
Shareholders' equity	360,782	360,266
	$634,433	$596,189
National's share of		
shareholders' equity	$146,964	$146,028

At December 31, 1980, the Company's share of the undistributed earnings of corporate associated companies was $30,909.

Investments in associated companies consist of interests in:

	% Owned	
	1980	1979
National Petro Chemicals Corporation, a domestic corporation	50	50
National Helium Corporation, a domestic corporation	50	50
U.S.I. Far East Corporation, a Taiwanese corporation	43	50
Unilever-Emery N.V., a Dutch corporation	—	50
Quimic S.A. de C.V., a Mexican corporation	49	49
Poliolefinas, S.A., a Brazilian corporation	28	28
United Polymers Corporation, a Taiwanese corporation	—	20
RMI Company, a domestic partnership	50	50
Syngas Company, a domestic partnership	33.6	33.3

As a result of the merger of United Polymers Corporation into U.S.I. Far East Corporation in June 1980, the Company's percentage investment in U.S.I. Far East was reduced from 50 to 43 per cent.

In December 1980, the Company sold its investment in Unilever-Emery N.V. to the other 50 per cent stockholder.

Income statement data	Year Ended December 31		
	1980	1979	1978
Revenues	$740,015	$619,228	$477,471
Net earnings	113,910	47,874	55,388
Distributions	74,262	55,781	36,709
National's share of earnings	39,381	25,744	26,075
National's share of distributions	34,910	24,901	15,450

Prior to 1980 the Syngas Company was in the formative stage and had no revenues. In 1980 Syngas became operational, supplying synthesis gas to the partner owners. Since the production of Syngas is purchased by the partner owners, the above income statement data for the year 1980 do not include any amounts with respect to Syngas. The Company's share of the 1980 results of operations of Syngas is included with costs and expenses in determining profits of the Chemical Division.

The Company includes its share of the income or loss and investment tax credits of the domestic partnerships, RMI Company and Syngas Company, in computing its taxable income. The resulting tax (expense) or benefit (except with respect to Syngas in 1980) is included in share of earnings of associated companies. Such (expense) benefit was ($15,272) in 1980, $1,337 in 1979 and $4,064 in 1978.

The Company is contingently liable in respect of indebtedness of certain of the associated companies for moneys borrowed. At December 31, 1980, the maximum amount of the Company's contingent liability was estimated at $30,350, assuming the other investor in one of the associated companies makes its required contribution should the liability arise.

X. STATEMENT OF CHANGES IN FINANCIAL POSITION

10.5. TRANSAMERICA CORPORATION

Treatment of gain/loss on sale in Statement of Changes in Financial Position. (Moderate: 60 minutes)

Transamerica is a diversified company with approximately 70 percent of its income derived from insurance and financial services. The company also provides travel services, including rentals, and owns a manufacturing subsidiary specializing in precision-engineered products.

In July 1981, the company sold its entertainment subsidiary, United Artists, to Metro-Goldwyn-Mayer Film Co. for $250 million cash plus $130 million to be received over a three-year period beginning in 1984. Apparently, the decision to sell United Artists was an outgrowth of the company's increased focus in 1981 on long-range strategic planning. The cash received from the sale was used to reduce notes and loans. (Extracted from chairman/president's message to stockholders, 1981.)

Study Transamerica's 1980–81 Consolidated Balance Sheet (assets only), 1979–81 Consolidated Statement of Income, Consolidated Statement of Changes in Financial Position, and Note H to the financial statements.

1. What was the pretax gain on the sale of United Artists to MGM, and how was this reported in the 1981 Statement of Income?

2. Provide a journal entry that would record all aspects of the sale. Assume that United Artists was a greater-than-50-percent-owned subsidiary with net assets other than Investments in Film Productions tied up as accounts receivable or payables. Assume also that the pretax loss of United Artists is attributable solely to amortization of film investments.

3. Why don't the proceeds from the sale show up in the Consolidated Statement of Changes in Financial Position? Revise the 1981 column of that statement to identify separately the proceeds and their application.

CONSOLIDATED BALANCE SHEET

Transamerica Corporation and Subsidiaries
December 31

Assets	1981	1980
Investments — principally of insurance subsidiaries:		
Equity securities — at market value (cost $152,404,000 in 1981 and $156,253,000 in 1980)	$ 129,128,000	$ 127,918,000
Fixed maturities — at amortized cost	2,219,931,000	2,351,373,000
Mortgage loans and real estate	1,415,341,000	1,367,971,000
Loans to life insurance policyholders	371,664,000	350,962,000
Short-term investments	276,955,000	138,871,000
	4,413,019,000	4,337,095,000
Finance receivables, of which $305,157,000 in 1981 and $354,234,000 in 1980 matures within one year	1,268,210,000	1,137,517,000
Less unearned discount ($71,638,000 in 1981 and $56,788,000 in 1980) and allowance for losses	113,544,000	94,690,000
	1,154,666,000	1,042,827,000
Cash, including temporary investments of $124,796,000 in 1981 and $116,897,000 in 1980	164,688,000	176,149,000
Trade and other accounts receivable	609,707,000	521,005,000
Insurance premiums in course of collection	282,963,000	281,092,000
Investment in film productions		280,839,000
Inventories of manufacturing subsidiaries	110,809,000	94,904,000
Property and equipment, less allowance for depreciation of $432,267,000 in 1981 and $357,928,000 in 1980:		
Land, buildings and equipment	364,497,000	345,101,000
Equipment held for lease	599,820,000	490,281,000
Aircraft and other flight equipment	312,731,000	265,862,000
Deferred policy acquisition costs of insurance subsidiaries	460,127,000	419,147,000
Separate accounts administered by life insurance subsidiaries	257,791,000	273,297,000
Excess of investments in subsidiaries over underlying net assets at date of investment — at amortized cost	122,614,000	134,970,000
Other assets	188,910,000	224,454,000
	$9,042,342,000	$8,887,023,000

Transamerica Corporation

CONSOLIDATED STATEMENT OF INCOME

Transamerica Corporation and Subsidiaries
Years ended December 31

Revenues	1981	1980	1979
Insurance premiums and other insurance income:			
Life insurance	$1,502,888,000	$1,499,769,000	$1,417,172,000
Property and casualty insurance	698,906,000	698,265,000	675,262,000
Title insurance	84,450,000	87,496,000	107,490,000
Investment income, exclusive of net gains on sales of investments	375,328,000	332,628,000	284,831,000
Finance charges and related income	279,479,000	219,689,000	196,382,000
Equipment leasing revenues	188,957,000	168,328,000	82,005,000
Airline revenues	328,548,000	348,708,000	267,332,000
Sales of manufactured products	436,832,000	379,313,000	328,522,000
Other	260,499,000	225,078,000	216,764,000
Total revenues	4,155,887,000	3,959,274,000	3,575,760,000
Expenses			
Life insurance benefits	1,381,623,000	1,359,965,000	1,289,646,000
Property and casualty insurance losses and loss adjustment expenses	506,187,000	468,449,000	442,748,000
Insurance commissions and other underwriting expenses	536,227,000	518,470,000	459,409,000
Equipment leasing operating and maintenance costs	115,176,000	99,046,000	41,684,000
Airline operating and maintenance costs	273,118,000	287,293,000	231,711,000
Cost of manufactured products sold	307,242,000	273,926,000	231,306,000
Cost of other products and services	151,264,000	166,094,000	149,472,000
Interest and debt expense	248,239,000	201,035,000	133,500,000
Other — principally administrative and general expenses	339,162,000	306,849,000	280,888,000
Total expenses	3,858,238,000	3,681,127,000	3,260,364,000
	297,649,000	278,147,000	315,396,000
Provision for income taxes	75,800,000	58,325,000	103,226,000
Operating income from continuing operations	221,849,000	219,822,000	212,170,000
Other Gains (Losses), After Taxes			
Gain on sale of entertainment subsidiary	140,000,000		
Provision for loss on planned sales of bonds owned by property and casualty insurance subsidiary	(121,871,000)		
Gains on sales of other investments	2,634,000	5,677,000	1,694,000
Operations of discontinued entertainment subsidiary	(18,129,000)	20,142,000	26,600,000
Foreign exchange translation adjustments	(1,147,000)	(662,000)	(262,000)
	1,487,000	25,157,000	28,032,000
Net income	$ 223,336,000	$ 244,979,000	$ 240,202,000
Earnings per share of common stock:			
Operating income from continuing operations	$3.43	$3.36	$3.24
Net income	$3.45	$3.75	$3.66

X. STATEMENT OF CHANGES IN FINANCIAL POSITION

CONSOLIDATED STATEMENT OF CHANGES IN FINANCIAL POSITION

Transamerica Corporation and Subsidiaries
Years ended December 31

Source of Funds	1981	1980	1979
From operations:			
Operating income from continuing operations	$ 221,849,000	$ 219,822,000	$ 212,170,000
Depreciation	117,955,000	102,165,000	66,708,000
Net change in other operating items:			
Accrued liabilities and income taxes	181,954,000	72,053,000	27,455,000
Insurance reserves and claims — net of deferred policy acquisition costs	119,586,000	230,285,000	383,059,000
Insurance premiums, trade and other receivables	(117,176,000)	(60,017,000)	(76,114,000)
Manufacturing inventories	(15,905,000)	(15,847,000)	(17,967,000)
	508,263,000	548,461,000	595,311,000
Other gains (losses)	1,487,000	25,157,000	28,032,000
Provision for loss on planned sales of bonds owned by property and casualty insurance subsidiary	121,871,000		
Net change in operating items of discontinued entertainment subsidiary	52,927,000	(33,826,000)	(24,974,000)
Total from operations	684,548,000	539,792,000	598,369,000
Proceeds from long-term debt financing	526,112,000	438,096,000	568,581,000
Increase in short-term notes and loans payable		194,068,000	90,913,000
Other	15,839,000	(19,579,000)	5,534,000
	$1,226,499,000	$1,152,377,000	$1,263,397,000

Application of Funds			
Dividends	$ 86,626,000	$ 78,409,000	$ 69,532,000
Payment of notes and loans	425,545,000	301,321,000	306,496,000
Addition to property and equipment	306,288,000	362,936,000	205,710,000
Addition to investments, principally of insurance subsidiaries	240,126,000	275,334,000	417,152,000
Purchase of Transamerica Interway Inc.			211,810,000
Increase in finance receivables	111,839,000	92,275,000	137,844,000
Cost of reacquired common stock	37,899,000	10,739,000	22,065,000
Increase in cash and temporary investments	18,176,000	31,363,000	(107,212,000)
	$1,226,499,000	$1,152,377,000	$1,263,397,000

Transamerica Corporation

Note H. Sale of Entertainment Subsidiary

On July 28, 1981, the Corporation sold the outstanding stock of United Artists Corporation, its wholly owned entertainment subsidiary, to Metro-Goldwyn-Mayer Film Co. for $380,000,000 in cash and notes. The following results of operations of United Artists through the date of sale, as well as the gain on sale of $140,000,000, after related taxes of $94,009,000, are included in other gains (losses).

	1981	1980	1979
Revenues	$230,662,000	$424,781,000	$468,887,000
Costs and expenses	269,886,000	398,679,000	420,847,000
Income tax provision (credit)	(21,095,000)	5,960,000	21,440,000
	$ (18,129,000)	$ 20,142,000	$ 26,600,000

11.1. CONAGRA, INC., AND SUBSIDIARIES

Accounting for transactions that affect stockholders' equity, purchase of companies, gain or loss on sale.
(Moderate: 60 minutes)

ConAgra, Inc., conducts operations across the food chain in agriculture, grain, and food. ConAgra manufactures and markets in agricultural chemicals, formula feeds and fertilizers, grain milling and merchandising, poultry products, frozen prepared foods, and seafood.

Study the relevant portions of ConAgra's financial statements.

1. Provide journal entries that would record all transactions affecting the Statement of Common Stockholders' Equity during the year ended May 31, 1981. (The account increased from $100,902,000 to $123,297,000 during this period.) Use "book value" methods.

2. Provide a journal entry that would record and account for all companies purchased in 1981—for a combined value of $74,424,000. (The $10,000,000 will be paid to Banquet Foods sometime in the future and only if certain conditions are met.)

3. Estimate the gain or loss on sale on Property, Plant, and Equipment sold or otherwise disposed during the year ended May 31, 1981. Make any assumptions you consider appropriate (e.g., you may wish to use "other—net" as a plug-item account).

Consolidated Financial Statements, ConAgra, Inc., and Subsidiaries

Consolidated Statements of Earnings

Dollars in thousands except per share amounts

	Fiscal years ended:		
	May 31, 1981	May 25, 1980	May 27, 1979
Revenues			
Net sales	**$1,376,808**	$842,905	$644,830
Other income	**5,193**	4,921	5,596
	1,382,001	847,826	650,426
Costs and Expenses			
Cost of goods sold	**1,220,213**	758,947	568,581
Selling, administrative and general expenses	**99,030**	53,391	39,370
Interest expense (Note 6)	**21,076**	13,382	7,391
Other expense	**3,482**	2,077	710
	1,343,801	827,797	616,052
Income before income taxes	**38,200**	20,029	34,374
Income taxes (Note 4)			
Current	**11,661**	(2,859)	13,657
Deferred	**(532)**	4,373	(317)
	11,129	1,514	13,340
Net income	**27,071**	18,515	21,034
Less preferred dividends	**388**	370	399
Net income available for common stock	**$ 26,683**	$ 18,145	$ 20,635
Income per common and common equivalent share			
Primary	**$ 2.21**	$ 1.55	$ 1.77
Fully diluted	**$ 2.16**	$ 1.50	$ 1.71
Weighted average number of common shares outstanding (000)			
Primary	**12,074**	11,706	11,626
Fully diluted	**12,561**	12,320	12,288

XI. STOCKHOLDERS' EQUITY

Consolidated Balance Sheets

Dollars in thousands

ASSETS	May 31, 1981	May 25, 1980
Current assets		
Cash	$ 26,292	$ 7,504
Receivables, less allowance for doubtful accounts of		
$5,971 and $5,207, respectively	140,377	87,627
Recoverable income taxes (Note 4)	834	8,404
Inventories		
Grain	24,780	32,206
Finished products and in process	150,834	93,605
Raw materials, containers and supplies	16,092	7,954
Advances on purchases	4,813	4,970
	196,519	138,735
Prepaid expenses	6,667	4,057
Total current assets	370,689	246,327
Other assets		
Investments in unconsolidated 50% or less owned		
foreign companies (Note 2)	8,174	3,592
Sundry investments, deposits and noncurrent receivables	4,901	4,980
Total other assets	13,075	8,572
Property, plant and equipment		
Land	6,891	5,380
Buildings, machinery and equipment	145,429	112,651
Furniture and fixtures	3,340	1,929
Autos, trucks, trailers, etc.	3,544	3,317
Construction in progress	4,034	8,105
	163,238	131,382
Less accumulated depreciation	54,704	43,749
Property, plant and equipment, net	108,534	87,633
Unamortized finance expense, etc.	1,245	535
Brands, trademarks and goodwill, at cost,		
less accumulated amortization	6,670	4,481
	$500,213	$347,548

LIABILITIES AND STOCKHOLDERS' EQUITY	May 31, 1981	May 25, 1980
Current liabilities		
Current installments of long-term debt	**$ 3,011**	$ 3,609
Accounts payable and accrued liabilities	**260,252**	163,450
Dividends payable	**2,493**	2,212
Income taxes (Note 4)	**10,104**	3,672
Total current liabilities	**275,860**	172,943
Long-term debt excluding current installments (Note 6)	**89,368**	65,047
Deferred income taxes (Note 4)	**3,012**	2,851
Commitments and contingencies (Notes 10 and 11)		
Preferred stockholders' equity		
Preferred shares subject to mandatory redemption (Notes 5 and 8)	**8,665**	4,470
Preferred shares subject to optional redemption (Notes 5 and 9)	**11**	1,335
Total preferred stockholders' equity	**8,676**	5,805
Common stockholders' equity (Notes 5 and 7)		
Common stock of $5 par value:		
Authorized 20,000,000 shares;		
issued 1981, 12,450,771; 1980, 11,895,784	**62,254**	29,739
Additional paid-in capital	**8**	6,643
Retained earnings	**62,557**	66,042
Less Treasury Stock, at cost:		
Common stock, 194,518 shares	**(1,522)**	(1,522)
Total common stockholders' equity	**123,297**	100,902
	$500,213	$347,548

XI. STOCKHOLDERS' EQUITY

Consolidated Statements of Changes in Financial Position

Dollars in thousands

	Fiscal years ended:		
	May 31, 1981	May 25, 1980	May 27, 1979
Funds provided			
Net income	$ 27,071	$ 18,515	$ 21,034
Items which do not use working capital			
Depreciation and amortization	12,323	7,672	5,928
Increase in noncurrent deferred income taxes	161	983	522
Working capital provided from operations	39,555	27,170	27,484
Proceeds from issuance and assumption of			
long-term debt	46,164	26,171	7,530
Issuance of preferred stock	7,000		
Proceeds from sale of property, plant and equipment	3,216	2,148	895
Fair market value of common stock issued in connection with			
the acquisition of Bow Wow Company, Incorporated			196
Issuance of common stock in connection with			
the senior management incentive plan		641	
Contracts to sell common shares under			
executive stock purchase plan	6	111	
Proceeds from exercise of employee stock options	517	104	112
Issuance of common stock for conversion of			
preferred stock—contra below	4,038	33	307
Total working capital provided	100,496	56,378	36,524
Funds used			
Additions to property, plant and equipment	15,891	22,818	17,589
Increase (decrease) in investment in unconsolidated			
50% or less owned foreign companies	4,582	(8,140)	7,975
Cash dividends	9,237	7,730	6,237
Repayment and current maturities of long-term debt	26,050	4,885	3,660
Redemption of preferred stock	100	26	776
Conversion of preferred stock—contra above	4,038	33	307
Purchase of common stock held in treasury		22	858
Acquisition of businesses, less net current assets			
acquired: 1981, $45,348; 1980, $7,334; 1979, $4,086			
Property, plant and equipment	20,002	7,526	715
Goodwill	835		1,955
Long-term liabilities assumed	(4,207)		
Other, net	2,153	711	2,372
Other items, net	370	724	1,285
Total working capital used	79,051	36,335	43,729
Net increase (decrease) in working capital	$ 21,445	$ 20,043	$ (7,205)
Consisting of			
Cash	$ 18,788	$ (2,300)	$ (6,579)
Receivables	52,750	4,029	39,561
Inventories	57,784	72,215	2,356
Current installments of long-term debt	598	(59)	(680)
Payables and other	(108,475)	(53,842)	(41,863)

Consolidated Statements of Common Stockholders' Equity

Dollars in thousands

	Common Stock	Additional Paid-In Capital	Retained Earnings	Treasury Stock	Total
Balance at May 28, 1978	$19,458	$15,417	$40,460	$ (642)	$ 74,693
Conversion of 6,143 shares of preferred stock into 55,162 shares of common stock	117	193			310
26,990 shares issued in connection with the acquisition of Bow Wow Company, Inc.	45	151			196
27,004 shares issued in connection with employee stock option plan	50	62			112
Three-for-two common stock split, 3,915,804 shares	9,790	(9,790)			
Cost of 102,784 shares of common stock held in treasury				(858)	(858)
Cash dividends:					
Preferred stock, all classes			(387)		(387)
Common stock, $.505 per share			(5,850)		(5,850)
Net income			21,034		21,034
Balance at May 27, 1979	$29,460	$ 6,033	$55,257	$(1,500)	$ 89,250
Conversion of 656 shares of preferred stock into 6,752 shares of common stock	17	16			33
25,124 shares issued in connection with employee stock option plan	63	41			104
Cost of 3,600 shares of common stock held in treasury				(22)	(22)
79,874 shares issued in connection with the senior management incentive plan	199	442			641
Contracts to sell 374,000 shares under executive stock purchase plan		111			111
Cash dividends:					
Preferred stock, all classes			(370)		(370)
Common stock, $.625 per share			(7,360)		(7,360)
Net income			18,515		18,515
Balance at May 25, 1980	$29,739	$ 6,643	$66,042	$(1,522)	$100,902
Conversion of 58,072 shares of preferred stock into 454,026 shares of common stock	1,143	2,895			4,038
100,200 shares issued in connection with employee stock option plan	383	134			517
Two-for-one common stock split, 6,197,685 shares	30,989	(9,670)	(21,319)		
Contracts to sell 10,000 shares under executive stock purchase plan		6			6
Cash dividends:					
Preferred stock, all classes			(400)		(400)
Common stock, $.73 per share			(8,837)		(8,837)
Net income			27,071		27,071
Balance at May 31, 1981	**$62,254**	**$ 8**	**$62,557**	**$(1,522)**	**$123,297**

XI. STOCKHOLDERS' EQUITY

2. Business Combinations

During the years ended May 31, 1981, May 25, 1980 and May 27, 1979, the company, in transactions recorded as purchases, acquired the following:

1981

The operating assets of Oklahoma-Kansas Grain Corporation, a grain and river terminal facility; Hess and Clark, Inc., an agricultural chemical company, and Singleton Packing Corp., a shrimp packing company; and 100 percent of the common stock of Banquet Foods Corporation, a frozen food company; and Interstate Terminals, Inc., a river grain facility; all for cash aggregating $59,250,000 and $7,000,000 of Class C, Series 2,5% preferred stock. The company is also required to pay an additional amount of up to $10,000,000 for Banquet Foods by January 1, 1985 if certain conditions specified in the acquisition agreement are met. In addition, the company acquired 50 percent of the outstanding capital stock of Bioter-Biona, S.A., a food company in Spain, for $8,174,000.

1980

On May 30, 1978, the company acquired a 49 percent interest in United Agri Products, Inc., engaged in the distribution of agricultural chemicals, for $6,038,000 in cash. The company also acquired, for $671,000, an option to purchase the remaining 51 percent interest. On May 28, 1979, the company exercised its option and acquired the remaining 51 percent interest for $7,190,000 in cash. The company is also required to pay an additional amount of up to $6,000,000 on or before June 1, 1983, if certain conditions specified in the acquisition agreement are met.

For the period ended May 27, 1979, the 49 percent investment was recorded as an investment in unconsolidated 50 percent or less owned companies. For the periods beginning after May 27, 1979, the financial position and results of operations of the acquired company are consolidated with ConAgra, Inc.

11.2. NATIONAL TECHNICAL SYSTEMS

Accounting for stock split or stock dividend, computation of primary earnings per share. (Moderate: 45 minutes)

National Technical Systems operates in three principal areas: scientific testing services, vocational schools and computer systems and services, and manufacturing and product development for amplifiers and energy-saving systems.

Study the company's 1980–82 Consolidated Statements of Earnings, 1980–82 Consolidated Statements of Stockholders' Equity, and notes on "Price Ranges of Common Stock" and "Stock Splits to Be Effected in the Form of Stock Dividends."

1. a. How many common shares were outstanding as of April 10, 1981, the date of record of the 66⅔ percent stock split?

   b. How many common shares were outstanding *after* February 5, 1982, assuming no other equity transactions took place between year-end and that date?

2. As of January 31, 1982, the firm had granted 262,000 options to purchase common stock, which were expected to provide cash proceeds of $382,000. Assume that the split shares could be purchased on the open market at $2.00 (on the average). Prove that primary earnings per share are $0.34 for 1982.

3. Using the 1981 and 1982 common stock price ranges, comment on the apparent economic impact of the April 10, 1981 (first-quarter fiscal year 1982) stock split.

CONSOLIDATED STATEMENTS OF EARNINGS
Years Ended January 31, 1982, 1981 and 1980

	1982	1981	1980
Revenues	$18,175,000	13,217,000	11,929,000
Cost of revenues	12,116,000	8,817,000	7,554,000
Gross profit	6,059,000	4,400,000	4,375,000
Selling, general and administrative expenses	4,780,000	3,702,000	3,213,000
Operating income	1,279,000	698,000	1,162,000
Other income (expense):			
Interest expense, net, less capitalized interest of $270,000 in 1982 (note 5)	(592,000)	(434,000)	(227,000)
Gain on dispositions of property and operations (notes 3 and 8)	314,000	208,000	112,000
	(278,000)	(226,000)	(115,000)
Earnings before income taxes	1,001,000	472,000	1,047,000
Income taxes (note 6)	294,000	93,000	480,000
Net earnings	$ 707,000	379,000	567,000
Earnings per common share after giving effect to stock split (note 2):			
Primary	$.34	.19	.26
Fully diluted	.33	.19	.26

CONSOLIDATED STATEMENTS OF STOCKHOLDERS' EQUITY
Years Ended January 31, 1982, 1981 and 1980

	Common Stock		Additional paid-in capital	Retained earnings	Total stockholders' equity
	Number of shares (note 2)	Amount			
Balance at January 31, 1979	844,000	$ 84,000	1,018,000	1,346,000	2,448,000
Net earnings	—	—	—	567,000	567,000
Purchase and retirement of common shares	(106,000)	(10,000)	(311,000)		(321,000)
Balance at January 31, 1980	738,000	74,000	707,000	1,913,000	2,694,000
Net earnings	—	—	—	379,000	379,000
Purchase and retirement of common shares	(6,000)	(1,000)	(18,000)	—	(19,000)
Balance at January 31, 1981	732,000	73,000	689,000	2,292,000	3,054,000
Net earnings	—	—	—	707,000	707,000
Stock options exercised	33,000	3,000	56,000	—	59,000
Stock split effected in the form of a stock dividend	495,000	50,000	(50,000)	—	—
Balance at January 31, 1982	1,260,000	$126,000	695,000	2,999,000	3,820,000

National Technical Systems

Price Ranges of Common Stock Fiscal Years Ended January 31, 1981 and 1982

The Company's Common Stock is traded in the over-the-counter market under the symbol "NTSC". The table of quotations below reflects inter-dealer prices without retail markups, markdowns or commissions, and does not necessarily reflect actual transactions during the Company's fiscal years ended January 31, 1982 and January 31, 1981.

1981*

	BID		ASKED	
	High	Low	High	Low
1st Quarter	2⅛	1¾	2½	2⅛
2nd Quarter	2	1¾	2¼	2
3rd Quarter	2⅛	1¾	2⅜	2
4th Quarter	1⅞	1¾	2⅛	2

1982

	BID		ASKED	
	High	Low	High	Low
1st Quarter*	3¼	1⅞	3⅝	2⅛
2nd Quarter	5	3⅛	5½	3⅝
3rd Quarter	4½	3⅝	5	4
4th Quarter	4⅜	3⅜	4⅝	3⅝

* Adjusted for a 66⅔ percent stock split effected in the form of a stock dividend on April 30, 1981. Prices have not been adjusted for the February 5, 1982 stock split.

(2) Stock Splits To Be Effected in the Form of Stock Dividends

On March 31, 1981, the Board of Directors approved a stock split to be effected in the form of a 66⅔% stock dividend of the Company's common stock to shareholders of record on April 10, 1981 and paid on April 30, 1981.

On December 14, 1981, the Board of Directors approved a stock split to be effected in the form of a 60% stock dividend of the Company's common stock to shareholders of record on January 18, 1982. The dividend is payable on February 5, 1982. Net earnings per share in the consolidated statements of earnings, stock options (note 8) and quarterly net earnings per share (note 10) have been restated to give effect to the stock splits.

11.3. PRETENDIX CORPORATION*

Computation of primary and fully diluted earnings per share. (Difficult: 75 minutes)

Pretendix Corporation's senior vice-president and treasurer, Mary Framingham, is at her wits' end. Her master's in business administration from a well-known business school in the East has enabled her to pull together all of Pretendix's figures for 1977 and 1978 except one—earnings per share applicable to common shares on a *fully diluted basis*. She knows she could call her friend William Golligee in head office, but since he is very busy working on a new merger plan with investment bankers, First Morgan Bros., she decides not to do so. Instead, she telephones her old friend Dave Purdy, who is currently enrolled at a graduate management school in the West.

"Dave, old chap, I'm having a little spot of bother with that nasty little fully diluted earnings-per-share calculation. How about a little help, for old time's sake?" Dave, a rather obliging fellow, responds: "OK, Mary, I'll do it, but this is the last time. Send me your financials and any other pertinent information by express mail and I'll get the numbers back to you by the end of the week."

So Mary collects the 1977–78 Earnings Statement, Consolidated Balance Sheet, Statement of Changes in Financial Position, Statement of Shareholders' Equity, and relevant notes on financing, long-term obligations, and shareholders' equity. Mary also includes a list of additional data that she thinks Dave will want to use in the calculations. The list includes the following:

---

*Pretendix Corporation's financial statements are those of a major U.S. corporation. While the various simplifying assumptions in this case mean that the actual company used different numbers in computing fully diluted earnings per share, the use of the *Opinion No. 15* procedures in this situation produces an identical result.

1. Average price at which options are exercisable, $11.10

2. Bank prime interest rate at date of issue (assume that all debentures were issued at par):
   - 6¾% convertible subordinated debentures, 8 percent
   - 8½% sinking fund debentures, 13 percent
   - 5% convertible subordinated debentures, 7 percent

3. Average market price of common stock, $15.56

   Year-end market price of common stock, $15.56

4. All payments to reduce long-term obligations took place on February 1, 1978 (i.e., the beginning of the fiscal year).

5. Current installments on long-term obligations relate to real estate subsidiaries' loans (not operating companies' debentures).

6. Use a 46 percent tax rate.

Dave receives the material next day. In order to get the job done in the minimum time, he uses the following approach. He first proves that primary earnings per share are $1.72 in order to familiarize himself with the figures. He then computes 1978 fully diluted earnings per share according to the Accounting Principles Board *Opinion No. 15*, "Earnings per share" (1969).

REQUIRED:

1. Prove that primary earnings per share were $1.72 in 1978.

2. Why are the stock options apparently not included in the calculation in part 1 above?

3. Compute the number of shares to be used in the denominator of your fully diluted earnings-per-share calculation (for 1978 only).

4. Compute the net earnings number after adjusting for common stock equivalents and other dilutive securities (for 1978 only).

5. Compute 1978 fully diluted earnings per share as part 4 divided by part 3.

PRETENDIX CORPORATION

Consolidated Earnings

Years ended January 28, 1979 and January 29, 1978
(in thousands except per share amounts)

	1978	1977*
Sales	$4,658,409	$4,035,369
Cost of goods sold	3,543,460	3,081,524
	1,114,949	953,845
Expenses —		
Selling, general and administrative	896,074	766,309
Depreciation and amortization	44,191	40,087
Interest, net of interest income of $5,649 and $2,400	18,500	18,542
	958,765	824,938
Earnings before income taxes	156,184	128,907
Income taxes	75,784	62,432
Net earnings	$ 80,400	$ 66,475
Earnings per share, adjusted for 3% stock dividend in 1978:		
Primary	$ 1.72	$ 1.41
Fully diluted	$ 1.64	$ 1.34

*Restated for pooling of interests and change in accounting for leases.
See financial review on pages 15 through 22.

Financial Review 1978

The statements compare our fiscal years 1978 and 1977 which are the 52 week periods ended January 28, 1979 and January 29, 1978. In the statements, dollar amounts are shown in thousands, but for easier reading in the financial review, they are shown in millions.

ACQUISITIONS

During the second quarter we acquired all of the outstanding shares of Prtdx Distributing Company, operator of family department stores and auto supply outlets, for 3,156,499 Prtdx common shares. Because this transaction was accounted for as a pooling of interests, the financial statements are presented as though PDC had been a subsidiary for both years. Sales and net earnings of PDC were $121.2 million and $6.0 million, respectively, for 1977 and $30.6 million and $1.1 million, respectively, for the three months of 1978 prior to acquisition.

In July 1978 we purchased all of the assets and liabilities of Pdx Packing Company, a manufacturer of luncheon meats, for 15,800 convertible preference shares. The net assets acquired are not material in the consolidated financial statements of Prtdx.

On March 1, 1979 we acquired substantially all of the assets and liabilities of PAGs Wholesale Company, operator of 48 supermarkets in western N.Z. The cost of the acquired company was $26 million consisting of $9 million in cash and 225,641 convertible preference shares. The acquisition will be accounted for as a purchase. Accordingly, the results of operations of PAG, Inc. will be included with those of Prtdx from the date of acquisition. Revenues and net earnings of PAG, Inc. for its year ended December 30, 1978 were $254 million and $3.5 million, respectively.

EARNINGS

Earnings per share for 1978 increased 22% over those of 1977 as restated for the pooling of interests and retroactive application of Financial Accounting Standards Board Statement No. 13, "Accounting for Leases." Primary earnings per share represent net earnings after preferred and preference dividends, divided by the weighted average number of common shares outstanding — 46,691,854 for 1978 and 46,379,267 for 1977 after restatement for the pooling and adjustments for stock dividends. Fully diluted earnings per share give effect to shares that may be issued for convertible securities and stock options where the effect is to dilute earnings per share.

INCOME TAXES

In addition to federal income taxes, Prtdx pays taxes on income to the various states in which it operates. Deferred income taxes result primarily from our use of accelerated depreciation and actual rentals for tax purposes, in contrast with straight-line

XI. STOCKHOLDERS' EQUITY

Consolidated Balance Sheet

At January 28, 1979 and January 29, 1978
(in thousands)

ASSETS	1978	1977*
Current assets:		
Cash and short-term securities	$ 37,541	$ 28,029
Receivables..	35,267	29,457
Inventories	475,584	388,760
Prepaid expenses and supplies	24,961	21,601
Reimbursable costs of property under development...................	6,950	39,594
Total current assets...	580,303	507,441
Property and equipment at depreciated cost:		
Operating companies	211,855	192,213
Real estate subsidiaries	111,969	69,856
	323,824	262,069
Property under capital leases, less $76,638 and $72,339 accumulated amortization	112,393	110,917
Licenses, receivables and other assets..............................	11,764	10,641
Excess of cost over net assets acquired	14,562	14,687
	$1,042,846	$905,755

*Restated for pooling of interests and change in accounting for leases.
See financial review on pages 15 through 22.

depreciation and capital lease amortization in the financial statements.

Other than the investment tax credit, the only significant difference between the federal statutory tax rate and the federal provision is the deduction allowed for state taxes on income.

PROVISION FOR INCOME TAXES

	1978		1977	
	Amount	% *	Amount	% *
Federal				
Current	$68.0	43.6	$58.5	45.4
Deferred	2.0	1.3	(1.0)	(.8)
Investment tax credits	(5.2)	(3.4)	(4.0)	(3.1)
Total federal	64.8	41.5	53.5	41.5
State				
Current	10.7	6.9	9.1	7.1
Deferred	.3	.1	(.2)	(.2)
Total state	11.0	7.0	8.9	6.9
Total income taxes	$75.8	48.5	$62.4	48.4

*Percent of earnings before income taxes

CAPITAL EXPENDITURES

Expenditures by operating companies for new facilities, equipment and improvements amounted to $57.2 million in 1978 compared with $52.1 million in 1977. In addition, our real estate subsidiaries invested $45.4 million in new properties during 1978, up from $8.8 million in 1977. Our investment in property and equipment at each yearend was as follows:

	Operating companies		Real estate subsidiaries	
	1978	1977	1978	1977
Buildings	$ 13.8	$ 12.7	$ 94.1	$ 57.8
Leasehold costs and improvements	48.0	42.5		
Fixtures and equipment	338.4	300.0	11.0	6.2
	400.2	355.2	105.1	64.0
Less - Accumulated depreciation and amortization	192.4	167.1	18.4	15.2
	207.8	188.1	86.7	48.8
Land	4.1	4.1	25.2	21.1
	$211.9	$192.2	$111.9	$ 69.9

The real estate subsidiaries are wholly owned by Prtdx, and their properties are leased to Prtdx. The properties have been financed through various institutional lenders with mortgages equal to the original investment and are pledged to secure the mortgage notes payable. This method of financing allows Prtdx to own selected properties with no initial down payment. At January 28, 1979, reimbursable costs of property under development include $1.7 million that will be held by consolidated real estate subsidiaries.

Consolidated Changes in Financial Position

Years ended January 28, 1979 and January 29, 1978
(in thousands)

SOURCES OF WORKING CAPITAL	1978	1977*
Operations:		
Net earnings	$ 80,400	$ 66,475
Expenses not affecting working capital:		
Depreciation and amortization	44,191	40,087
Deferred income taxes	4,329	1,720
	128,920	108,282
Issuance of preference shares	1,185	
Disposition of property and equipment	4,326	3,393
Disposition of property under capital leases	314	317
Conversion of convertible securities and exercise of stock options	9,079	1,170
Long-term borrowings:		
Operating companies	948	6,532
Real estate subsidiaries	45,365	8,761
Capital lease obligations	9,315	10,909
Total sources	199,452	139,364
USES OF WORKING CAPITAL		
Cash dividends	37,576	30,696
Additions to property and equipment:		
Operating companies	57,184	52,100
Real estate subsidiaries	45,365	8,761
Additions to property under capital leases	9,315	10,909
Reduction of long-term obligations	12,429	8,624
Reduction of capital lease obligations	6,357	6,369
Conversion of convertible securities	7,020	500
Redemption of preferred shares	39	14,377
Increase in licenses, receivables and other assets	1,245	146
Total uses	176,530	132,482
Working capital increase	$ 22,922	$ 6,882

ANALYSIS OF WORKING CAPITAL CHANGES

	1978	1977*
Increase (decrease) in current assets:		
Cash and short-term securities	$ 9,512	$(5,375)
Receivables	5,810	(1,671)
Inventories	86,824	36,254
Prepaid expenses and supplies	3,360	3,564
Reimbursable costs of property under development	(32,644)	20,336
	72,862	53,108
(Increase) decrease in current liabilities:		
Accounts payable	(25,994)	(20,409)
Current notes payable	(2,318)	(3,895)
Current instalments on long-term obligations	402	1,175
Current portion of capital lease obligations	(107)	(421)
Accrued liabilities	(24,138)	(19,831)
Accrued income taxes	2,215	(2,845)
	(49,940)	(46,226)
Working capital increase	22,922	6,882
Working capital beginning of year	167,499	160,617
Working capital end of year	$190,421	$167,499

*Restated for pooling of interests and change in accounting for leases.

XI. STOCKHOLDERS' EQUITY

LIABILITIES AND SHAREHOLDERS' EQUITY

	1978	1977*
Current liabilities:		
Accounts payable	$ 213,938	$187,944
Current notes payable	6,213	3,895
Current instalments on long-term obligations	3,632	4,034
Current portion of capital lease obligations	5,939	5,832
Accrued liabilities	131,048	106,910
Accrued income taxes	29,112	31,327
Total current liabilities	389,882	339,942
Long-term obligations - instalments due after one year:		
Operating companies	59,937	72,172
Real estate subsidiaries	113,476	71,775
Capital lease obligations	129,627	126,669
Deferred income taxes	15,573	11,244
Contingencies - Litigation		
Shareholders' equity:		
Preferred and preference shares, authorized 100,000 shares, $50 par value; 1,000,000 shares without par value (liquidation value $3,316 and $4,426)	2,921	4,426
Common shares, authorized 100,000,000 shares, $1.25 par value	58,922	56,474
Capital in excess of par value of shares issued	156,303	132,666
Retained earnings	116,205	90,387
Total shareholders' equity	334,351	283,953
	$1,042,846	$905,755

FINANCING

In addition to working capital supplied by operations, Prtdx provides for its expansion program through various short-term and long-term borrowings.

Short-Term Borrowing

The maximum monthend borrowing was $7.4 million during 1978 and $19.4 million during 1977. Average borrowings outstanding were not significant during either year; the average interest rate was 9.8% in 1978 and 7.7% in 1977. During 1978 and 1977 Prtdx Distributing Company maintained a $4.5 million line of credit, which it has now terminated.

Long-Term Obligations

The 1978 year end balances, excluding $3.6 million current installments, are:

Operating companies:	
6¾% convertible subordinated debentures, due in 2000	$ 35.8
8½% sinking fund debentures, due in 1996	21.0
5% convertible subordinated debentures, due in 1993	.3
Other	2.8
	$ 59.9
Real estate subsidiaries:	
5⅛% to 9¾% mortgage notes	$113.5

The 6¾% convertible subordinated debentures were issued in July 1975 to provide funds for our capital expenditure program. They are callable at prices decreasing from 105.40% in 1979 to 100% after July 15, 1995 and require annual sinking fund deposits of $2.2 million beginning July 15, 1986. The debentures are convertible into 71 common shares for each $1 thousand of principal. The 8½% sinking fund debentures, which were issued in 1971, are callable at prices decreasing from 105.10% of face value in 1979 to 100% in 1991 and require annual sinking fund deposits of $1.25 million through 1996. The 5% convertible debentures, which were issued in 1968, are convertible into 123 common shares for each $1 thousand of principal and are callable at prices decreasing from 102.75% of face value in 1979 to 100% in 1990.

Required sinking fund deposits and principal payments on long-term debt in each of the four years after 1979 are:

Fiscal year	Operating companies	Real estate subsidiaries
1980	$1.9	$3.1
1981	1.7	3.3
1982	1.6	3.5
1983	1.5	3.8

Consolidated Shareholders' Equity

(shares and amounts in thousands)

	Preferred and preference shares		Common shares		Capital in excess of par value of shares issued	Retained earnings
	Shares	Amount	Shares	Amount		
Balance, January 30, 1977:						
As previously reported	95	$ 4,773	40,786	$50,982	$118,698	$ 77,972
Adjustment to reflect 1978 pooling of interests	143	14,338	3,156	3,946	(800)	1,358
Adjustment to reflect lease capitalization.						(9,578)
As restated	238	19,111	43,942	54,928	117,898	69,752
Net earnings for 1977*						66,475
Dividends:						
Preferred and preference						(200)
Common —						
Cash, 71¢ a share						(29,565)
Common shares, 3% (at approximate market value)			1,134	1,418	13,726	(15,144)
By subsidiary before pooling						(931)
Redemption of preferred shares by subsidiary before pooling.	(143)	(14,338)				
Conversion of convertible securities and exercise of stock options	(7)	(347)	103	128	1,042	
Balance, January 29, 1978	88	4,426	45,179	56,474	132,666	90,387
Net earnings for 1978						80,400
Dividends:						
Preferred and preference						(168)
Common —						
Cash, 83¢ a share						(37,408)
Common shares, 3% (at approximate market value)			1,262	1,578	15,428	(17,006)
Issuance of preference shares for Regal acquisition	16	1,185				
Conversion of convertible securities and exercise of stock options	(54)	(2,690)	696	870	8,209	
Balance, January 28, 1979	50	$ 2,921	47,137	$58,922	$156,303	$116,205

*Restated for pooling of interests and change in accounting for leases.

SHAREHOLDERS' EQUITY

Preferred and Preference Shares, issued in current and prior years' acquisitions, are entitled to one vote each and substantially all are convertible into common shares; 15,800 are redeemable at $100 a share and all others at $50 a share after various stipulated dates. If all conversion privileges are exercised, 181,023 additional common shares will be issued.

Stock Option Plan: In May 1978 shareholders approved a stock option plan for employees. (Under the 1969 qualified stock option plan no additional options could be granted after December 31, 1978). Under the 1978 plan, options for 2,500,000 common shares may be granted. Options have been granted to employees under both plans to purchase common shares at a price not less than 100% of the fair market value at date of grant. Options may not be exercised within two years from the date of grant; expire five years (1969 plan) and seven years (1978 plan) from the date of grant; and terminate, except to a limited extent in the event of retirement or death of the optionee, upon termination of employment. The 1978 plan provides that the Management Compensation Committee of the Board of Directors, at its discretion, may settle the whole or any part of an exercisable instalment of an option granted under the 1978 plan by offering payment in common shares, or in common shares and cash, in exchange for the surrender of such instalment or partial instalment. No more than one half of any settlement offer may be in cash. The amount of any settlement offered shall be the lesser of the option price or the excess of the fair market value of the shares over the option price. Charges to compensation expense for the estimated amount which will be paid in future years to employees who elect to settle options amounted to $0.5 million during 1978.

STOCK OPTION ACTIVITY	1978	1977
Options outstanding at beginning of year	1,076,922	1,142,080
Adjustment for 3% stock dividend	30,030	30,873
Granted at $14.75 to $15.38 per share in 1978 and $13.23 to $15.29 per share in 1977	612,350	141,850
Exercised at $7.11 to $14.02 in 1978 and $7.11 to $15.91 in 1977	(204,293)	(61,434)
Terminated	(84,929)	(176,447)
Options outstanding at end of year	1,430,080	1,076,922

Of the options outstanding at the end of 1978, 431,267 were exercisable at $7.11 to $15.10 per share. Options for 1,897,650 shares are available for future grants.

At January 28, 1979, 4,186,895 authorized but unissued common shares were reserved for issuance upon conversion of convertible securities and exercise of stock options outstanding.

LONG-TERM LEASES

Most of our stores and some of our other facilities are leased from outside parties. Many of the leases have renewal options for periods ranging from five to thirty years. Some give us the option to buy the property at certain times during the initial lease term for approximately its estimated fair market value at that time, and some require Prtdx to pay taxes and insurance on the leased property.

In 1978 Prtdx changed its accounting for leases to conform with the provisions of Financial Accounting Statement No. 13 (FAS 13), "Accounting for Leases", and restated prior years' financial statements. Under the new method, leases defined as "capital leases" by FAS 13 are recorded as an asset and the related liability as a long-term obligation.

The accounting change decreased 1978 net earnings by $0.8 million and previously reported 1977 net earnings by the same amount. Retained earnings for years prior to 1977 were reduced $9.6 million by the retroactive application of FAS 13.

Future minimum lease payments under capital and operating leases as of January 28, 1979 are as follows:

Fiscal year	Operating leases	Capital leases
1979	$ 44.4	$ 17.8
1980	43.1	17.4
1981	41.7	16.6
1982	40.3	16.1
1983	39.2	15.7
Thereafter	484.6	209.9
Total minimum rent	$693.3	293.5
Executory costs		(1.8)
Imputed interest		(156.1)
Present value of net minimum lease payments including $5.9 million classified as current portion of capital lease obligations		$135.6

RENT EXPENSE	1978	1977
Minimum rent under operating leases	$46.7	$39.9
Additional rent based on sales under all leases	9.8	7.6
	$56.5	$47.5

PENSION PLANS

Prtdx pays for various retirement plans covering most employees who are under collective bargaining agreements.

We also have trusteed, non-contributory pension plans covering most other employees. Costs for these plans are determined by independent actuaries. The amount included in expense was $3.3 million in 1978 and $2.6 million in 1977.

INCENTIVE COMPENSATION PLANS

Prtdx has incentive compensation plans for store management and other management personnel covering more than 3,000 employees. Provision for payments to be made under the plans is based on pretax earnings in excess of a specified return on capital employed in Prtdx operations. The aggregate provision under both plans was $13 million in 1978 and $12 million in 1977.

SEGMENT INFORMATION

Intersegment sales are not material. Entering into the determination of pretax earnings are general corporate expenses and net interest expense arising from general corporate debt and investments totaling $2.6 million in 1978 and $6.3 million in 1977. These expenses are allocated to food stores, department stores, specialty stores and automotive based on sales or assets employed, according to the nature of the expense. These expenses are not allocated to the fabric and restaurant subsidiaries.

12.1. RELIANCE ELECTRIC COMPANY*

Ratio analysis, projection of future cash flow, calculation of present value of assets and stockholders' equity, efficient markets hypothesis. (Moderate: 120 minutes)

This case uses ratio analysis to address certain valuation issues related to the late-1979 merger between the Reliance Electric Company and Exxon Corporation. Specifically, Reliance's 1978 financial statements are analyzed in order to derive accounting data relevant to an independent valuation of Reliance's common stock.

RELEVANT BACKGROUND

Although the first news of a possible merger came on May 18, 1979, it was not until May 25, 1979, that Exxon (through a subsidiary called Enco Corporation) announced its intention to make a cash tender offer of $72.00 per share for Reliance's common stock and $202.72 per share for the Series A preferred stock. The closing common stock prices for Reliance were $34.50 and $48.25 on May 17, 1979 and May 24, 1979, respectively. By November 2, 1979, the price had risen to $69.50 per share.

Exxon's reason for seeking to acquire Reliance was that it needed manufacturing and marketing expertise to fully develop and exploit a new alternating current synthesizer that would supposedly revolutionize the industry for electric motors, producing—among other things—massive energy savings.

Study Reliance's 1977–78 Consolidated Balance Sheets and the Five-Year Financial Summary (from 1974 to 1978).

---

*David Bauer, Royee Chen, Kevin Fong, Judith Jones, and Alison Kirby assisted in the preparation of this case.

1. Calculate:

   a. Percentage growth in Earnings Applicable to Common Stock for 1976–77 and 1977–78.

   b. Dividend payout ratio for 1977 and 1978 (based on primary earnings per share).

   c. Percentage growth in Net Sales for 1976–77 and 1977–78.

   d. Ratio of Earnings before Income Taxes plus Interest Expense to Sales for the years 1977 and 1978.

   e. Ratio of Actual Taxes Paid to Earnings before Income Taxes (assume that Actual Taxes Paid equals Income Tax Expense less Change in Deferred Income Tax liability) for 1978 only.

   f. Ratio of 1976 and 1977 Capital Expenditures (net of Depreciation) to Change in Sales for 1977 and 1978, respectively.

   g. Ratio of Change in Working Capital (Current Assets less Current Liabilities) to Change in Sales for 1977 and 1978.

   h. Ratio of Common Stock Price (high) to Fully Diluted Earnings per Share for 1977 and 1978.

2. Use the information derived in part 1 to compute the cash flow for periods $t = 1,2,....,10$ according to the following formula (period $1 = 1979$):

$$C_t = S_{t-1} (1 + g)(p)(1 - T) - (S_t - S_{t-1})(f + w)$$

   where

   C_t = cash flow for period t
   S_{t-1} = net sales for period $t - 1$
   g = ratio (c), based on 1978 data
   p = ratio (d), based on 1978 data
   T = ratio (e), based on 1978 data
   f = ratio (f), based on 1978 data
   w = ratio (g), based on 1978 data

3. a. Compute the present value of cash flows $C_1, C_2,...,C_{10}$ discounted at an assumed rate of 12 percent. Assume that the net cash flows are received at the end of each year.

   b. Assume that Year 10 operating earnings after taxes [i.e., $OE_{10} = S_9 (1 + g)(p)(1 - T)$] will continue indefinitely at a constant amount. Compute the present value of operating earnings $OE_{11},...,OE_\infty$ assuming a discount rate of 12 percent. (Note: $OE_{10} = OE_{11}$.)

4. Combine the present values in parts 3a and 3b and, with appropriate subtractions for debt (at book value), calculate the present value of one share of the outstanding common stock of the Reliance Company.[1]

5. Use the information derived in part 1 above to compute dividends per share (D_t) for periods $t = 1,2,...,5$ plus a terminal per share price at the end of period 5 (TP_5), where

$D_t = E_t \times$ (dividend payout = ratio (b) for 1978, assume constant)

$E_t =$ earnings applicable to common for period t divided by the number of common shares outstanding at year-end (assume constant at 15,401,000 shares)

$E_t = E_{t-1} \times$ (earnings growth = ratio (a) for 1978, assume constant)

$TP_5 = E_5 \times$ (terminal price-earnings ratio = ratio (h) for 1978, assume constant)

6. Compute the present value of the sum of dividends per share, D_t, for $t = 1,...,5$ plus terminal stock price (TP_5), assuming a discount rate of 14 percent.[2]

7. What discount rate makes the present value of future dividends plus terminal stock price equal to (a) $34.50 and (b) $72.00?

---

[1]The steps taken in parts 2, 3, and 4 are in essence an application of the discounted-cash-flow equity valuation model. See, for example, A. Rappaport, "Strategic Analysis for More Profitable Acquisitions," *Harvard Business Review*, July–August 1979, pp. 99–110.

[2]The steps taken in parts 5, 6, and 7 are in essence an application of a dividend/earnings equity valuation model. See, for example, D. F. Hawkins and W. J. Campbell, *Equity Valuation: Models, Analysis, and Implications* (New York: Financial Executives Research Foundation, 1978), Chap. 3.

Consolidated Balance Sheets

RELIANCE ELECTRIC

	Year Ended Oct. 31	
	1978	1977
	(Thousands of Dollars)	
ASSETS		
CURRENT ASSETS		
Cash	**$ 10,405**	$ 10,123
Short-term investments	**30,044**	43,570
Trade accounts receivable	**175,437**	144,608
Inventories	**189,065**	159,629
Deferred taxes	**19,714**	13,907
TOTAL CURRENT ASSETS	**424,665**	371,837
INVESTMENTS AND OTHER ASSETS		
Affiliated companies	**3,503**	2,938
Costs of businesses over net assets acquired	**7,572**	8,157
Deposits and deferred items	**15,177**	14,832
	26,252	25,927
PROPERTY, PLANT AND EQUIPMENT		
Land	**8,383**	7,450
Buildings	**82,892**	76,575
Machinery and equipment	**213,071**	187,264
	304,346	271,289
Less allowances for depreciation	**142,015**	127,406
	162,331	143,883
	$613,248	$541,647
LIABILITIES AND STOCKHOLDERS' EQUITY		
CURRENT LIABILITIES		
Notes payable	**$ 4,084**	$ 2,304
Trade accounts payable	**49,751**	45,417
Compensation and employee benefits	**38,122**	29,149
Other liabilities and accrued items	**47,477**	37,208
Customer advances	**14,593**	12,120
Income taxes	**13,626**	21,121
Current maturities of long-term debt	**1,009**	1,431
TOTAL CURRENT LIABILITIES	**168,662**	148,750
LONG-TERM DEBT	**99,395**	94,910
OTHER LONG-TERM LIABILITIES	**7,971**	6,945
DEFERRED INCOME TAXES	**13,167**	9,637
STOCKHOLDERS' EQUITY	**324,053**	281,405
	$613,248	$541,647

Five Year Financial Summary

RELIANCE ELECTRIC

(Dollars in thousands, where applicable)

			Year Ended October 31		
	1978	1977	1976	1975	1974
Statements of Consolidated Earnings*					
Net sales	$ 96,264	$829,139	$712,007	$680,384	$624,930
Costs and expenses:					
Cost of products sold	657,681	564,254	485,477	478,449	447,661
Selling, administrative and general expenses	158,040	134,437	118,079	112,483	100,223
Depreciation	19,548	16,698	14,031	12,107	9,898
Interest expense	8,577	8,124	8,772	9,082	7,987
	843,846	723,513	626,359	612,121	565,769
EARNINGS BEFORE INCOME TAXES	122,418	105,626	85,648	68,263	59,161
Income taxes	57,770	52,110	41,893	31,910	27,420
NET EARNINGS	64,648	53,516	43,755	36,353	31,741
Dividend requirements on Serial Preferred Stock	(1,081)	(1,861)	(3,359)	(4,527)	(4,631)
NET EARNINGS APPLICABLE TO COMMON STOCK	$ 63,567	$ 51,655	$ 40,396	$ 31,826	$ 27,110
Net earnings per common share:					
Primary	$ 4.18	$ 3.63	$ 3.26	$ 2.87	$ 2.55
Fully diluted	3.96	3.32	2.72	2.32	2.07
Cash dividends per common share	1.40	1.15	1.025	.875	.80

*Years prior to 1977 restated for pooling of interests.

315

		Year Ended October 31			
	1978	1977	1976	1975	1974
Financial Position—historical					
Current Assets	$ **424,665**	$371,837	$311,163	$288,401	$269,496
Current Liabilities	**168,662**	148,750	124,420	110,669	141,980
Working Capital	**256,003**	223,087	186,743	177,732	127,516
Current Ratio	**2.52**	2.50	2.50	2.61	1.90
Long-term Debt	**99,395**	94,910	92,304	92,341	52,988
Stockholders' Equity	**324,053**	281,405	222,037	192,501	168,177
Debt to Total Capital	**23.5%**	25.2%	29.4%	32.4%	24.0%
Property, Plant & Equipment—Net	**162,331**	143,883	119,861	107,811	93,544
Total Assets	**613,248**	541,647	454,473	409,435	375,702
Per Share Common Stock Data—historical					
Primary Earnings	$ **4.18**	$ 3.63	$ 3.60	$ 3.20	$ 2.67
Fully Diluted Earnings	**3.96**	3.32	2.92	2.48	2.10
Dividends Paid	**1.40**	1.15	1.025	.875	.80
Dividends to Fully Diluted Earnings	**35.4%**	34.6%	35.1%	35.3%	38.1%
Stockholders' Equity	**20.91**	19.04	17.87	18.54	16.67
Stock Price (Range) (High–Low)	**$41–27⅜**	$35½–29¼	$35–18	$18⅝–10¼	$23⅝–9¼
Other Items—historical					
Incoming Orders	**$1,048,000**	$869,000	$671,000	$566,000	$721,000
Order Backlog	**$ 292,000**	$221,000	$214,000	$222,000	$315,000
Product Development and Application Engineering	$ **36,541**	$ 30,290	$ 26,532	$ 24,446	$ 21,706
Capital Expenditures	$ **33,552**	$ 33,434	$ 24,269	$ 23,155	$ 23,726
Number of Employees—Worldwide	**21,717**	20,416	19,454	17,585	20,069
Number of Stockholders	**14,035**	14,401	14,607	16,785	15,639
Number of Common Shares Outstanding at Year-end (thousands)	**15,401**	14,556	12,044	9,582	9,177

A: ASSIGNMENT OF CASES TO CHAPTERS OF SELECTED TEXTBOOKS

1. Paul Danos and Eugene A. Imhoff, Jr., *Intermediate Accounting*. Englewood Cliffs, N.J.: Prentice-Hall, 1983.

Text Chapter	Appropriate Cases	Text Chapter	Appropriate Cases
1	1.2, 1.3	14	9.1–9.9
2	1.1	15	7.1–7.3
3	1.4, 1.5	16	6.4
4	1.6	17	8.1–8.7
5	5.6	18	6.1–6.3
6	5.2, 5.3	19	7.4
7	2.1	20/21	11.1, 11.2
8	2.2, 2.3	22	11.3
9	2.4	23	3.5
10	2.5, 2.6	24	5.4, 5.5
11	3.1, 3.2	25	10.1–10.5
12	3.3, 3.4	26	5.1
13	4.1–4.6	27	12.1

2. Charles T. Horngren, *Introduction to Financial Accounting*, 2nd ed. Englewood Cliffs, N.J.: Prentice-Hall, 1984.

Text Chapter	Appropriate Cases	Text Chapter	Appropriate Cases
1	1.1–1.3	9	3.1–3.4, 4.2, 4.4–4.6
2	1.4	10	3.5, 6.1–6.5, 7.1–7.4
3	4.1, 4.3	11	11.1–11.3
4	2.3	12	9.1–9.8
5	1.5	13	8.1–8.7
6	2.2	14	2.1, 5.1–5.6
7	2.4–2.6	15	1.6, 10.1–10.3
8	—	16	10.4, 10.5, 12.1

3. Michael H. Granof, *Financial Accounting: Principles and Issues*, 2nd ed. Englewood Cliffs, N.J.: Prentice-Hall, 1980.

Text Chapter	Appropriate Cases	Text Chapter	Appropriate Cases
1	1.2, 1.3	9	3.1–3.5, 4.2, 4.4–4.6
2	1.1, 1.4	10	6.1–6.5, 7.1–7.4, 8.1–8.7
3	1.5	11/12	11.1–11.3
4	4.1	13	9.1–9.8
5	2.3, 4.3	14	1.6, 10.1–10.3
6	2.1, 5.6	15	10.4, 10.5, 12.1
7	2.2	16	5.1–5.5
8	2.4–2.6		

B: CHECK FIGURES FOR SELECTED CASES

SECTION I

1.1. No. 4a: $1,162,000

1.2. At end of year: J.P.'s owner's equity, 72,000 barrels; Ronnie's total assets, 118,000 barrels

1.3. Net income: Igor, 122 bushels

1.4. Closing balance, cash, $12,215

1.5. Total assets, December 31, 1980, $110,192,000

1.6. Letters: *d*, $4,521,000; *h*, $39,761,000

SECTION II

2.1. No. 4: $110,870,593

2.2. No. 1: $1,096,299

2.3. No. 3: $9,831,867

2.4. No. 1: *e*, $227 million; *g*, ($10.7 million)

2.5. No. 2: $4,903.5 million (ignoring taxes on gain)

2.6. No. 2a: 1976 inventories higher by $49,788,076; 1975 retained earnings higher by $105,466,988 (ignoring taxes)
No. 6a: ($30,913,000)

SECTION III

3.1. No. 2: $23,008,000

3.2. Current assets increased by $155,897,000 ($132,808,000 + $23,089,000)

3.3. No. 2b: $136,794,000

3.4. No. 5: ($55,000)

3.5. No. 2: 1979 net income before taxes on income, ($1,593,000); 1978 net income before taxes on income, $33,015,000

SECTION IV

4.1. No. 1: Restated 1980 net earnings, $137,376,000

4.2. No. 2: Beginning of second quarter

4.3. No. 1: TriStar inventory, 12/31/72, $959 million; TriStar inventory, 12/31/73, $1,160 million

4.5. No. 1: Current profits reduced to $252.6 million loss

4.6. No. 2: Net earnings before taxes: $1,259.7 million on straight-line basis; $1,177.8 million on sum-of-years'-digits basis

SECTION V

5.1. No. 3: $129,099,000

5.3. No. 2: $25,202 million

5.4. Net income before both accounting changes for 1981, $579.6 million

5.5. No. 3: Lower by $449 million

5.6. No. 1: $7,715.27

SECTION VI

6.1. No. 2: $17,221.51

6.2. No. 2: $19,915

SECTION VII

7.1. No. 3: 1980, $5,206,000; 1981, $9,041,000

7.2. No. 2a: $6.1 million increase; No. 2b: $4.4 million decrease

7.3. No. 3: $198.2 million

7.4. No. 2: F = $8,616 million; No. 4: $365.6 million increase

SECTION VIII

8.1. No. 4: 1981 net earnings restated for: Credit = ($223.4 million); Sears = $407.0 million

8.3. No. 1: $436.5 million

8.4. Northwest No. 3: 1979 net earnings (restated) $45,079,000 United No. 1: $31,600,000

8.6. Restated 1980 earnings, $50,269,000

9.1. No. 1: $4,328,000

9.2. No. 3: 1980 net earnings (cost method), $7,827,000

9.4. No. 1: Other assets (as a plug item), $8,210,000

9.5. No. 3: Estimated goodwill if purchase, $141.0 million

9.7. No. 4: Net income after adjustment for profits and gains for Consolidated Aluminum Company, $69,334,000

9.8. No. 3: $570.9 million

SECTION X

10.1. No. 3: $138,754,000

10.2. No. 4: Cash = $275.5 million

10.3. No. 3: $380,224,000

10.4. No. 1d: $134,910,000

10.5. No. 2: Accounts payable reduction, $95,624,000

SECTION XI

11.1. No. 3: Gain on sale, $547,000

11.2. No. 1b: 2,016,000

11.3. No. 4: $81,713,000

SECTION XII

12.1. No. 2: $CF_1 = \$27,559,000$; $CF_2 = \$32,106,000$
No. 5: Terminal price = $120.78